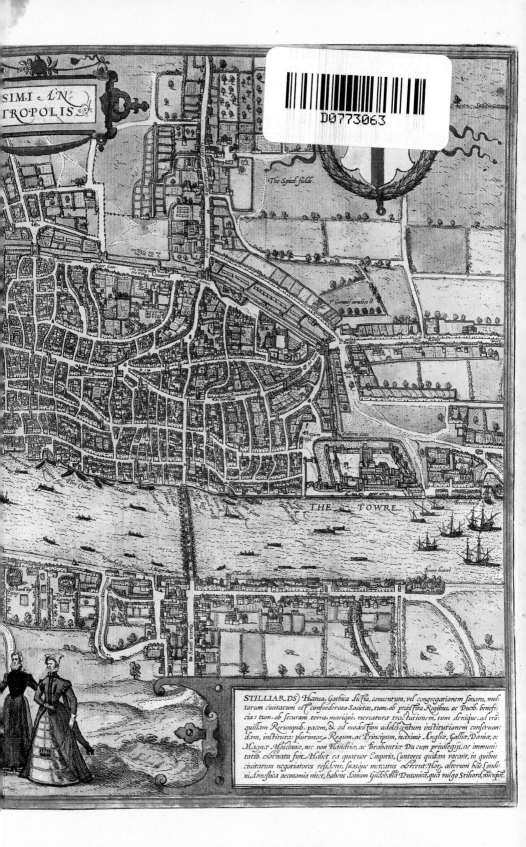

THE CITY
ON THE
THAMES

THE CITY
ON THE
THAMES

THE CREATION OF A WORLD CAPITAL:
A HISTORY OF LONDON

SIMON JENKINS

PEGASUS BOOKS
NEW YORK LONDON

THE CITY ON THE THAMES

Pegasus Books Ltd.
148 W 37th Street, 13th Floor
New York, NY 10018

Copyright © 2020 Simon Jenkins

First Pegasus Books cloth edition September 2020

ISBN: 978-1-64313-552-6

10 9 8 7 6 5 4 3 2 1

Printed in the United States of America
Distributed by Simon & Schuster
www.pegasusbooks.com

For Hannah

Contents

List of Illustrations

Section 2

Section 3

Section 4

Maps

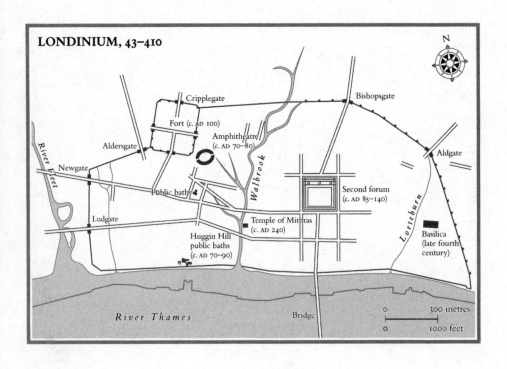

LONDINIUM, 43–410

N

Cripplegate

Fort (c. AD 100)

Aldersgate

Amphitheatre (c. AD 70–80)

River Fleet

Newgate

Public baths

Walbrook

Bishopsgate

Aldgate

Second forum (c. AD 85–140)

Temple of Mithras (c. AD 240)

Lorteburn

Ludgate

Huggin Hill public baths (c. AD 70–90)

Basilica (late fourth century)

River Thames

Bridge

0   300 metres

0   1000 feet

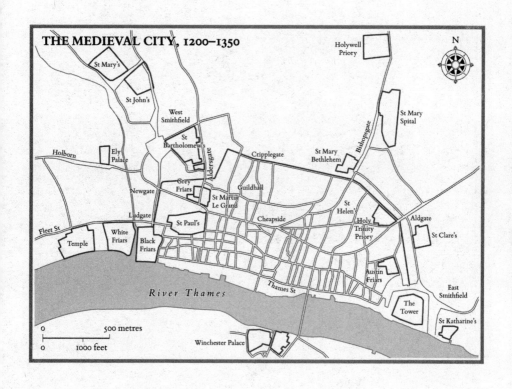

THE MEDIEVAL CITY, 1200–1350

Holywell
Priory

St Mary's

St John's

West
Smithfield

St Bartholomew's

Holborn

Ely
Palace

Cripplegate

St Mary
Bethlehem

St Mary
Spital

Bishopsgate

Aldersgate

Newgate

Grey
Friars

St Martin
Le Grand

Guildhall

St
Helen's

Ludgate

St Paul's

Cheapside

Holy
Trinity
Priory

Aldgate

St Clare's

Fleet St

White
Friars

Black
Friars

Temple

Austin
Friars

East
Smithfield

Thames St

The
Tower

St Katharine's

River Thames

0   500 metres

0   1000 feet

Winchester Palace

N

THE CITY OF LONDON,
as shown on Civitas Londinum, a woodcut map of London, c.1560

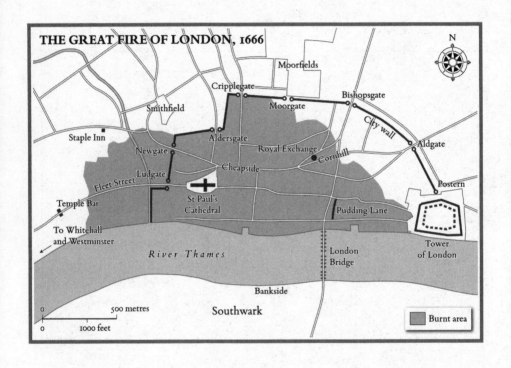

THE GREAT FIRE OF LONDON, 1666

N

Moorfields

Cripplegate

Bishopsgate

Smithfield

Moorgate

City wall

Aldersgate

Royal Exchange

Aldgate

Staple Inn

Newgate

Cornhill

Cheapside

Postern

Ludgate

Fleet Street

St Paul's
Cathedral

Temple Bar

Pudding Lane

To Whitehall
and Westminster

River Thames

London
Bridge

Tower
of London

Bankside

500 metres

Southwark

1000 feet

Burnt area

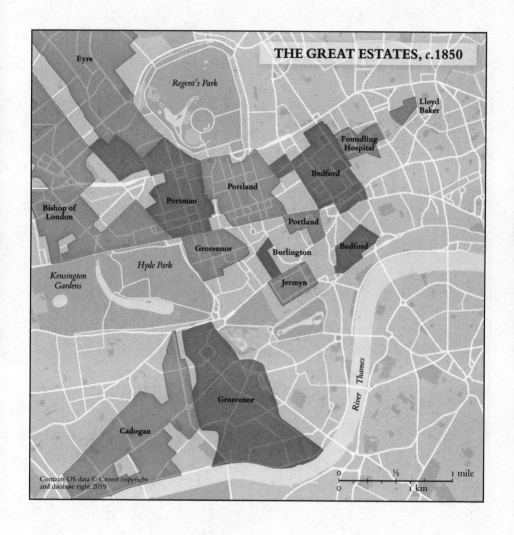

THE GREAT ESTATES, *c.*1850

Eyre

Regent's Park

Lloyd
Baker

Foundling
Hospital

Portland

Bedford

Portman

Portland

Bishop of
London

Portland

Bedford

Grosvenor

Burlington

Hyde Park

Jermyn

Kensington
Gardens

Grosvenor

River Thames

Cadogan

Contains OS data © Crown copyright
and database right 2019

0   ½   1 mile

0   1 km

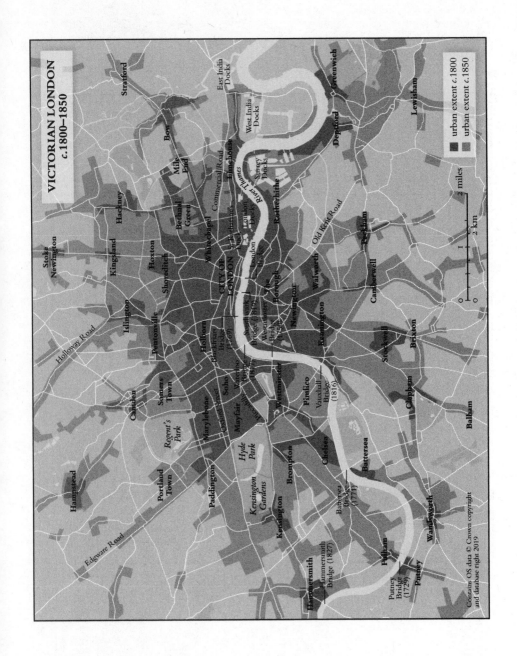

VICTORIAN LONDON
c.1800–1850

Legend:
- urban extent c.1800
- urban extent c.1850

0 2 miles
0 2 km

Contains OS data © Crown copyright and database right 2019

Labels:
Hampstead · Stoke Newington · Stratford · Bow · Hackney · Kingsland · Holloway Road · Islington · Hoxton · Shoreditch · Bethnal Green · Mile End · Commercial Road · Whitechapel · East India Docks · West India Docks · Greenwich · Lewisham · Deptford · Rotherhithe · Surrey Docks · London Docks · River Thames · Limehouse · City of London · Pentonville · Holborn · Camden · Somers Town · Regent's Park · Marylebone · Portland Town · Edgware Road · Paddington · Hyde Park · Kensington Gardens · Mayfair · Soho · Blackfriars Bridge (1769) · Southwark Bridge (1819) · London Bridge · The Borough · Newington · Walworth · Camberwell · Peckham · Old Kent Road · Westminster Bridge (1750) · Westminster · Pimlico · Vauxhall Bridge (1816) · Kennington · Stockwell · Brixton · Clapham · Balham · Battersea · Chelsea · Brompton · Kensington · Waterloo Bridge (1817) · Battersea Bridge (1771) · Hammersmith Bridge (1827) · Hammersmith · Fulham · Wandsworth · Putney · Putney Bridge (1729)

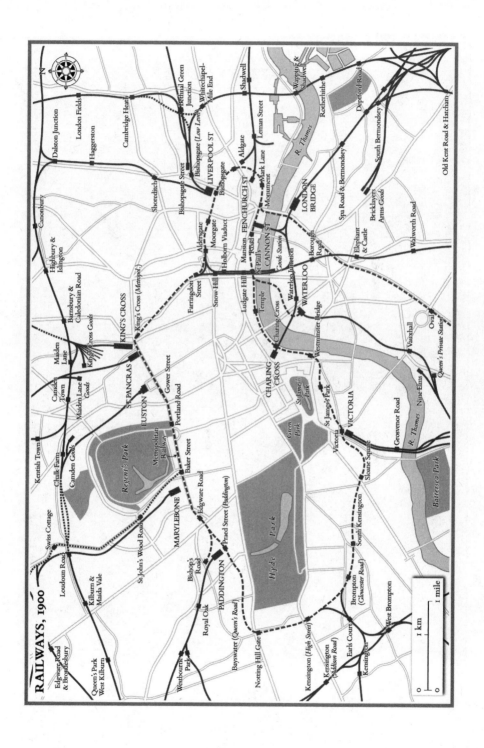

RAILWAYS, 1900

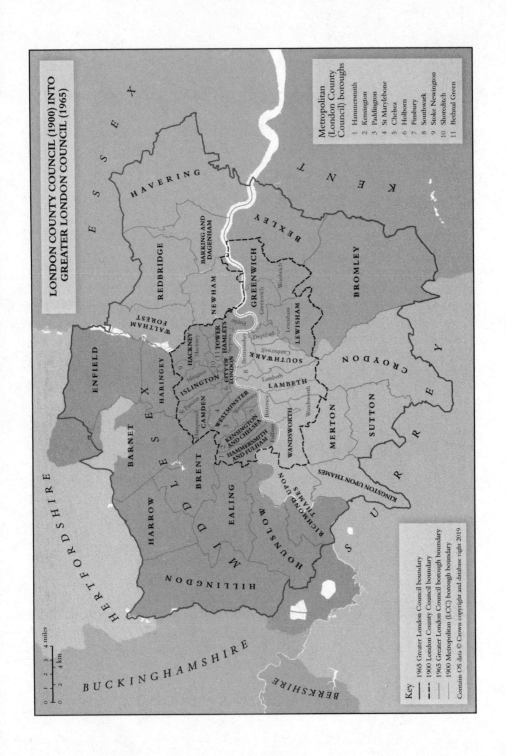

LONDON COUNTY COUNCIL (1900) INTO GREATER LONDON COUNCIL (1965)

Metropolitan
(London County
Council) boroughs

1 Hammersmith
2 Kensington
3 Paddington
4 St Marylebone
5 Chelsea
6 Holborn
7 Finsbury
8 Southwark
9 Stoke Newington
10 Shoreditch
11 Bethnal Green

E S S E X

K E N T

HAVERING

REDBRIDGE

BARKING AND DAGENHAM

WALTHAM FOREST

NEWHAM

GREENWICH

Woolwich

BEXLEY

BROMLEY

ENFIELD

HARINGEY

HACKNEY
Hackney

ISLINGTON
Islington

9

10 11 TOWER HAMLETS
CITY OF LONDON
Poplar

Bermondsey
Deptford
Lewisham

LEWISHAM

Greenwich

SOUTHWARK
Camberwell

CROYDON

BARNET

M I D D L E S E X

St Pancras

CAMDEN

WESTMINSTER
Hampstead
Westminster

2 3 4

5

Battersea

LAMBETH
Lambeth

Wandsworth

MERTON

SUTTON

KENSINGTON AND CHELSEA

HAMMERSMITH AND FULHAM
Fulham

WANDSWORTH

KINGSTON UPON THAMES

HARROW

BRENT

EALING

HOUNSLOW

RICHMOND UPON THAMES

HILLINGDON

S U R R E Y

H E R T F O R D S H I R E

B U C K I N G H A M S H I R E

B E R K S H I R E

Key
— 1965 Greater London Council boundary
-ı-ı- 1900 London County Council boundary
— 1965 Greater London Council borough boundary
— 1900 Metropolitan (LCC) borough boundary
Contains OS data © Crown copyright and database right 2019

0 1 2 3 4 miles
0 2 4 km

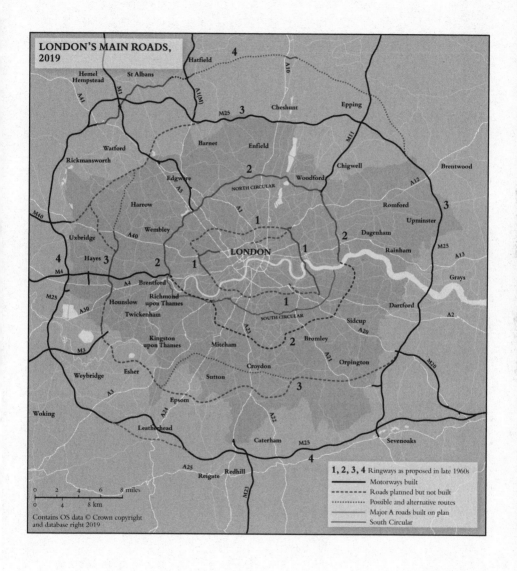

LONDON'S MAIN ROADS, 2019

Hemel Hempstead
St Albans
Hatfield **4**
A10
A41
M1
A1(M)
M25 **3**
Cheshunt
Epping
Watford
Barnet
Enfield
Rickmansworth
Chigwell
Brentwood
Edgware
Woodford
A12
A8
NORTH CIRCULAR **2**
Romford
3
Harrow
A1
Upminster
Wembley
1
M25
A13
A40
2
Dagenham
M40
Uxbridge
1
Rainham
Grays
4
Hayes **3**
2
1
M4
A4
Brentford
Dartford
A2
M25
Richmond upon Thames
1
A30
Hounslow
Sidcup
SOUTH CIRCULAR
A20
M3
Twickenham
Bromley
2
Kingston upon Thames
Mitcham
Orpington
M20
Weybridge
Esher
Croydon
A21
Sutton
3
A3
Epsom
Woking
Leatherhead
Caterham
M25
Sevenoaks
A22
A25
4
Reigate
Redhill
M23

1, 2, 3, 4 Ringways as proposed in late 1960s
——— Motorways built
- - - - Roads planned but not built
·········· Possible and alternative routes
——— Major A roads built on plan
——— South Circular

0   2   4   6   8 miles
0   4   8 km

Contains OS data © Crown copyright and database right 2019

POPULATION, 1801–2019

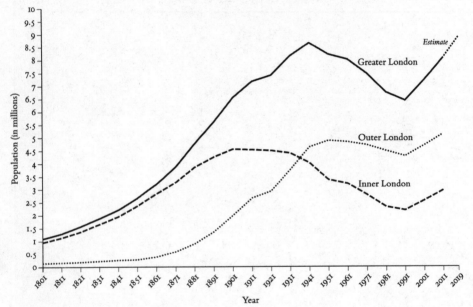

THE CITY
ON THE
THAMES

Introduction

The view of London from Waterloo Bridge is of a mess – an eccentric, unplanned, maddening, exhilarating mess. I have seen it evolving all my life, and still struggle to understand what moves it. This book is a record of that struggle. Founded in Roman times and refounded by Anglo-Saxons, London has grown relentlessly ever since. By the eighteenth century it was the biggest metropolis in Europe and by the nineteenth the biggest in the world. After the Second World War, London was thought to have reached its limits and began a period of decline. Yet by the turn of the twenty-first century, it had resumed its rise, sucking in people, money and talent from across the nation, the continent, the world. Its population is expected to surpass 9 million by 2025. Of one thing I am now sure: London has a life of its own.

For most of history there has been a London and a Westminster, two civic entities serving distinct purposes, one economic the other political. The tension between the two is a recurring theme of this book. The first medieval metropolis reached a crisis in the seventeenth century, with the Civil War, the Great Plague and the Great Fire. From this it emerged into the 'golden age' of eighteenth-century renewal and intellectual fertility. This was followed by the upheaval brought by the railways and a resulting explosion of suburban growth, on a par with no other city on earth. London reached an imperial apotheosis at the turn of the twentieth century, and survived bombing in two world wars during it, after which it entered a period of decline and confusion. In the new millennium it has surged forward into new prosperity as a global financial centre, but the arguments over where it should grow, how it should look and to whom it 'belongs' remain unresolved.

This book is chiefly concerned with the evolution of London's appearance, why it looks as it does today, more variegated and visually anarchic than any comparable city. All histories have their roots in geography. London's physical evolution has been intimately related to its location and topography. Its people and their activities change with the generations, but the city's fabric has been a continuous link between past and present.

Wherever people congregate there is potential for unrest but, over the two millennia of its existence, London's conflicts have been remarkably peaceful. Fewer people have died from political violence in its streets than in any of the world's other great cities. Its struggles have been organic, deriving from the nature of its growth, the forces of the market place and attempts to plan or regulate that market. That those attempts have largely failed is the outstanding fact of this story. London has long been its own master. When it has been traumatized – by Boudicca's revolt, Norman conquest, Henrician Reformation, plague, fire or bombs – it has put its head down and minded its own business, with extraordinary success.

Most histories of London set it in isolation from the nation of which it is the capital. I have tried to set it in its national, and to an extent international, context. It was always careful in holding itself aloof from events affecting the rest of the country, but its role in the Civil War and again in the nineteenth-century battles for reform was critical. The London mob had a voice of its own, which should not be underestimated simply because it was so rarely violent.

Beyond the City and Westminster, the task of defining London becomes ever harder. The Victorian Walter Besant wrote of two Londons about which 'no one knows and no one is curious': east London and south London. Both were larger than Manchester, yet millions of those who lived there never crossed the boundary between them. East London was a working-class city almost entirely apart, while the nearest south London came to a civic monument, said Besant, was the Elephant and Castle pub – now alas gone. In the past two centuries a third London has arisen, even less conspicuous. It is the silent, anonymous, railway-created suburban metropolis, which in the half-century from 1880 expanded London's land area six times over. Depending on definition, it comprises up to 80 per cent of the city. I have tried to do it justice.

London as a whole has never, at least until the twenty-first century, been self-governing in the sense of having a unified executive authority responsible for all or most of its public services. Indeed it has been perennially apathetic. The answer to the question why has London been politically inert compared with Paris, Berlin, Vienna or St Petersburg has lain partly in its playing host to an emergent national democracy. I believe another reason is geography. Cities are pressurized boilers whose safety valve is space. Whenever London seemed about to burst at its seams, it went on a building spree. Its nineteenth-century slums were terrible, but they were modest compared with those of Paris. And their outlet was the railway, always easing the city into the accessible acres of Middlesex, Essex, Surrey and Kent. An 1854 Royal Commission wearily described the capital as 'a province covered with houses'. When Karl Marx pondered London's poor, and gazed out over its quietly dignified streets and squares, he despaired of their revolutionary potential.

Of the conflicts mentioned above, the most serious and least recorded, and the one to which I devote most attention, is that covering the third quarter of the twentieth century. The Blitz destroyed a lot of the City and some of the East End, but the damage was minor compared with the destruction inflicted by the bulldozers of London's post-war governors. A drive through inner suburbia today navigates a ghost map of mostly working-class streets lying lost beneath council estates and tower blocks. Absolutist architects sought to rebuild from the ground up, imposing their own ideological and aesthetic template on a living, breathing city. By the time they had stopped, through antipathy and lack of resources, much of what was predominantly Victorian London had been devastated – though mercifully far from all.

As history approaches the present, the narrative is inevitably coloured by contemporary experience. I have lived in London since infancy, in four of its boroughs, three of them north and one south of the river. The Greeks held that, for the polis to survive, its citizens should participate in its government. I have never held elected office, but have spent my life writing about every facet of the capital, and served on bodies involved in its transport, housing, planning, arts and conservation.* I have edited a London morning and evening newspaper (*The Times* and the *Evening Standard*), been a juryman three times and a school governor twice. Activism has been a constant theme, and I now pass through the city like a veteran soldier, bearing daily witness to past victories and defeats. It can be elating and depressing.

My interest in London's appearance is specific and deliberate. It is for the London of all time, not the same London but the same sort of London. Battles over gentrification, poverty, schooling and public housing are real and important, but I believe urban politics should never privilege the current generation. We have a right to be heard. But the city we briefly inhabit will survive, and what matters is the city we pass on to the future. I shudder to think what generations to come will say of our handling of London's skyline

---

* The Boards of British Rail, Transport for London, Museum of London, South Bank, Old Vic, Somerset House, Paddington Housing, English Heritage, National Trust, Save Britain's Heritage, the Twentieth Century Society.

just as we shudder at what our parents and grandparents did after the Second World War. We must remember that in choosing the London we want, we decide in the name of others.

Curiosity is the best approach to history. I try to answer questions that have always intrigued me, and I hope intrigue others. Why has the City of London been always so different from Westminster? Why does south London – just a hundred yards across the river – seem so utterly different, almost provincial? Why are London's inner neighbourhoods so diverse, its outer suburbs so uniform? How did the terrace house become the favoured style of living, for old and young, rich and poor, and why are modern planners so hostile to so popular a building form – including one that appeals to most architects? Why are London's tall buildings scattered so randomly?

I struggle to stay dispassionate. If love can be applied to a place shared with 9 million others, then I love London. I find absence from it distressing, and returning to it uplifting. Its celebrated views, from Parliament Hill, Waterloo Bridge and Greenwich, always thrill me. Its disappointments are mortifying but its joys a delight. London never betrays its vocation to surprise. It has that greatest of human virtues: never to be dull.

I

Londinium
43–410

Old Father Thames

Most cities start with water. Where there is river, lake or sea there is trade, and where there is high ground along a shore, people put down roots and begin to deal. Before London ever existed, humans occupied the Thames valley, digging ditches, raising earthworks, killing wild animals, cultivating crops, leaving clay pots and metal objects. But they never took their eye off the river.

The Thames was not a placid stream. It was a tidal torrent twice its present width, running far inland. From earliest times it was, like most rivers, regarded as sacred. Its personification as Father Thames, a name possibly derived from a Celtic root for darkness, assumed a Neptune-like old man with flowing locks. Offerings were made to the river's gods, of pots, axes, swords, money, much as lovers continue to toss coins into fountains for good luck. At some turning point in my own life, I remember crossing Waterloo Bridge and looking down into the river below. Some primal instinct made me throw a coin into the water.

In prehistory there was no London, just a twin-bosomed hill. The best way to sense its rise and fall is by riding a bicycle, preferably at night, west from the Tower of London. The contour rises up Tower Hill and along Eastcheap and Cannon Street, from where lanes run steeply down to the Thames. Cannon Street clearly dips in the middle, where it crosses the course of the old Walbrook before rising again to the second 'bosom' at St Paul's. Further lanes descend to the river below Carter Lane.

Beyond the cathedral, Ludgate Hill falls steeply to cross the old Fleet river, now a buried relief sewer. The route rises again up Fleet Street, to reach what was a stretch of shingle recalled in the name of the Strand. Here lies the Aldwych – Saxon for old port – of the post-Roman settlement known as Lundenwic, roughly the present Covent Garden. At Trafalgar Square, we can dip towards the marshes of Westminster, or bear right up Haymarket to the higher land of Soho. We may not have seen old London, but we have felt it in our legs.

A map in the Museum of London of this landscape in prehistoric times shows flint axes, bones and human skulls littered among the remains of mammoth, rhinoceros, bison and bear. The nearest so-called 'camps' were on more fertile ground upstream, at Uxbridge, Staines, Carshalton and Heathrow. By the first millennium BC, simple field systems appear, including one south of the river in Southwark. A fine Bronze Age shield was found at Battersea, at a probable early crossing of the river.

The Thames appears to have been a boundary between late Iron Age tribes of unknown origin. The river would have formed a natural conduit for trade between the North Sea and the interior. As for the name London, there are a dozen theories, the most plausible being from the Celtic *lond*, for wild, or from *plowonida*, for fast stream. The medieval historian Geoffrey of Monmouth, mimicking Rome, declared London to have been founded by 'Brutus', a Trojan descendant of Rome's Aeneas. Even in myth, London was seen as bonded with 'Europa'.

City of Rome

Julius Caesar's two expeditions to Britain in 55 and 54 BC left no trace on the London area. The first was merely a landing in Kent, the second a massive invasion of 800 ships, making it the most numerous maritime crossing of the Channel, albeit in the other direction, until D-Day. It defeated a British force under Cassivellaunus, crossed the Thames and reached into Middlesex. Where the crossing took place and what the invasion achieved is unclear. It appears to have been no more than a show of strength. Caesar left neither a base nor troops, and retreated to Gaul.

The return of the Romans in AD 43 during the reign of Emperor Claudius was more emphatic. An army under Aulus Plautius landed at Richborough on the Kent coast and marched up the Thames shore. They would probably have crossed the river onto high land opposite Southwark on their way to the British fortress of Colchester. Whether the hill was already occupied by traders we do not know. Its settlement soon became Londinium.

The crossing point grew swiftly on either side of the Walbrook stream. Like all Roman towns, it was planned as a formal grid of streets, oriented on a road leading east to the British city of Colchester and north-west up Watling Street (the present Edgware Road) to St Albans. In its centre was an open space or forum, on the site of the present Leadenhall market. West of the Walbrook was an amphitheatre, found in 1988 in Guildhall Yard.

The streets were built Roman-style with mostly rectangular houses, though there were also some round dwellings, presumably for the native population. Along the river front were wharves to receive ships and supplies. Tacitus remarked that it was 'not dignified by the title colony [like Colchester] and was mainly peopled by merchants'. This is supported by the discovery in 2010 of wax tablets under the Bloomberg building dating from AD 57, indicating trading activity as well as schooling and judiciary.

This first London survived just seventeen years. In 60, the Iceni of Norfolk and the Trinovantes of Essex rose in revolt under the Iceni queen, Boudicca, when the Roman governor, Suetonius, sought to absorb the Iceni into his province on the death of Boudicca's husband, an ally of Rome. For reasons that remain obscure, Boudicca was flogged and her daughters raped. In retaliation, the warrior queen assembled a large army, destroyed the Romans' base at Colchester and then attacked them in London and St Albans.

Suetonius's troops were campaigning in Wales at the time, leaving him defenceless. Those citizens who did not flee with him were massacred and the city was razed to the ground (an ash layer of this date has been discovered by archaeologists). Contemporary estimates of 40,000 dead seem exaggerated, but indicate the size to which London had grown in under two decades of occupation. By the following year, Suetonius had gathered his forces and returned to defeat and then kill Boudicca.

Such was London's strategic importance that it swiftly recovered its status as the biggest town in Britain, capital of what was now the prized Roman province of Britannia. The Walbrook brought fresh water from Finsbury and carried waste down into the Thames. Roman villas fronted the main streets. Warehouses lined the quayside. The first wooden bridge across the Thames to Southwark was built early in the Roman occupation. Wooden piles were discovered in 1981 a hundred yards east of the present London Bridge, dated to AD 80–90. This enabled Watling Street from St Albans to cross the river to Kent and Dover, while Ermine Street ran north up modern Kingsland Road to York. They are still the only streets in London to run dead straight for miles. As for the bridge, it was to be the symbol of London's identity for centuries.

Over the course of the second century Londinium continued to grow, surviving an extensive fire in *c.*120. Under Emperor Hadrian, who is believed to have visited it in 122, a fort for 1,000 troops was built in the north-west corner, today's Barbican. In addition, a semi-circular stone wall was erected in the early third century stretching two miles from the present Tower of London to the mouth of the Fleet at Blackfriars, punctuated at Ludgate, Newgate, Bishopsgate and Aldgate. A kink in the north-west corner marked the presence of the old Cripplegate fort. With adjustments, this wall forms the basic boundary of the City of London to this day. Meanwhile, the forum was extended to become the largest north of the Alps, overlooked by a basilica or administration building which excavation suggests was longer even than the present St Paul's Cathedral.

Gradually suburbs grew beyond the walls, along modern-day Fleet Street and Holborn, Aldgate and south of the bridge in Southwark. By the end of the first century Londinium is estimated to have reached its population peak, with some 60,000 inhabitants, in Roman terms a major metropolis. Of its society little is known, though the best evocation of the Roman city is the display in the Museum of London in the Barbican. The museum offers a tableau of luxurious domestic comforts, with mosaic floors, painted saloons, baths and courtyards. What is significant from DNA analysis is that this London had a highly cosmopolitan population drawn from across the Roman empire, including the Mediterranean and northern Europe. These people would have worshipped their gods in temples and shrines, giving offerings on the banks of the Thames and the Walbrook. The most prominent so far found is to the god Mithras, built near the Walbrook in *c.*240. Guesses have been made that St Paul's might cover the site of another temple, perhaps to the goddess Diana.

Retreat and disappearance

The reason for the decay of Londinium in the fifth and sixth centuries is the great mystery of London's past. Its population had already started to decline by 150. It is possible that southern Britannia was mostly peaceable, and the capital needed no resident legion, soldiers being mostly billeted on the Welsh and Scottish borders. People appear to have drifted away. The emergent 'Romano-British' culture dispersed to towns and villas located across the adjacent slopes of Kent, Surrey and the Thames valley, as they are today. London was an important port, but much of the province's trade could be transported by water round the coast.

As imperial security started to disintegrate, distant provinces such as Britain became vulnerable to 'barbarian' incursions – notably from Angles and Saxons – and their governments to mutinous generals. A full-scale rebellion under Carausius in 286 required a 'reconquest' of Britain in 293 by Constantius Chlorus, father of Constantine the Great. This led to a revival of building, though not for long. Soon after 300 there are clear signs of a city losing its purpose. Buildings emptied, public baths fell into disuse and even the forum became derelict.

The arrival of Christianity in northern Europe *c.*300 may have been marked by a church near Tower Hill. A council held at Arles in France in 314 was attended by a bishop called Restitutus 'from Londinium'. But by the end of the century, archaeology indicates a sudden decline. London may have become unpleasant, half-ruined, polluted, unpoliced and cursed with plagues. It may have been that newcomers preferred to settle on healthier, more open ground to the west.

All we do know is that the year 410 signalled doom. The Roman empire was threatened on many fronts by invading barbarians, with Rome itself sacked that year by Alaric the Visigoth. The twenty-six-year-old emperor, Honorius, withdrew legions from the empire's periphery, including Britain. To emissaries pleading for help against Germanic tribes, the emperor declared that for 'the security of his possessions in Gaul, Italy and Spain, he renounces the imperial claim over Britain'. Its counties and garrisons 'are forthwith independent . . . and should fall to their own defences'. It was the first Brexit.

While Romano-British culture continued elsewhere in Britannia, it seems that in Londinium there was an abrupt abandonment. How many Romans stayed behind, what language they spoke or why they left the security of a walled enclosure is a mystery. All detritus of coins, goods and refuse disappears. There was no cataclysmic event, just a city that gives all the appearances of its inhabitants having packed up and departed. The archaeological record has London covered in a layer of dark earth, usually a sign of land reverting to rubble and soil. This vacant London seems to have lasted two centuries, a lost settlement on a hill, like Old Sarum in Wiltshire, Archaeologists suggest that untraceable activity, possibly civic or religious ceremonial, may have continued within the walls. It was clearly enough to support the site's revival two centuries later, but otherwise there was nothing.

As a boy I tried to walk the circumference of this long-lost city. It was a fruitless venture. A portion of Roman wall survives opposite the Tower and another along Cooper's Row to the north. A bastion overlaid with medieval brick is preserved in the Barbican, along London Wall, and another in a Barbican car park. These are mere fragments. Public baths lurk under Huggin Hill off Queen Victoria Street, where they were fed by chains of buckets. Their wall is still visible in the delightful pocket park of Cleary Garden. The baths themselves, among the best relics of Roman London, were partly filled in during the 1960s so offices could be developed above them.

Other baths, occasionally accessible, remain under a building opposite Billingsgate. Less remains of the old amphitheatre on the site of the present Guildhall.

In 1954 a temple to Mithras emerged on the bank of the Walbrook during the building of Bucklersbury House. It caused great excitement, though not enough to leave it in situ. The jumble of stones was relocated to a forecourt in Queen Victoria Street. Redevelopment in 2017 for the Bloomberg Centre returned the stones to their original location, but this entailed their encasement in a darkened box in a modern basement as what looks like an abstract sculpture. Better would have been a rebuilt temple in an envisaged setting, like the recreated Viking street in York's Coppergate. Roman London remains a lost and curious place, an alien implant from a distant land, rendered insignificant by its sudden disappearance.

2

Saxon City
410–1066

Lundenwic interlude

The term Dark Ages to describe the period after the decline of
Rome is disliked by historians. It suggests they are not on the job.
Yet it well characterizes London after its abandonment by Rome.
Vagrants, drovers and market gardeners may have used the site,
but for almost two centuries the archaeological cupboard contains
only discarded items and no sign of settlement, no coins, pottery,
refuse or datable woodwork in the relevant archaeological strata.
Perhaps most telling is the fate of the Roman street grid. Even
where old towns decline, paths tend to remain, but in London the
grid itself vanished.

In the sixth and seventh centuries the Saxon kingdoms of Kent,
Essex and Mercia were coming into being, with the Thames as a
natural boundary between them. The contemporary Jarrow his-
torian Bede and the *Anglo-Saxon Chronicle* both refer to a new 'east
Saxon' trading base by the seventh century. This became known as
Lundenwic, or London port/market, and was later referred to as the
Aldwych – note the definite article – the old port. Here was surely the
location of London's missing link.

In 1985 a sort of confirmation emerged in excavations in the Covent
Garden area north of the Strand. Two archaeologists, Alan Vince
and Martin Biddle, working on different sites, discovered a wealth
of finds dating from the abandonment of London. It seems that in

the fifth century the river bank upstream of the Roman city took over as the base for river-borne trade, with the shingle beach as its landing. There is no evidence of wharves at Lundenwic or of stone structures. Only the wooden posts of a possible trading hall have been discovered, appropriately under the present Covent Garden market.

For these new Londoners, the old city to the east must have seemed a ghostly ruin, perhaps to be visited only on special occasions. The author Simon Young in *AD 500* imagines a visit by a Greek/Byzantine embassy to London, apparently seeking to resume authority over Britain in the name of Byzantium after the sack of Rome in 410. They find a few hundred residents still within the walls, ruled by a council of elderly Latin-speaking patricians with some Saxon mercenaries. The idea is mildly plausible, but of evidence there is none.

Rebirth of Christianity

If there is one imperial glue that outlasts military power, it is that of faith. The most likely survivors in the deserted city would have been relics of Christianity from the Roman occupation. The empire had been officially Christian for a century before 410, and a few hardy Romano-Britons would surely have tramped from Lundenwic over the Fleet Bridge and up Ludgate Hill to their family altars, even if the new, possibly pagan, London authorities disapproved.

Who these authorities were, and where they came from, is not known. It has always been assumed that the Britons of England's south-east, many of them now 'Romano-Britons', were Brythonic-speaking Celts of Belgic origin. There are fragmentary written references to them as 'Britons' attacked by Jutes, one of many Germanic incursions into Britain following the departure of Rome.

There is mention of them seeking refuge within the old walls in *c*.457. Others dispute this concept of a sudden Saxon invasion of a Celtic England. The eastern littoral of the British Isles had been settled by German tribes from across the North Sea. The Iceni and Trinovantes of East Anglia and the tribes of Kent may even have spoken a Germanic tongue, different from the Brythonic of the western/northern areas of the islands. Place names round London are overwhelmingly Saxon, not Brythonic. There are no -abers, -tors or -thorpes, but rather Saxon suffixes, -wic for port, -sey for island, -ham and -ton for homestead. Greenwich, Dulwich, Bermondsey, Battersea, Clapham, Streatham, Kensington and Dalston are Saxon. East Anglia and the south-east had long been settled by legionary veterans from Germany. Of 'British' Celts there is no trace.

At the end of the sixth century the clouds roll back and a new notable date emerges. Augustine's mission to Canterbury in 597 began England's march towards a new Rome, that of the Catholic church. Augustine converted the king of Kent, Aethelbert (*r. c*.589–616), to Christianity, but his pope, Gregory the Great, significantly ordered that a new English bishopric be divided between York and London. The settlement was subject to Essex, whose king, Saebert, was Aethelbert's nephew and owed allegiance to him. Since Saebert now converted to Christianity, London's bishopric was ostensibly assured. In 604 a letter from Pope Gregory appointed Mellitus as first Bishop of London, and he in turn founded St Paul's Cathedral, possibly on the site of a Roman temple or even church.

However, Mellitus did not enjoy a secure episcopacy. On Saebert's death in 616 Essex passed to the probably pagan King Redwald (in office *c*.600–24) and Kent's authority declined. Following an argument over Mellitus's refusal to give communion to unbaptized Londoners, he was expelled – the first sign of what became London's instinct for independence. Forced to take refuge in Gaul, Mellitus returned in 619 but only to become the third Archbishop of Canterbury. It was thus Canterbury, in the heart of Christianized Kent, and not Gregory's choice of London, which duly became the headquarters of the English church, and remained so for all time.

Christianity appears to have revived in Essex with the arrival of Cedd of Lindisfarne as London's bishop (654–64). A missionary sent south from Northumbria, Cedd founded a monastery at Bradwell in Essex that still sits in glorious isolation in a field near a deserted stretch of coast. It is among the most moving and unknown relics of early Christianity in England. Cedd was succeeded by Wine (666–72), previously bishop of both Dorchester and Winchester, and then by Erconwald (675–93), officially London's patron saint. The settlement was by now under the midlands kingdom of Mercia and remained so into the ninth century, notably under King Offa (757–96).

For Offa, whose capital was at Tamworth, London offered an outlet to the continent and to diplomatic relations with Charlemagne and the Franks. The old city had clearly been reoccupied and was drawing population back within its walls. Offa is thought to have had a pied-à-terre of sorts on the site of the Roman fort, with St Alban Wood Street (near the Barbican) suggested as his chapel.

Saxons and Danes

Within years of Offa's death in 796 and that of Charlemagne in 814, a new threat appeared on Europe's northern horizon. London's trading status made it vulnerable to Viking raids down the east coast. At the end of his life, Charlemagne had declared himself 'overwhelmed with sorrow as I look forward, and see what evils the Northmen will bring upon my offspring and their people'. The first Danish attack on London came in the 830s, and in 851 the city was occupied and put to fire and the sword, but Aethelwulf, king of Wessex (839–58) and Alfred the Great's father, hit back with a victory leading to 'the greatest slaughter of a heathen host heard of to that day', according to the *Chronicle*. However, London found little security until Alfred's defeat of the Danes in 878 at the Battle of Edington in Wiltshire. He occupied London in 886, and the Danes were forced back to the so-called Danelaw territory of East Anglia and Northumbria.

Of the London rebuilt by Alfred the Great (871–99) we have scant knowledge. Though clearly a trading post of some importance, it was a vulnerable frontier town at the northern extremity of Wessex, long pulverized and impoverished by the Danes. The Danelaw itself began at the River Lea, just four miles east of the city. None the less, Alfred restored the walls and refounded it as one of his Saxon burghs (fortified towns). Trade with the continent resumed in earnest. Quays were allocated for specific goods, from Normandy, Flanders, Germany and the Baltic ports. Alfred also formalized London's markets on a new street pattern. The chief markets were at East Cheap, Poultry and Cheapside.

Alfred appears to have devised a street pattern quite different from that of Londinium, presumably one emerging from custom and practice over intervening time. Cheapside and Gracechurch Street survived of the old Roman cross routes. Otherwise, streets, lanes, courts and alleys appeared wherever they could be squeezed between plots of land. As rights of way, they acquired an almost sacred protection that still endures. Alfred's meandering streets are the sole remaining relics of ancient London acknowledged by the City's surveyors. Skyscrapers may demolish buildings and deface views, but even the mightiest must be shoehorned into ground plans ordained by King Alfred. In the heart of today's capital, we can still see the spectral outline of a Saxon map.

London government emerged from a council of elders, with

public meetings or 'folkmoots', apparently originating in Germanic tribal gatherings. These met in what remained of the old Roman amphitheatre. Attendance was notionally compulsory for all free citizens. Regular courts known as 'hustings' also met, usually to determine commercial affairs, which may explain the use of a Danish word for them. Alfred also divided the city into wards, each with subordinate church parishes, responsible for local order and what passed for welfare. Each ward had to contribute men and money to the city's defence. These institutions developed slowly over the centuries, but London was already enjoying a degree of self-government in embryo.

The city did not stay secure for long. Danish attacks continued throughout the tenth century. The city within the walls was able to repulse most of them, but invaders frequently had to be bought off by Danegeld. In 1002, Ethelred 'the Unready' (978–1016) sought to deter these attacks by ordering the slaughter of all Danes within his domain, the so-called St Brice's Day massacre. The dead appear to have included the sister of the Danish king, Swein Forkbeard, the most considerable of the Viking leaders. He was unlikely to be deterred.

London was the only English settlement able to mount armed resistance to the Danes, but it too fell to Swein. In 1014 Ethelred called for help in its recapture from Olaf II, Christian king of Norway and no friend of Denmark. In a possibly legendary incident, Olaf's ships undermined the supports of London Bridge and brought it down, thus enabling him to sail upstream and retake the city from Swein. The collapse of the bridge as implying London's salvation is a possible origin of the nursery rhyme 'London Bridge is Falling Down'. A Norse saga continues the rhyme, 'Gold is won and bright renown,/ Shields resounding, war-horns sounding . . ./ Odin makes our Olaf win.' But London remained vulnerable and in 1015 Swein's son and successor, Cnut, invaded with a large force and, a year later, entered London as king of England (1018–35). The city became part of Cnut's Scandinavian empire until his death.

Under the Saxons, English kings had regarded Winchester as politically their principal city, where they were crowned and buried, and where they kept their treasury. Under Cnut, London took the lead. Its trading importance made it a centre of financial activity, including the collection of taxes and the minting of money. London also financed Cnut's army. In return, trade with the Baltic States and Scandinavia prospered, reaching across the North and Baltic seas to the great rivers of Russia, and down them to Kiev, the Black Sea and Byzantium.

Cnut's empire was Christian and loyal to Rome. The number of churches in London is thought to have grown to twenty-five by the time of his death, including possibly six later dedicated to the city's saviour Olaf, the Norwegian king turned saint, as well as one to St Magnus Martyr (Olaf's son). Tooley Street in Southwark is derived, distantly, from St Olaf. St Clement Danes may have served a Danish garrison or Danish traders outside the walls in the Aldwych. The names are rare glimpses of this alien period, in a city located far from the centre of its adopted empire.

A second city rises in the west

Cnut's death in 1035 led eventually to the crown passing to his stepson, Edward the Confessor (1042–66). Edward had been brought up in France by his mother, Emma of Normandy, wife to both Ethelred (Edward's father) and then to Cnut. He was as foreign to the people of London as had been Cnut. He spoke Norman French and brought with him the customs and fashions of his Normandy upbringing. Most significant, he made his base not in the Saxon city of London but upstream of the Aldwych at a small Benedictine abbey – so small as to be called a 'monasteriolum' – on the marsh-land of Thorney Island.

Here Edward built his 'west minster' in the new Romanesque style, importing as Archbishop of Canterbury Robert from Jumi-èges in Normandy. At ninety-eight metres long the minster was bigger than any known Norman church of the time. Adjacent to it, a new monastery was constructed, and to the east Edward built himself a riverside palace for his court. The old royal enclave within London by St Paul's was given to the monastery of St Martin-le-Grand, founded *c*.1056. This single decision, to locate the apex of English power outside London, was the most critical in the city's history. It created what became a second capital, a political focus separate from the seat of business and commerce. It was inevitable that this separation, of French-speaking court from Anglo-Danish commercial centre, would lead to conflict between the two. It soon did.

In 1051 Edward's leading counsellor and power broker, the Anglo-Dane Godwin of Wessex, was driven into exile by Edward's predominantly Norman council, the witan. A year later Godwin returned on a tide of anti-Norman sentiment, and his son Harold became army commander and de facto ruler of the kingdom. On Edward's death in 1066, Harold was declared his successor. He had no other claim beyond being the queen's brother and commander of the army. William, Duke of Normandy, claimed that Edward had promised him the succession, and that Harold had consented to this when marooned in Normandy some years earlier. A con-tested succession was certain.

Of London in these early Middle Ages hardly more survives than of Roman Londinium. There are pre-Conquest fragments in All Hal-lows by the Tower and recent archaeology has found original stonework from the monastic quarters south of Westminster Abbey. What remains most clearly is London's spine, the two-mile thoroughfare that winds from the present City, across the valley of the Fleet and along the Strand to Westminster. From the founding of Edward's abbey, this route became the actual and metaphorical conduit between power and money. It was never rebuilt as a grand avenue, ceremonial or otherwise. It was just an ordinary street. Yet from the earliest muddy track to its status as artery of empire, it stretched like taut elastic along the bank of the Thames. It is the route of today's No. 11 bus, and I find it impossible to journey it without sensing its political tension.

London's story now becomes a tale of two cities, each with different preoccupations, tribes, interests, establishments and styles of government. While Westminster would wield monarchical authority, London held the power of the purse and the market economy. Neither was ever to triumph over the other, though in the evolution of the capital the market mostly came out on top. As the senior partner, the City of London was accorded the honour of a capital C. From now on I refer to it simply as 'the City', and Westminster as Westminster, though it too later became a 'city'.

3

Medieval Metropolis
1066–1348

Norman Conquest

As soon as the witan in London proclaimed Harold king, he was challenged by two rivals, Harald Hardrada, king of Norway, and William of Normandy, direct descendant of the Danish Rollo, original Viking colonizer of this part of France. Both claimants prepared to invade and seize the crown. Harold overwhelmed and killed Hardrada outside York later that same year, but he then had to race south to confront William, who had landed at Pevensey in Sussex. He left London before assembling his full army, and was subsequently defeated and killed by William's cavalry at Hastings in October 1066, forever the most famous date in England's history.

The Battle of Hastings, portrayed in school histories as the English against the French, was essentially between two equally tenuous claimants to the English throne, one Anglo-Dane and one Danish-Norman. The struggle marked the true emergence of Charlemagne's 'men of the north' onto the European stage. After Hastings, William marched towards London, nervous of its formidable defences. He burned Southwark but was unable to cross the Thames, detouring upstream as far as Wallingford before turning east, destroying towns and villages as he went. At Berkhamsted he finally received the submission of London's leading citizens – including Harold's teenage heir Edgar – as being 'of necessity'. He promised 'to be a gracious lord'. As for submission, the *Anglo-Saxon Chronicle* remarked that 'it was a great piece of folly that they had not done it earlier'.

William was crowned on Christmas Day 1066, stressing his legitimacy by holding the coronation in Edward's Westminster Abbey and not at Winchester. His Norman nobles now needed their reward, as they had regarded his invasion as a private affair, beyond their obligation of feudal duty. To win their support, William had promised them access to the wealth of Saxon England. Initially this was by means of fines from those who had fought with Harold, but it developed into the greatest land transfer in England's history. An estimated 95 per cent of provincial England south of the Tees was to pass from the Saxon nobility and church to the Norman invaders. Some 4,000 earls, thanes and abbots gave way to 200 Norman barons. All was recorded in the Domesday Book of 1086. When the north-east rebelled, appalling repression was visited on them, the 'harrowing of the north'.

London was the exception. English uprisings were stimulated over the next two years, primarily by 'the loss of their patrimonies', but there was little such trouble from London. Specifically excluded from William's depredations, it was granted a charter honouring its customary rights and protections. William declared the security of Londoners' property by inheritance, and affirmed, 'I will not suffer that any man do you wrong.' London's autonomy was thus entrenched by virtue of William's shrewd diplomacy. Its Saxon aldermen and folkmoot were acknowledged, and its subdivision into wards and parishes was by now established. It could choose its own sheriffs and impose its own regulations, most importantly on trade. Though French monasteries seized formerly Saxon ones, the recorded names of prominent London landowners remained Saxon well into the next century.

City of business

In truth London's personality was already cosmopolitan. It had been founded by Latin-speaking continentals, succeeded by German-speaking Anglo-Saxons and Norse-speaking Danes. It now owed fealty to French-speaking Normans. The city's population was some 25,000, on a par with Brussels and Ghent though a fraction of Paris's 100,000. And was prosperous. The names of its streets reflected their trading prominence, not just traditional markets for cloth, bread, poultry, fish and sea coal, but imports of silk, leather, furs and precious metals. It had its Fish Street and Poultry. The grandest merchants were the mercers, grocers, drapers and vintners.

From these markets emerged monopolies and guilds, with complex entry requirements, apprenticeships and regulations, guarding quality and excluding outsiders – except those with money or business to trade. They had their 'misteries' or craftsmanship rules, to which old Fleet Street printers used to refer in my youth. They were not just business and craft fraternities but, for their members, disbursers of cradle-to-grave welfare. Since guild admission also led eventually to the freedom of the city, the guilds in effect ordered the civic franchise and dominated governance.

London's bargain with the Norman state was thus forged in the early days of the conquest. It gave William revenue through taxes, and received in return autonomy over its affairs. While William acknowledged the bargain, he left the City in no doubt of his supremacy. He had three castles built on the City perimeter, Montfichet by Ludgate, Baynard's at the mouth of the Fleet and, in the seaward corner, a formidable tower, initially of wood but later of stone, daubed with lime and called the White Tower. This last remained outside the City's jurisdiction, but its very existence acknowledged London as a state within a state. Baynard's and

Montfichet were demolished under King John in the thirteenth century and the land given to Blackfriars' monastery. Today's Black Friar pub, in resplendent art nouveau, marks the spot.

Crucial to William's conquest had been the support of the pope, whose emblem he carried into battle at Hastings. He repaid that support in full. England saw an astonishing burst of ecclesiastical as well as military construction. Over the next half century, the Normans were to rebuild nearly every Saxon cathedral, abbey and church. They built new castles and monasteries and imported knights and abbots to populate them, creating a new aristocracy. The old Saxon St Paul's was rebuilt after a fire in 1087 and emerged as one of the longest cathedrals in Europe. In 1097 William's son Rufus constructed a great hall at Westminster, again said to be the largest in existence at the time. With a later roof, it remains as a testament to eleventh-century engineering. Nothing in Europe's history was to compare with this orgy of construction. Churches, castles and private houses, once built of wood, were now re-built of stone, much of it brought from Normandy.

While Londoners were sceptical of the authority of kings, they were not sceptical of the church. They might be independent, raucous, money-grabbing, often violent, but they were devout. Norman London saw 126 churches built, plus thirteen chapels in monastic houses. New foundations were often just a hundred yards apart, each with its own allegiance to bishops, barons, merchants and guilds, all eager for a City foothold.

Abbeys were founded near Bishopsgate and Aldgate. In 1123 the priory of St Bartholomew rose on the 'smooth-field' (hence Smithfield) outside the city's north-west wall. The crusader knights of St John of Jerusalem arrived at Clerkenwell *c.*1145 and never left. Today their society runs ambulances. Their companions, the Knights Templar, settled off Fleet Street, but were suppressed and their wealth seized in the fourteenth century. Their estate now hosts lawyers, but its round church, based on Jerusalem's Holy Sepulchre, still stands. St Mary Spital and St Mary Bethlehem followed to the north. South of the site of London Bridge, monastic foundations had long existed in Bermondsey and Southwark.

This coalition of church and lay authority determined the politics of the City throughout the Middle Ages. When the crown was disputed, as during the Anarchy of Stephen and Matilda (1135–53), the City's folkmoot decided for Stephen, though Matilda was crowned in Winchester. In the conflict over church authority between Henry II and Becket, London declined to take sides. Though Becket was a Londoner – a chapel on London Bridge was later dedicated to him – the city had no dog in his fight. London instinctively held aloof from political conflict, unless there was an outcome from which it might take advantage.

As the twelfth century progressed, the City developed a governing council of the twenty-four ward aldermen. Power within the metropolis rested not in any monarch, warlord or military institution but was, in effect, that of organized commerce. A council of aldermen imposed a ban on thatch as a roof covering, and required alehouses, much given to fires, to be of stone. London Bridge was reconstructed in stone in 1209, to the design of a priest, Peter Colechurch. This was a glory of the City and wonder of medieval engineering. It was of nineteen pointed arches erected on 'starlings' or footings twenty feet wide dug into the river bed and reinforced over the centuries, turning the stream into a virtual waterfall with each turn of the tide. A wider twentieth arch was crossed by a drawbridge. The bridge was remarkably strong, as evidenced later when it supported houses of up to five storeys. With much repair, it survived into the 1820s.

In 1189 London chose its first mayor, a French term derived from the 'major' domo or senior official in a lord's castle. The holder of the title until 1212 was Henry Fitz-Ailwyn. On him fell the task of raising 'a king's ransom' for the release of Richard the Lionheart from Austrian captivity after the Third Crusade. On Richard's death, King John (1199–1216) formally conferred on the City the right to elect a mayor, in the hope of securing City support against the barons, many of whom were in open revolt over taxation and the war in France. It was a futile hope. The City sided with the barons at Runnymede over Magna Carta, winning a series of explicit liberties and freedoms. Clause 41 declared: 'All merchants shall have safety and security in coming into England, and going out of England, and in staying and in travelling through England, as well by land as by water, to buy and sell, without any unjust exactions, according to ancient and right customs.' Europe was to be a single market and the king was not to exploit his power to make treaties and award licences to their disadvantage.

As in that other great city of commerce, Venice, too much power vested for long in one individual was thought bad for business, and mayoral tenure was eventually limited to just a year. Eligible voters were 'discreet and powerful citizens . . . wealthier and wiser men as of old accustomed'. Holders of the office tended to come from established aldermanic families, themselves related to the leading guilds. It was oligarchy, not democracy. The City would 'present' its mayor to the king in an annual gesture of homage, with the guilds processing out of the City down the Strand to Westminster in what is still the Lord Mayor's 'Show'. Rules of precedence were often contested. The feud between the merchant tailors and skinners over who should occupy sixth place in the procession is the putative source of 'being at sixes and sevens'. It was resolved in 1515 with an agreement to alternate annually (as they still do). The show was notionally a display of submission, but in reality one of conspicuous consumption. It was the power of wealth flaunted before the seat of political power, the City's annual exercise in flexing its muscles.

Henry III: a dangerous rebellion

London did not enjoy being paymaster to Plantagenet monarchs, not least for their costly warmongering and interference with trade. The disputes of Henry II, the ransoming of his son, Richard I, and King John's no less expensive defeats in France and war with the barons were all bad for business. The subsequent reign of Henry III (1216–72) was also a source of continual discord. He was French-educated and regarded London as a cultural backwater, much in need of new continental architecture and fashion. He was keen to play a role in European politics, and encouraged new monastic orders from the continent – the Dominicans in 1221 and the Franciscans in 1224. When, in 1236, Henry married the thirteen-year-old Eleanor of Provence, the girl arrived in London attended by the French king and 'all the chivalry and beauty of the south of France, a stately train of nobles, ladies, minstrels and jongleurs', records the chronicler. Many of these expected to be offered English manors and bishoprics.

Eleanor's arrival brought out London's most xenophobic gestures. Her barge was pelted with rotten food as it passed upriver. The barons and the City protested at the court's use of 'alien' Provençal in place of the 'English tongue' – by which they meant Norman French. Londoners were not appeased by Henry giving them their first zoo, located at the Tower and including a bear, a rhinoceros, an elephant, lions and snakes. Visitors were admitted on payment of a cat or dog as food for the animals.

Henry was obsessed with his distant ancestor, the equally Francophile Edward the Confessor. This led him to rebuild Westminster Abbey as a shrine to his forebear as well as a tomb for himself and his family, all in the new French gothic style. It was a project requiring extortionate taxing not just of the City but of the court. Henry declared there should be no 'weighing of the costs, past or future, so long as it prove worthy of and acceptable to God and St Peter'. This view of public expenditure, common to later monarchs and some governments, was not shared by the City.

Henry's decision in 1245 to hold two annual fairs in Westminster was viewed by the city's merchants as a hostile act. Guild members rioted in the streets and sent armed bands in support of Simon de Montfort's uprising against the king. In the Battle of Lewes in 1264, de Montfort was triumphant and Henry was captured. The following year saw the first autonomous parliament summoned to Westminster, though it dissolved in chaos. Disorder and persecution became widespread and 400 Jews were killed by a mob in one unprovoked massacre. A chronicler, Thomas Wykes, was appalled. Though they 'had not the mark of our faith', he wrote, 'it was an inhuman and impious deed to slay them without cause'.

The City for once had misread the political mood, and suffered dearly for its support for de Montfort, after whose defeat at Evesham in 1265 sixty of its leading citizens were stripped of their property. Fines were widely imposed, though many were later rescinded. After Henry's death, the aldermen were understandably scrupulous in celebrating Edward I's 1272 coronation in lavish style. At a banquet staged at Westminster Hall were consumed swans, peacocks, pike, eel and salmon, as well as sixty cattle and forty pigs. In the City, the fountains of Cheapside ran alternately with red and white wine.

A diverging metropolis

Despite this reception, Edward initiated an era in which City and monarch were frequently in conflict. He reinforced the Tower, outlawed many restrictive guild practices and inserted his own sheriffs in the Guildhall to keep order. City justice was brought within the jurisdiction of the royal courts. The king also demanded the opening of the aldermanic council to a wider constituency of middling tradesmen. He wielded his power by issuing trading licences to alien merchants, much to the City's displeasure. Then, in 1290, Edward expelled all Jews from England, forcing them to surrender their loans to the crown. With few exceptions, they did not return until Oliver Cromwell's day, almost four centuries later. The Jews were replaced in part by an inflow of Italian bankers, who gave their name to Lombard Street. Merchants of the Hanseatic League were also granted their own fortified enclave at the Steelyard on the Thames waterfront.

As was to happen periodically throughout London's history, a trauma in relations with the monarch had the effect of refreshing and updating the City's restrictive practices and galvanizing competition. The chief product underpinning the London economy, and indeed that of England, was now wool. This had traditionally passed through London to the 'staples' or markets of the continent, but these markets were being accessed by ships sailing from Hull, Boston in Lincolnshire, King's Lynn and Southampton, many sailing direct to Flanders. Permits and taxes on this trade were a royal prerogative.

The consequence was to strengthen the barter of money for power, between the City and the monarch. Edward I was a warrior king and needed money for his battles, particularly in Wales and Scotland. He summoned periodic parliaments to raise funds, giving that body a degree of leverage over him. These taxes placed the City in a position to barter rights and privileges with Westminster. As a result, throughout the fourteenth century, the three Edwards had to negotiate London's loyalty. The costly belligerence of the Plantagenets was a crucial factor in the emergence of these two countervailing centres of power in England's constitution. The monarch was not independently rich.

4

The Age of Chaucer and Whittington
1348–1485

Plague and rebellion

We have no map or image of medieval London and must construct an impression of it from later evidence. Likewise the size of its population, believed to be around 80,000, is guesswork. It was still smaller than Paris and European cities such as Amsterdam, Venice and Naples. Constantinople had over 400,000. London remained a walled settlement of mostly wood-framed buildings on brick foundations. Only the grandest houses and churches were of stone. Alleys and courtyards ran with sewage and the air was filled with noxious smells, little eased by a primitive 'night-soil' clearance. The prevalence of disease kept life expectancy low, at roughly thirty during the Middle Ages, and only constant inward immigration prevented the population from falling. London remained a place of upward social mobility, of adventure and opportunity, and although living conditions could be appalling, few Londoners starved.

From disease there was no escape. A virulent plague out of Asia arrived in Europe, probably in Genoese ships, in 1347 and was in England by the autumn of 1348. Known as the Black Death, it stayed a year before abating, returning in milder form in 1361. About a half of Londoners are thought to have died, with as many as sixty bodies a day arriving at Smithfield's plague pits alone. The ground level of churchyards rose across London. A chronicle says of the affliction that many 'who were attacked in the morning it carried out of human affairs before noon; none whom it willed to die did it permit to live longer than three or four days'. Priests called on citizens to repent their sins, and bequests poured into chantry chapels.

The consequences were drastic, though as so often in national crises, in London not lastingly so. There was an acute shortage of labour and wages rose despite laws banning their increase. It was said the masons at Westminster Abbey were doubling their pre-plague rates. Those employing carters, glove-makers, farriers and even domestic servants found them demanding 'immeasurably more than they have been wont to take' before the time of the pestilence. There was, however, a welcome relief from overcrowding.

Edward III responded to the plague by allowing provincial and alien merchants to trade within the City's jurisdiction. A debilitated City short of labour could do little other than concede. Restrictive practices were eased. Immigrant Italians, Flemings and Hanseatics might be regularly attacked by City gangs, but they were vital in assisting London's recovery. They also brought with them loans for the king's continued war in France, a venture now in disarray and unpopular with the City and provincial aristocracy alike – at least when failing to deliver victories and booty.

The City's government was now regularized. The twenty-five-man aldermanic council was selected, usually for life, from the established members of the twelve principal guilds. Though this oligarchy would develop strong personalities, family power rarely ran for long, if only because the City's business was constantly replenished with new blood – a crucial difference between an essentially sea-going commercial city and the land-based economies of continental Europe. London had no Montagues and Capulets, no Guelphs and Ghibellines, though the changing nature of guild craftsmanship produced frequent conflicts, sometimes spilling into the streets.

Below the aldermanic court was the Common Council, composed

of a hundred representatives of twenty-five wards, who over time became ever more boisterous and influential. Its members controlled entry to the freedom of the City and were the focus of guild lobbying and regulation. The Common Council did not rule the City, but it had by custom to be consulted on decisions by the aldermanic court, especially on matters of money. The lesser guilds were well 'below the salt' on banquet days, but as the City grew increasingly diverse, guild membership stretched into the poorer sections of the community. By the late fourteenth century it is believed to have embraced three-quarters of the male population.

The plague had rendered all these groups better paid, more secure and more assertive. It was inevitable that in time they would prove susceptible to popular leadership. A draper on the Common Council, John de Northampton, was a natural rabble-rouser who rose to become an alderman and mouthpiece for the lesser guilds and what amounted to the City 'mob'. Relations between the City and the crown became more vexed when Edward III died and his grandson, the ten-year-old Richard II (1377–99), ascended the throne.

Matters reached a crisis when some of Northampton's supporters took the side of Wat Tyler's peasants when they arrived in the City from Canterbury in June 1381 and ran riot in their revolt for higher wages. Three days of violence saw widespread burning of houses and monasteries, as well as the murder of those familiar targets of London hooligans, aliens. But the ward militias saw to it that Tyler's rioters found their victims mostly outside the City walls. They were told to target the Archbishop of Canterbury's Lambeth Palace, lawyers in the Temple, John of Gaunt's Savoy Palace and the Newgate and Marshalsea prisons.

When finally the rebels were met and appeased by the now teenage king, it was the mayor who killed Tyler and the City militias who rounded up his followers and sent them home. Northampton went on to become mayor himself, showing once more the City's talent in switching allegiance to back the winning horse. But the revolt was evidence of a new source of power in London, that of the popular mob. How to respond to and police that mob was to be crucial in guiding the city through troubled times to come. Westminster Abbey's portrait of Richard in 1390, looking pensive and desperately vulnerable at twenty-three, is the first of an English monarch that is possibly a likeness.

Chaucer's London

If London at the time of the Peasants' Revolt was a closed book, it was soon dramatically opened. Geoffrey Chaucer was a government official and courtier during the unsettled reigns of Edward III and Richard II. He was a diplomat, sent on missions to the continent, where he met Petrarch and Boccaccio. He rose to be MP for Kent, comptroller of customs and clerk of the king's works. He married John of Gaunt's sister-in-law, Philippa Roet. Chaucer was in every sense a member of the medieval establishment. Yet he was driven from an early age to write, and became the first English poet to create a window on the world around him in all its richness.

In describing the England of his age, Chaucer fastened on the device of a diverse group of pilgrims telling their tales as they set out from Southwark one Easter for Canterbury. *The Canterbury Tales* was written during the 1380s and left unfinished and unpublished on Chaucer's death in 1400. None of the pilgrims was either high- or low-born, rather they were the emergent middle class of late-medieval England: a knight, a lawyer, a merchant, a miller, a prioress, some thirty in total. The characterization is astonishingly vivid.

The merchant talks of little but his money and cuckolds. The Wife of Bath is an independent soul, telling of her four husbands and her interest in clothes, magic, gossip and the status of women. The knight relates how he 'spent all Monday at a joust and dance/ And the high services of Venus'. But he goes to bed early so as to be refreshed 'to witness a great fight' on the morrow. The 'revelling apprentice' in the Cook's Tale is 'as full of love and womanizing as the hive is full of honey'. He completes his apprenticeship only so his master can be rid of him, and goes off with a friend on an orgy of fornication.

These people emerge from the Tales not as caricatures, locked in a superstitious past, but of all time, funny, cynical, worldly, sceptical, socially self-conscious. The Canterbury pilgrimage is a medieval package tour to a fashionable destination. Sex is an obsession. The pilgrims seem uninhibited in attacking the mores of the day, including the church, authority and the antics of their contemporaries, young and old. They are independent-minded citizens of an open society.

London's streets were also places of constant festival and diversion. Prostitution was ubiquitous, reflected in such corners as Puppekirty (or 'poke-skirt') Lane, and even Gropecunt Lane (now sadly vanished beneath an office block off Cheapside). Chaucer's city could also turn nasty. Aliens might be feted one day and beaten the next. Of the annual Bartholomew Fair Wordsworth asked, 'What say you then/ To times when half the city shall break out/ Full of one passion – vengeance, rage, or fear –/ To executions, to a street on fire,/ Mobs, riots, or rejoicings?'

I have long sought other cities that might convey some impression of Chaucer's London. The nearest I can imagine is the squalor of 1970s Calcutta, transplanted into the physical streets of modern York. Perhaps it is more reliable to inspect the paintings of Carpaccio and his contemporaries of fifteenth-century Venice. Carpaccio's depiction of the 'Miracle of the True Cross' (in the Accademia) must be akin to such festivities in London, a crowded parade of brightly costumed young and old, rich and poor, pious and profane, above all confident and ostentatious. That surely is Chaucer's London.

Church and politics

A distinguishing feature of London at this time is the status of the church. It owned a quarter of the City and most of the suburban land, and played an important role in both parliament and local administration. It taught London's children, fed its poor and cared for its sick. However, the pope was then resident in Avignon, under the protection of the French, with whom England was supposedly at war. Londoners were thus understandably responsive to critics of church corruption and dogma, such as John Wycliffe and his Lollards. Wycliffe opposed papal hierarchy, the sale of indulgences and the extreme veneration of saints. He derided clerical indolence. Faith, said Wycliffe, was to be found solely in the Bible, a message taken up over the coming century by early voices of the Reformation, such as Jan Hus in Prague and Martin Luther in Worms.

Wycliffe's challenge to the authority of the church found a ready audience among not just ordinary citizens but also leading figures such as Chaucer and John of Gaunt. However, Lollardy did not long outlive its leader. Londoners might be open-minded, but they were not religious radicals. The crown was not enamoured of Lollardy, and the City, in a period of troubled relations with Westminster, was not inclined to contest the issue. It also had a new personality to succeed Northampton, the remarkable Richard Whittington.

The son of a Gloucestershire landowner, Whittington was a typical new Londoner. A mercer by trade and supplier to Richard II, he was mayor a most unusual four times between 1397 and 1419. His subsequent pantomime celebrity is a mystery. He was not poor and did not leave London via Highgate, let alone with a cat given to chasing Moorish rats. What Whittington did become was a crucial diplomat and a favourite of the king, to whom he lent copiously against the security of royal jewels and wool taxes. He went on to perform the same service for Henry IV and Henry V, flattering the monarchy while guarding the City's interest.

Whittington would have been among those who welcomed Henry V back to London after his victory at Agincourt in 1415. An anonymous record has Henry feted at Blackheath, then passing through a City decorated with tapestries and towers, in each niche of which 'was a beautiful girl in the posture of a statue; in their hands were golden cups from which they very lightly puffed gold leaf on the king's head as he rode by . . . Wine flowed from the channels and cocks of the conduit.' The City never skimped on style.

Whittington's later fame almost certainly rested on another City tradition, that wealth derived from its commerce should be returned to it. Lacking an heir, his benefactions were unequalled in value. He rebuilt the Guildhall, drained slums round Billingsgate and financed help for unmarried mothers at St Thomas' hospital and a college of priests. He also built a public lavatory by the river with 128 seats – known as Whittington's Longhouse – flushed regularly by the tide. Whittington Hospital in Highgate was not his, but commemorates the legend of his turning back to the City on hearing the bells of Bow church.

The withering of the Hundred Years War and its mutation into a more savage civil conflict for the crown between Yorkists and Lancastrians caused the City distress but not disaster. The City mostly supported the Yorkists, and was openly for Edward IV. But when he died in 1483 and Henry Tudor triumphed over Richard III at Bosworth Field two years later, London was content. It welcomed Henry VII at Shoreditch with a procession of trumpeters, poets and a gift of a thousand marks. It was now a Tudor city.

Epitaph on a medieval city

The mayor and aldermen who greeted Henry VII after Bosworth represented a city still on the fringes of a new Europe, one of Renaissance and religious Reformation. Its population slowly recovered from the Black Death – regaining its pre-plague total at the end of the century – but did not compare with Paris, still four times its size. Its trade depended heavily on wool, and its labour supply on migrants from provincial England. Studies of names and dialects at the time suggest that Londoners still spoke an East Anglian version of Anglo-Saxon until well into the fourteenth century, but then shifted to the 'east Midlands' dialect. Records suggest that, after the plague, a quarter of those admitted to the freedom of the City came from Yorkshire and points north.

In the economy of Europe, London was still an outlier. In matters of trade, it was junior partner to Antwerp. The latter's buildings were more magnificent, its merchants wealthier and its seafarers more adventurous. Unlike Venice, England had no trading outposts. Pre-Columbian rumours of transatlantic voyages make reference to 'lands the Bristol captains know' but not those of London. Antwerp printed more books in English than did London. England could boast Thomas More and play host to Erasmus, but it had no painter to match Dürer or Cranach, no architects to match Brunelleschi or Bramante. While Florence was revelling in the architecture of the Renaissance, London's was displaying the final flourish of medieval gothic, the Perpendicular style. Henry VII's chapel at Westminster, built in 1503 and designed by an unknown hand, remains a masterpiece of European architecture, but it was far from the European mainstream.

London did, however, possess two ingredients that were to be essential for its long-term growth. It had abundant land beyond its walls, and it had political stability to allow the exploitation of that land. Unlike cities on the continent, it was free from the threat of siege. Walls built by the Romans, reinforced by Alfred and patched up thereafter, were largely administrative. Citizens with money could escape London's cramped and noisome streets to colonize the countryside round about. Nor did commercial power exist cheek-by-jowl with political power. Each estate of the realm had its own geography. London's history is at root the history of its land.

While the City might enjoy independence under royal charters going back to the Conquest, Westminster was virtually beyond any jurisdiction. Its population was no more than 3,000 in the fifteenth century, consisting almost entirely of crown servants and clerics. Only when parliaments were summoned, usually when the king needed money, was the enclave flooded with peers, bishops, MPs and their retinues, clamouring for inns and supplies. The old abbey, which owned and thus administered two-thirds of Westminster's land, grew rich on the proceeds. As the court expanded, many services were unsure where to set up business. In 1476 William Caxton established his celebrated press near Westminster Abbey, to be near the headquarters of the church and away from the guild restrictions of the City printers. Other publishers moved to the vicinity of another church, St Paul's, where they stayed until the Blitz.

As far back as the twelfth century, Thomas Becket's secretary, William Fitzstephen, had noted that 'almost all the bishops, abbots and magnates' occupied what were later to be over thirty mansions or so-called inns along the banks of the Thames. London's river became a grand avenue of dignitaries, easier of access than the crowded streets behind. The monarch was at Westminster. The archbishops of Canterbury and York had their respective palaces at Lambeth and York Place (later Whitehall). The Bishop of Winchester was also over the river in Southwark.

Along the Strand were the mansions of the bishops of Durham,

Carlyle, Worcester, Salisbury, and Bath and Wells. Only a strip of land next to York Place was doggedly retained by a commoner, Adam Scot, later to be called 'Scotsland' and eventually Scotland Yard (which had nothing to do with Scotland). Immediately west of the Fleet river was a neighbourhood of inns for lawyers, conveniently between the City and the courts at Westminster. Some of these inns grew in size to acquire quadrangles and halls in the manner of Oxford colleges, of which four, the Inner and Outer Temples, Lincoln's Inn and Gray's Inn remain today.

To the east of the City was the hospital of St Katharine, with next door the forgotten abbey of 'Eastminster', founded by Edward III in 1350 in gratitude for his rescue from a storm at sea. It never rivalled Westminster and was later supplanted by the Royal Mint. On the south side of the river east of Southwark spread the extensive once-Benedictine abbey of Bermondsey, its foundation recorded as being in the eighth century. Round these institutions grew up shanty towns of brewers, slaughterers, tanners, lime- and tile-makers, and the ever expanding business of the sea. Shipbuilders and suppliers stretched from Wapping towards Shadwell, their rigging fashioned in Cable Street. The divide between London's rich and poor districts was becoming entrenched, and was only to deepen.

Henry VII (1485–1509) initiated the Tudor dynasty. Eager to establish its European status, he married his son Arthur to Catherine of Aragon, daughter of Ferdinand and Isabella of Spain, and thus brought the English royal family within the penumbra of the Holy Roman Empire. When Arthur died young – the king was so distressed he did not attend the funeral – the succession passed to his brother, who became Henry VIII and promptly married his brother's widow. Theirs was initially a happy partnership, but Catherine's failure to bear a son would lead to the greatest upheaval in London's history since the Norman conquest.

5

Tudor London
1485–1603

Reformation capital

The opening years of Henry VIII's reign were prosperous and peaceful. He married Catherine a fortnight before his coronation in June 1509, and they lived extravagantly on the full treasury left by Henry's father. The young king was an athlete and a scholar, fully engaged with the religious controversies now consuming much of the European church. The queen was intelligent and active, having served as Spanish ambassador to London. A happy window on the city was offered by a fellow ambassador, the Scottish poet William Dunbar, who wrote home in 1501: 'London, thou art the flower of Cities all . . ./ Strong be thy walls that about thee stand . . . / Blythe be thy churches, well sounding be thy bells;/ Rich be thy merchants in substance that excels;/ Fair be their wives, right lovesome, white and small.' Dunbar clearly regarded London as a good posting.

Early in the king's reign the affairs of state were mostly left to an ambitious royal counsellor, Thomas Wolsey, Archbishop of York and later Cardinal. But as Wolsey schooled Henry in statecraft, the young king's ambitions were stirred and his reach became greater than his grasp. He was drawn to the old bugbear of English kings, war with France. Two campaigns in 1512 and 1513, aimed at securing for Henry the former English possession of Aquitaine, were unsuccessful. They led to desultory diplomacy against France by

Wolsey, in league with the Holy Roman Empire of Charles V, nephew of Henry's consort. In 1520 Henry attempted reconciliation with France's monarch, Francis I, at a most sensational display of kingly vanity, the Field of the Cloth of Gold outside Calais, attended by 6,000 retainers. To enhance his status, he demanded he be addressed in future no longer as 'your grace' but as 'your majesty', a title retained by the royal family ever since.

Despite the preaching of Wycliffe a century earlier, London had been a bystander in the early surging of Reformation in northern Europe. Henry had been a loyal Catholic, standing aloof from the emerging Protestantism. When Luther declared his defection from Rome at Wittenberg in 1517, Henry took the pope's cause against him, and was rewarded by Rome with the title Defender of the Faith, which bizarrely still adorns British coins as Fid Def. The Lord Chancellor, Sir Thomas More, persecuted Protestants and burned them at the stake. William Tyndale had to flee to Germany to undertake his Bible translation, published in Germany and Antwerp in 1525. When a copy was smuggled into England it was burned and he was condemned as a heretic.

Yet all Henry's faith could not withstand his overriding obsession with his lack of a son, compounded by his affair with Anne Boleyn, begun in 1526, and his need for a divorce from Catherine. The last required permission from the pope, but since he was currently a virtual prisoner of Charles V, Catherine's nephew, it was refused. England's breach with Rome was thus initially not theological but personal and institutional. The Act of Supremacy of 1534 put Henry at the head of the church in England, 'recognizing no superior on earth but only God'. Thomas More, adamantly opposed to the legislation, was executed a year later – and canonized by Rome. London became a Protestant city almost by accident, but Protestant it most emphatically was.

Dissolution of the monasteries

Henry now proceeded with the consequences of his decision, and they were much to his – and the City's – advantage. By 1536 Henry and his new chancellor, Thomas Cromwell, had dissolved all abbeys, priories and monasteries and ejected their monks and nuns. Both the land and the wealth of 800–900 institutions nationwide were seized, with the king pocketing the proceeds or distributing them to courtiers and supporters. Historians have calculated that, by the early sixteenth century, as much as a third of property in the City and almost all of Westminster was in the hands of religious organizations. Dissolution included thirty-nine religious houses in London, of which twenty-three were within the City. The most determined resistance was from the monks of the Charterhouse, eighteen of whom were eventually executed for defying the king. They were duly made saints by the Catholic church.

Almost overnight, the City and its surrounding land saw a transfer of ownership and wealth on a scale not witnessed even during the Norman conquest. While much of this wealth outside London passed directly to the king's treasury, property in and around the City passed to aristocrats, merchants and cronies of the monarch. The king took Wolsey's York Place on the river – he had already taken his Hampton Court – with the intention of building there a new Whitehall palace. The inns of the bishops of Chester and Worcester were demolished for the king's later brother-in-law Edward Seymour, later the Duke of Somerset, and Somerset House arose in their place. The inn of the Bishop of Bath and Wells went to the Duke of Norfolk, of Carlyle at the old convent garden to the Earl of Bedford and of Salisbury to the Earl of Dorset. The abbots of Glastonbury, Lewes, Malmesbury, Peterborough and Cirencester all lost their London houses. Holy Trinity Priory at Aldgate went to the Lord Chancellor, Thomas Audley. The great abbey of Bermondsey, seven centuries old, was demolished and saw three owners in thirty years.

For the City the dissolution presented both an opportunity and a crisis. While poor relief was strictly a parish responsibility, the monasteries had dispensed extensive charity in the fields of education, sickness, disability and destitution. Deputations from the City pleaded with the king that, whatever he did to the monasteries, he should leave their charities alone, or at least give them to the City. Otherwise 'the poor, sick, blind, aged and impotent . . . were lying in the street, offending every clean person passing by with their filthy and nasty savours'.

To this the king mostly acceded. In 1547 Christ's Hospital became a charity for orphans and the Charterhouse eventually became an almshouse, as it remains today. St Thomas' and St Bartholomew's continued as hospitals, which is why Henry's statue curiously adorns Bart's gatehouse in Smithfield. When the latter's priory was transferred to the City, the expected care home for a hundred paupers turned out to be derelict, with 'three or four harlots then lying in childbed'. Bridewell was built by Henry as a royal palace, but was later given to the City as a refuge for vagrant youths and petty crooks, a primitive workhouse. Schools sprang up to replace monastic ones. That at St Paul's was reopened in 1510. The Mercers founded a school in 1541 and the Merchant Taylors in 1561. Christ's Hospital and Charterhouse later added schools to their existing charities.

Of more lasting importance was Henry's seizure of church lands to add to his London hunting estate. Present-day Green Park, St James's Park, Hyde Park, Kensington Gardens and Regent's Park were acquired – and saved – in this way. Given the rapacious nature of subsequent property development, it is very possible that London would have had no central parks had it not been for Anne Boleyn and her husband's love of hunting. Even now, central London has less open space than any comparable European capital.

A city paved with gold

On the deaths of Henry and of his short-lived son, Edward VI, London sat out the counter-reformation of his Catholic daughter Mary (1553–58). There was always a strongly Catholic section of the City's population, as there was a determined Protestant one. In 1554 apprentices hurled snowballs at the Catholic Philip II of Spain's entourage when he came to marry Mary, and incidentally claim the throne of England. Yet there was no uprising when 300 Protestants were burned on Tower Hill on Mary's instructions. In matters of faith, London's longstanding open door seemed to have bred tolerance even of intolerance. After Mary's death, the *Book of Martyrs* by the Protestant historian John Foxe became the best-selling volume of the age after the Bible.

The coronation of Elizabeth I (1558–1603) brought London a hesitant stability. The queen's chief counsellor, Lord Burghley, was a master diplomat in handling relations between the City and the crown, aided by his mistress's admirably frugal lifestyle. Meanwhile, the City property market continued to digest Henry's dissolution. The Venetian ambassador reported that it was 'much disfigured by the ruins of a multitude of churches and monasteries, belonging heretofore to friars and nuns'. Another recorded that 'by reason of the late dissolution of religious houses, many houses stood vacant, and not any man desirous to take them'. The market was like a reservoir half emptied of water and taking time to refill. After the dissolution around 60,000 people were living in the City itself, out of a (greater) London population of some 100,000. By 1600 the occupation of monastic property saw the City rise to 100,000, with London overall at 180,000. The City still had the majority, but only just.

London during Elizabeth's reign was increasingly conditioned by events abroad. In 1572 France's Catherine of Medici precipitated the St Bartholomew's Day massacre of Protestants, sending thousands of Huguenots (French Protestants) fleeing to London for refuge. They were mostly skilled craftsmen and traders, swiftly assimilated into the city economy. Four years later, Spain's imposition of a Catholic inquisition on Flanders led to the sacking of Antwerp in a 'Spanish fury' and the killing of 7,000 of its citizens. Antwerp had long been London's commercial partner and rival, and again the beneficiary of a Catholic persecution was London. A decade later, the city's image of robust independence was reinforced by the failure of Philip II's Spanish Armada in 1588, and the end of his attempt to bring England under the papacy.

These continental developments steered English foreign policy in new directions, towards the New World so far seen as the preserve of Spain, Portugal and the Netherlands. While Elizabeth's rivals sought to impose their beliefs on other Europeans, her ships set their sails to the winds of trade. Francis Drake had circumnavigated the world in 1577–80 and claimed California for the English crown. He and his fellow mariners were encouraged to pursue every opportunity for exploration and profit, a pursuit which after the Armada degenerated into little short of piracy. Philip put a bounty of £6 million in today's money on Drake's head. Under Elizabeth, England took its first steps from offshore island to overseas empire, while the ever cautious Burghley pleaded in vain for the return of stolen loot to Spain.

Typical of a City merchant ready for such opportunities was Richard Gresham, a mercer from Norfolk, who by the age of twenty-five was already lending money to Henry VIII. He became an alderman, mayor and MP. At the dissolution, Gresham was entrusted with the negotiations mentioned above to secure the priory hospitals for the City. His son, Sir Thomas Gresham, became crown agent and ambassador in Antwerp. He exceeded his father in wealth and was a financial manipulator without scruple, regarded even in his day as a swindler and debaser of currency. Despite this, all four Tudors – Henry, Edward, Mary and Elizabeth – relied on him to manage their loans.

Gresham oversaw a crucial moment in London's development, its succession to Antwerp as commercial hub of northern Europe. He was against the City's xenophobia, pleading with the queen to admit Flemish refugees from Spanish persecution, as it would 'much profitte the citie'. Gresham proposed a London bourse to outdo Antwerp's. Designed by Flemish architects and using Flemish stone and glass, the Royal Exchange opened in 1571, topped by the Gresham family emblem of a grasshopper. The exchange, with its covered colonnade, was London's first civic building in a Renaissance style. Its arcades could accommodate 4,000 merchants and included 160 lock-up stalls.

Gresham was the first in a line of talented money managers gradually to cement London's position as Europe's premier financial centre. Elizabeth referred to him as a 'necessary evil', and was happy to visit him at his Middlesex seat of Osterley. Once at supper she was said to have remarked how much better the courtyard would look with a wall across it. By morning, one had appeared. It was declared proof, not of Gresham's love of his queen, but of his claim that 'money commands all things'. He founded a college, Gresham's College, a rival to Oxford and Cambridge and later a model for the Royal Society. On his death in 1579 the college was based at his Bishopsgate mansion. It now lives on in lectures at Barnard's Inn Hall in Holborn.

The City was by now taking its first steps from being a trader of produce to being a purveyor of credit, in effect a buyer and seller of money. Credit was based on trust, on faith in the honouring of debts, and this involved a network of men who knew and could depend on each other. Crucial to this was the City's stable political structure, contrasted with the ever-changing personality of the monarchy upriver – and beyond its boundaries. At its apex was not a single figure but two dozen aldermen, reinforced by kinship and life tenure. But though a clique, they were an open clique, constantly refreshed by ambitious young men from the provinces such as Whittington and Gresham.

Throughout the turbulent sixteenth century, London could well have become a hotbed of dissent and revolt. Yet even during the Henrician Reformation and the Marian counter-reformation, it drew back. As the social historian Roy Porter wrote, 'The absence of grass-roots rebellion suggests that, though run by the rich, City institutions were seen not as alien and despotic but as, in some measure, responsible and responsive.' Above all, 'London was conspicuously governed by Londoners.' In other words, the first shoots of a sort of democracy were as critical for making money as for political stability.

First glimpse of a metropolis

In 1550 there appeared the first authentic view of London, sketched over seven sheets by a Flemish eye-witness, Anthonis van den Wyngaerde, a specialist in European panoramas. Based on his walks through the capital's streets, he depicted the city in an arc from Westminster Abbey round to the distant towers of Greenwich, as viewed from a 'bird's eye' over Southwark. This was soon followed by the first true map, a 'copperplate' made anonymously and printed in Antwerp in 1559. It was used as the source for a new map published by Frans Hogenberg in 1574, and is thought to have been the basis for the well-known 'Woodcut' map of London by Ralph Agas and others well into the seventeenth century. They are replicated in an imaging of Tudor London by means of a digital fly-through by De Montfort University, a brilliant evocation of a medieval city.

These works show London as it was between the dissolution and the start of the Stuart era. The horizon is still dominated by churches, with St Paul's towering over them. The architecture is virtually untouched by the Renaissance. Mansions have gothic facades while streets are lined with oversailed and gabled houses. There is none of the formal planning, the straight streets, ornamental gardens and classical facades appearing in Rome and Paris at the time. Only Cheapside is clearly recognizable as a thoroughfare. London Bridge features strongly, still with its ghoulish row of traitor's heads on sticks.

Beyond the city walls, the built-up area is chiefly confined to Southwark – brought within the City's jurisdiction after 1550 – and the districts of Farringdon, Clerkenwell and Holborn. Beyond is open country. Cows stroll down Borough High Street while archers practise in the fields of Finsbury, surrounded by market gardens. To the west, Lambeth Palace is set amid farmland; to the east, the river winds past scattered bankside settlements to reach the gothic towers of the royal palace of Placentia at Greenwich. Here both Henry VIII and Elizabeth were born and spent their summers.

As is apparent from Wyngaerde and Hogenberg, apart from Westminster Abbey and St Paul's, sixteenth-century London had few of the adornments of a great capital. It would not have impressed a well-travelled foreigner. There was no royal estate set about with avenues and ornate facades. Henry VIII had built Nonsuch Palace at Ewell in Surrey, an attempt to imitate Francis's Fontainebleau, but it was far out of town and it decayed and was eventually demolished. Elizabeth built no new palace, content with Whitehall, Greenwich and Richmond. Her creativity went into extravagant make-up and costumes. She left it to her courtiers to spend their money – much of it formerly monastic – on 'prodigy houses' in the English Renaissance style, notably those by Robert Smythson at Hardwick, Wollaton and Longleat. Elizabeth merely invited herself to stay, costing her nothing but crippling her hosts with expense.

London's strongest suit was literature. Here the Renaissance came to roost in the poetry of Edmund Spenser, the plays of Christopher Marlowe and Ben Jonson and, above all, the writings of William Shakespeare, whose poems were as celebrated in his lifetime as his plays. But, unlike books, plays needed theatres, and these were disliked by the City authorities for their rowdy crowds and general disturbance. According to one bid to have them suppressed they were 'nothing but profane fables, lascivious matters, cozening devices and scurrilous behaviours'. The City banned theatres from its jurisdiction and petitioned for their suppression, forcing them outside it walls, notably to the liberty beyond the ward boundary of Southwark, alongside the Thames. An exception was a company of royal choristers based at Blackfriars, notorious for kidnapping boys for training.

A joiner, James Burbage, built the first wooden theatre in Finsbury Fields in Shoreditch in 1576, calling it The Theatre. This was followed by the adjacent Curtain and by Philip Henslowe's Rose in Southwark in 1587, where bull- and bear-baiting pits were already established. The Rose was recorded as staging some 300 performances of thirty-six plays in the single year of 1595. Burbage's company had tried to move from Shoreditch to Blackfriars in 1596, but was forced to close. He moved his building, stick by stick, to Southwark and reopened it as the Globe in 1599. This became home to Shakespeare's company, the Lord Chamberlain's Men, and Burbage's son Richard became the star of Shakespeare's productions. Both theatres, in keen competition, proved highly vulnerable to fires and were often rebuilt.

The theatre was a popular as well as a literary phenomenon. Even the relatively poor could afford the few pence admission. The playwright Thomas Dekker was careful to applaud both his rich patrons and the 'groundling and gallery-commoner' on whom his income depended. They embraced carters and porters, papists and Puritans, gallants and prostitutes, with frequent fights between them all. Shows included bear-baiting, circus acts and displays of freaks. The theatre was a place not just of entertainment but also of social mixing, its writers, promoters and performers a bridge between aristocracy, gentry and the crowd. Perhaps as a result, the Privy Council was nervous about regulating or censoring it. Eventually Southwark declined, as the more liberal Stuarts welcomed drama to the court and Westminster. But 'south of the river' merits a salute, home for a while to London's indiscipline, recreation and genius.

John Stow's City

By the end of Elizabeth's reign it was estimated that half the wealthiest Londoners were living outside the walls. Some were to the north in Finsbury but most were in Farringdon to the west. A hundred and twenty-one were listed as having 'country seats', in effect second homes. Largely through the dissolution and dispersal of ecclesiastical wealth, London was acquiring a middle class, independent of both the court and the church. The visiting Duke of Württemberg wrote home that Londoners 'are magnificently apparelled and are extremely proud and overbearing, and because the greater part, especially trades people, seldom go into other countries, but always remain in their houses in the city attending to their business, they care little for foreigners, but scoff and laugh at them'. As for London's womenfolk, they 'have much more liberty than perhaps in any place. They also know well how to make use of it, for they go dressed out in exceedingly fine clothes and give all their attention to ruffs and stuffs.'

The first detailed survey of the metropolis, ward by ward and street by street, came from the antiquarian John Stow in 1598. He ventured into what were now the City's suburbs, north, south, east and west. He found new buildings obliterating open spaces, and alleys 'pestered with small tenements and homely cottages . . . by men that more regard their own private gain than the common good of the city'. Times to Stow were never what they used to be. His London was 'the most scoffing, respectless and unthankful age that ever was'. Its growth had to stop if it was to remain a habitable metropolis, a litany of woe that would echo throughout London's subsequent history.

Stow saw migrants everywhere. 'The gentlemen of all shires do fly and flock to this city, the younger sort of them to see and show vanity, the elder . . . to find a quick and ready market.' Even the traffic evokes a moan. 'The world runs on wheels, with many whose parents were glad to go on foot.' Stow was London's first urban economist. He could see that a rising population in the capital would induce 'the loss and decay of many or most of the ancient cities and towns and markets within this realm'. London was damaging trade in the provinces, and he proposed that some trades be forcibly dispersed to other towns.

Yet even Stow had to acknowledge that nothing could counter the pull of the monarch's court, 'which is nowadays much more numerous and gallant than in ancient times'. When the Earl of Salisbury came to town, he would bring with him 'a hundred men on horses'. It was said that Stow's 'only pains and care was to write truth'. Pleas towards the end of his life to Elizabeth's successor, James I, for a pension produced only a permit to 'seek voluntary contribution and kind gratuity from his subjects'. In other words,

Stow could beg. His memorial in St Andrew Undershaft has him holding a quill, which whenever it disintegrates is carefully replaced. The reporter's pen shall never die.

The dawn of planning

Tudor London tried and mostly failed to replace the welfare functions that had been supplied, if half-heartedly, by the monasteries. A few civic hospitals and some parochial charities were not enough for an ever rising population. Some remedial, if ruthless, action was taken. Vagrants, including abandoned children, were regularly rounded up and put in the Bridewell hostel, from where some were deported to Virginia. Then, in 1576, a first compulsory local 'rate' for the poor was ordered to be levied by what were now over a hundred City parishes. This first step towards civic welfare placed formal responsibility on parishes for their sick and destitute, a burden the new rate could not possibly bear.

In 1580 came London's first serious attempt at planning control. Elizabeth issued a proclamation against any further construction within three miles of the City gates, an early green belt. It forbade subletting or 'suffering any more families than one only to be placed, or to inhabit from henceforth, in any house'. There were also orders against new building deep into Middlesex. Despite the most draconian punishments, these edicts were ineffective. They increased overcrowding wherever an owner thought profit outbid the risk of prosecution.

Soon the authorities capitulated, and multi-occupancy was allowed on payment to the crown of a 'subsidy'. Government was thus given a vested interest in breaching its own regulations. Elizabeth was no more ready to confront this conflict than any of her successors – down to the present day. At the end of her reign, she complained that 'notwithstanding her gracious and princely commandment . . . yet it falleth out, by the covetous and insatiable dispositions of some persons, who without any respect of the common good and public profit of the realm, do only regard their own particular lucre'. The queen attacked the negligence of her own officers who 'ought to see the said proclamation duly performed'.

By the 1590s, partly as a result of the damage to trade by the Spanish wars, London was suffering economic recession. Landlords who had acquired former monastic sites had mostly not made them mansions for the rich, but had crammed them with tenements for poorer citizens. Provincial newcomers had driven down wages but they, along with harvest failures, had sent food prices soaring. They rose 40 per cent in Elizabeth's last decade and, for the first time in living memory, London experienced food riots. In the dying years of Tudor London, a new reality began to dawn. As Stow warned, a free market in people and property exerted a pressure to expand the city that not even the monarch had the power to resist. Government might propose, but London's property market would dispose.

6

Stuarts and Rebellion
1603–1660

Divine bureaucracy

The arrival in London from Scotland of James I (1603–25) offered liberation from the Puritan ethos of Elizabeth's declining years. Despite his traumatic upbringing – his father murdered and his mother, Mary Queen of Scots, executed – James was a scholarly, stylish and innovative monarch. Author of a number of books on theology and philosophy, he sponsored a new translation of the Bible, the King James version, and welcomed Shakespeare's players into his court. They became the King's Men, and opened a second theatre at Blackfriars.

James's arrival, and his specific ideas on kingship, initiated a new concept of a capital city. Elizabeth's monarchy had been medieval and personal, based on her physical presence on constant tour through her realm – at least its safer southern half. Day-to-day authority was exercised in London by her Privy Council and elsewhere by plenipotentiary magnates. When in London, her government as such comprised no more than a thousand officials, including those of the exchequer and the courts.

Under James, the metropolis grew, not only absolutely but relative to the rest of the country. Over the course of the sixteenth and seventeenth centuries, it was to rise from the fifth or sixth largest city in Europe to second after Constantinople. In 1500 it had been three times the size of its nearest English rivals, Norwich and Bristol.

Under the Stuarts it became at least ten times larger, until by 1680 two out of every three English town-dwellers lived in London.

The scale of this growth has puzzled historians. It could no longer be attributed purely to the City's trading economy and must have been due to the new responsibilities attaching to its status as capital of England and home of its administration. The king saw monarchy as not just divinely ordained, but as standing at the apex of a creative bureaucracy. He roughly doubled the London civil service, attracting lawyers, contractors, place-seekers, supplicants and sycophants, all eager to attend on the king. These people had to be housed, fed, served and entertained. London was flooded with Porter's cast list: chaplains, physicians, tutors, musicians, painters, notaries, scriveners, secretaries, ushers, heralds, minstrels, jewellers, book-sellers, peruke-makers, grooms and engravers.

For this new population London at least had space. The chief brake on migration into most European cities was the awfulness of living in them. In London the City was no exception. One house in Dowgate ward was found to contain eleven married couples and fifteen single persons. Another in Silver Street had ten families in ten rooms, most also with lodgers. None had sewers, refuse of all sorts being simply tipped into the street, hoping for the night-soil collectors to gather it. What was different in London was that those with money could escape, at least to points north and west. And westwards lay the magnet of regality, the seduction of court life. Where money migrated, so did money's acolytes.

A better place to live

In 1615 James appointed a young Welshman named Inigo Jones as Surveyor of the King's Works. Jones had travelled to Italy, there acquiring a taste not for the eccentricities of Mannerism and baroque, but for a reversion to the classicism of Serlio and Palladio. Royal patronage set aside the Elizabethan Renaissance and adopted Italian Palladianism. The result was two buildings in that style: the Queen's House in Greenwich (1616) for James's wife, Anne of Denmark, and a new Banqueting House for Whitehall Palace, completed in 1619. Miraculously, both are still standing, their revolutionary presence camouflaged by the buildings round them, designed in the classical style for which they had supplied the original inspiration.

Less restrained were James's excursions into male fashion. The Stuart court saw an outbreak of competitive dandyism, in the bizarre costumes depicted in portraits by William Larkin and Daniel Mytens. The sensational full-length paintings of courtiers by Larkin, now in Kenwood House, might have been ripped from a Jacobean *Vogue*. The extravagance was prodigious. In five years, the king was reported to have bought 180 suits and 2,000 pairs of gloves. To show them off, he opened Hyde Park to the public as a place of promenade for himself and his court.

Despite doing his best to fuel the attractions of London life, James was soon converted to Elizabeth's desire to curb it. A hundred peers (two-thirds of the total) were now estimated to be living much of the year 'in town', and James warned against 'the swarms of gentry who, through the instigation of their wives and to new-model and fashion their daughters . . . did neglect their country hospitality'. They 'cumber the city, a general nuisance'. A single meeting of parliament – usually to raise funds for the king's expenditures – was calculated to bring 1,800 people to Westminster. It became a suburb of inns.

The king was adamant that 'our City of London is become next the greatest in the Christian world, and it is more than time that there be an utter cessation of new building'. An edict of 1625 restraining growth stipulated that unlicensed new houses be demolished up to five miles from the City gates, and their builders jailed. This could apply as long as seven years after construction. Their materials should be sold to benefit the poor. Alternatively, paupers could inhabit any house left unoccupied for five years – a policy of killing two birds with one stone that merits revival. The king also extended his patronage to public works. Smithfield market was to be paved and Moorfields laid out as gardens. Water conduits were constructed, fountains set up and hospitals restored. As for any new building, it was 'by final and peremptory commandment' to stop. There was no mention of reducing court extravagance.

Countervailing these measures was James's descent into debt. He was soon attracted to the same 'subsidies' as had undermined Elizabeth's policy. Payments for licences were now called 'fines'. A lengthening queue of landowners proved eager to pay them, mostly men who had come into church property on the dissolution. They were ready to profit from provincial courtiers and wealthy Londoners desperate to escape what one contemporary, William Petty, called the 'fumes, steams and stinks of the whole easterly pyle', the City.

First off the mark was the Earl of Salisbury, awarded a licence in 1609 to develop his land round St Martin's Lane, north of the present Trafalgar Square. No sooner were houses built than the king was complaining of sewage flowing downhill into his palace at Whitehall. Salisbury family names are recalled in today's Cecil Court and Cranbourn Street. Salisbury also built shops along the Strand, modelled on Gresham's Exchange in the City. It swiftly became the Bond Street of its day.

An aesthetic crown

James's fiscal extravagance was inherited by his son, Charles I (1625–49) and was to blight what soon became a disastrous reign. A now strongly Protestant London did not warm to his Catholic wife, Henrietta Maria of France. She arrived for her coronation in 1626 at the age of fifteen, with a retinue of two hundred priests and retainers and with trunks laden with diamonds, pearls and embroidered dresses, carried by caparisoned horses. She processed at once to Tyburn to pray for the souls of Catholic martyrs executed by the Tudors.

Charles's relations with parliament primarily over money became ever more difficult, culminating in 1628 in the Petition of Right and parliament denying the king funds for more than a year. Charles in turn attempted to levy his own tax, ship money, which proved uncollectable. The resulting 'tyranny' was to last until the crisis of 1640.

Throughout this period of mounting political tension, London prospered. Following Salisbury's development above St Martin-in-the-Fields, the Earl of Bedford in 1630 sought a licence to build houses on adjacent land, site of the former convent garden north of the Strand. The Privy Council had required him to pave and maintain the lane known as Long Acre to its north, which Bedford thought unfair unless he could build houses to compensate. He was no friend of the king, being a champion of the Petition of Right, and he gained building permission only after an exorbitant payment of £2,000 (£250,000 today). The permission included a requirement that Bedford build a new church and a square, and both had to be designed by Inigo Jones, the king's surveyor. Of the church, an angry Bedford reputedly told Jones that he 'would not have it much better than a barn'. Jones retorted it would be 'the handsomest barn in England'.

The faintly barn-like facade now fills the west side of Covent Garden piazza, which was designed on the classical lines of Paris's Place des Vosges. Bedford dutifully named the surrounding streets after his and the king's family, hence Russell Street, James Street, King Street and even Henrietta Street. The earl sought more profit by letting out the square itself, not as a public amenity but as a fruit and vegetable market. This severely detracted from the estate's value, and it soon became a red-light district. The market survived into the 1970s.

Next forward in 1638 was a builder, William Newton, who bought land in the fields west of Lincoln's Inn. The Lincoln's Inn benchers were furious, in 1643 securing a halt on the grounds that the building was purely for Newton's 'own private lucre'. The king's court of the Star Chamber, effectively his cabinet, gave permission, but as with Bedford only on condition that the designer was Jones and a portion of the fields be left open, to 'frustrate the covetous and greedy endeavours of such persons as daily seek to fill up that small remainder of air in those parts with unnecessary and unprofitable buildings'.

In these cases, the view of the Star Chamber was clear and enlightened. The development of the West End was not to imitate the City. The permit for Covent Garden stipulated layout, designer and church. That for Lincoln's Inn Fields was equally clear, that London should be protected from developers, and 'unnecessary and unprofitable' building be stopped – unprofitable to the community, that is. Building, in other words, would be required to meet some concept of public benefit, in architectural quality and amenity. This set a standard that was later reflected in the conduct of the great London estates and in successive building regulations. Numbers 59–60 Lincoln's Inn Field, presumably by Jones, still survive and the fields are an early triumph for London planning. The Stuarts were remarkable in their feel for the city they ruled.

Charles left London another lasting legacy. He was an exceptional patron of art, amassing unquestionably the finest collection of paintings in the history of the crown, and employing as his court painter Anthony van Dyck, an outstanding pupil of Rubens. Royal palaces were now filled with works by Dürer, Leonardo, Mantegna, Holbein, Titian, Tintoretto and Rubens. While they were a target for dispersal under Cromwell, those sold were mostly recovered at the Restoration, to form the core of the present royal collection.

In 1647 a gifted Bohemian artist, Wenceslaus Hollar, arrived in London to escape the Thirty Years War (1618–48). He drew a series of sketches of the city from the tower of Southwark priory church (now cathedral), which he worked into a tableau, first published the same year. It depicts a metropolis much altered from that of Wyngaerde a century before. The old City is now enveloped by suburbs, notably a much-expanded Southwark in the foreground. Westminster is dominated by St Stephen's Chapel, the Great Hall and the Abbey, still with fields beyond. But the focus of a new London is clearly moving west. Hollar's is the last reasonably accurate view we have of old London before the Great Fire of 1666.

The Civil War

The crown under the Stuarts had co-existed uneasily with the City. When parliament refused the monarch money, the City stepped in with loans. The monarch reciprocated by showering honours on its leaders, and by respecting its autonomy. This bargain began to erode under Charles. Initially, the City's aldermanic leadership favoured a stable crown, understandably since the crown usually owed it money. The City was also host to a persistent pro-Catholic and therefore pro-Charles undercurrent. But such leadership was adrift of opinion on the Common Council, which was strongly opposed to the king's autocratic counsellor, Thomas Wentworth, 1st Earl of Strafford. A new parliament in 1640 – to become the Long Parliament – presented Charles with a Grand Remonstrance, re-asserting the 1628 Petition of Right. Among other failings, it protested against the crown's abuse of London building licences, expressed as 'the sale of pretended nuisances', as being in practice taxation beyond parliament's control. Charles rejected the remonstrance, and relations between king and both the City and parliament deteriorated. London in the winter of 1640 saw the re-emergence of street politics – including of the so-called 'mob' – barely experienced since the Peasants' Revolt. The Common Council, not the aldermen, became the voice of London.

As the crisis mounted during 1641, crowds would regularly march across London to Westminster, to heckle and harangue parliament and harass its members, and even the royal family, in the street. The 'December days' of that year brought the people of London the closest they had ever come to open revolt. A crowd of apprentices and labourers, fired up by Puritan preachers, presented a petition at Westminster demanding that bishops be excluded from parliament. The crowd attacked the Archbishop of Canterbury and occupied Westminster Abbey, destroying 'popist' relics.

A week later Charles tried and failed to arrest five MPs on grounds of treason. The MPs took refuge, significantly, in the Guildhall in the City. The king followed them there, but was 'frighted by the burghers'. A pro-royalist lord mayor was imprisoned in the Tower. As the king fled to Windsor, the City did what it had not done since the days of Henry III, and sided formally with forces in opposition to the monarch. The City contributed to parliament's army against the king, and the two were united in open rebellion. England was at civil war.

London in 1642 saw something unwitnessed since ancient times: its citizens preparing for a siege. With news of a royal army marching on the capital, an anonymous contemporary wrote that 'each day Londoners marched out with shovels and banners, tailors and watermen alongside gentlemen vintners and lawyers . . . from ladies down to oyster wenches, laboured the pioneers in the trenches.' Within weeks, eighteen miles of earth ramparts and trenches encircled the city, dotted with twenty-four forts. The ramparts passed north round the City from the Tower, through Holborn and modern Oxford Street and down across the present Hyde Park Corner and Victoria to Westminster Abbey. One fort is recalled in Mayfair's Mount Street, named after 'Oliver's Mount'.

The Civil War was a desperate and often desultory affair. At first London's militia, the 'trained bands' drawn from the City's wards, formed the core of the parliamentary army. In 1643, after the indecisive Battle of Newbury, the City's troops returned home to be greeted by the mayor and aldermen at Temple Bar in Fleet Street, who 'entertained us joyfully, many thousands bidding us welcome home and blessing God for . . . delivering us from the rage and insolence of our adversaries'. But by the end of 1643, with royalist forces no longer threatening London, the City's soldiers were unreliable and prone to desert. London sentiment turned so against the war that parliament had to rely on Oliver Cromwell's quasi-professional New Model Army, drawn mostly from East Anglia. By 1647 voices within the City were calling for the return of the king. Only the arrival in London of Cromwell's army put a stop to that prospect.

The reality is that London, as ever, was ambivalent. It was mainly Puritan in sympathy and hostile to many Anglican church institutions, in particular bishops. To the parliamentarian John Milton, London was 'a city of refuge, a mansion house of liberty, encompassed and surrounded by His [God's] protection'. A few guilds even supported the Levellers, whose demands for religious tolerance and universal franchise presaged the revolutions of the nineteenth century. The Levellers' leader, John Lilburne, was a Londoner. But though the City's four MPs were Puritans, an entrenched peace movement kept up pressure for a settlement. As the war neared its end in 1648, London petitioned for the freeing of the captured king, backed by aldermen eager for peace and a return to trade.

Rise and fall of the Commonwealth

Continental Europe at the time had passed through a trauma unprecedented since the Black Death. For a century since the rise of Lutheranism, religious conflict had rolled back and forth, mostly in the German-speaking regions, and in 1618 exploded in the Thirty Years War. Much of northern Europe, both towns and countryside, reverted to conditions not experienced since the Middle Ages. By 1648, an exhausted continent pinned its hopes on the Peace of Westphalia and on the promise of a new era of tolerance across Europe. In comparison, England's civil war was modest, and in essence, political rather than religious. London's wish was now that the dispute between monarch and parliament could be resolved without further bloodshed.

It was not to be. In 1649 the high court of parliament judged Charles I guilty of treason, and ordered his execution. Cromwell feared obstruction and even riots if he tried to convey the king through the City to the Tower Hill scaffold, and duly erected a makeshift one outside the Whitehall banqueting house. The king's execution saw little rejoicing. One onlooker from Oxford University wrote, 'The blow I saw given . . . at the instant whereof I remember well there was such a groan by the thousands there present as I never heard before and desire I may never hear again.' Cromwell himself could only reflect on its 'grim necessity'.

The ensuing Commonwealth (1649–60) saw London fragment into Protestant diversity, with chapels springing up not just for Presbyterians and Baptists, but for Independents, Congregationalists, Quakers, Ranters, even 'Muggletonians'. In 1652 Cromwell declared war on the Netherlands, following the resurgence of Dutch trade with Spain after the Peace of Westphalia. But even trade wars were not to the City's liking as they meant higher taxes.

Equally unpopular was Cromwell's 1655 invitation of Jews back to the City from across Europe, for the first time since their expulsion by Edward I. Anti-Semitism was allied to resistance to competition, but Cromwell needed Jewish money, and soon a community of some 400 had been re-established in the vicinity of Bevis Marks, to remain ever since.

Apart from the banning of Christmas, church music and theatrical performances, London was spared the more draconian Puritan regime visited on some of the provinces. The diarist John Evelyn was briefly arrested for celebrating Christmas, but he recounted an enjoyable day in the park, with a rope-dancer, a bearded lady and a coach race. The portrayal of the Interregnum as a cultural desert is now discredited. Cromwell himself patronized London's first opera performed in English and with women singers, *The Siege of Rhodes*. A Committee of the Council for the Advancement of Musicke was established, perhaps England's original Arts Council. London's first coffee house opened in 1653.

The continued vitality of life in the capital was illustrated by the need to regulate the booming market in hackney carriages. A 1654 ordinance tried to combat 'the many inconveniences that do daily arise by reason of the late increase and great irregularity of hackney coaches and hackney coachmen'. The latter were legendary for rudeness and bad behaviour. Just 200 licences were issued, but this was soon doubled.

When Cromwell died, having appointed his son Richard to succeed him, the resulting vacuum in authority alarmed the City. Control defaulted to the army, but it had no clear leader. Cromwell's governor in Scotland, General Monck, duly marched his army south, but rather than take office, he consulted what remained of the Long Parliament, where he found a firm consensus in favour of a restoration of the king. Strict conditions ordaining the Sovereignty of Parliament were agreed with the exiled Charles II under the 1660 Declaration of Breda.

True to form, the City turned out in force to welcome the Restoration, with 20,000 of Cromwell's Ironsides on parade on Blackheath. Evelyn saw them 'brandishing their swords and shouting with inexpressible joy; the ways strewn with flowers, the bells ringing, the streets hung with tapestry, the fountains running with wine'. As the king crossed London Bridge and passed through the City on his way to Westminster, 'above a hundred proper maids in white garments with flaskets full of flowers and sweet herbs strewed the way before him as he rode'.

In 1641 the City of London had been divided between rebels and loyalists, with the former uppermost. It had opted for rebellion against the crown, and then expressed itself forcefully for compromise. The City was rarely as powerful as it was during the Civil War. Its 'mob' had taken daily to the streets, marching to the fount of government power in Westminster. It terrified the king and his family, and strengthened the will of parliament. London was a peaceful city, but the threat of violence lay never far below the surface. As the king declared war, it was London that financed parliament's army and that of Cromwell.

The historian Thomas Babington Macaulay later concluded that, 'but for the hostility of the City, Charles I would never have been vanquished, and without the help of the City, Charles II could never have been restored'. It was as if London's instinct for its own interest enabled it to judge a cautious but insistent path through periods of upheaval and danger. It was not shrill for long in the cause of Protestantism or Catholicism, any more than for parliament or the crown. The City perpetrated revolution, but once revolution had made its point, common sense dictated caution and retreat. Always money talked. A new monarch, with his power appropriately curtailed, was the best way forward. It was time to return to business.

7

Restoration, Calamity, Recovery
1660–1688

Lightness after dark

Charles II (1660–85) made an immediate impression. The new king's public persona could hardly have been more different from that of his father, let alone Cromwell's. His was a revolution of personality. A debonair, six-foot extrovert, he had spent his exile amid the hospitable French and Dutch courts. He was a libertine, a patron of the arts and sciences and an avid commissioner of public works, the downside of which was a Stuart weakness for extravagance. The barrenness of his wife, Catherine of Braganza, was his implausible excuse for at least seven mistresses, by whom he had fourteen known children. He ennobled nearly all of them.

King Charles would perambulate London's parks with several of the spaniels forever associated with him, chatting amiably to passers-by. He became the 'Merrie Monarch', the first to associate with his subjects in the streets of his capital, and thus able to share, in moments of crisis, something of their misery. According to one biographer, Ronald Hutton, Charles was a playboy ruler, 'naughty but nice, the hero of all who prized urbanity, tolerance, good humour, and the pursuit of pleasure above the more earnest, sober, or material virtues'. They are qualities not to be underrated as an accompaniment to power.

The king ordered fun and learning in equal measure. A Theatre Royal was opened in Drury Lane and a Duke of York's Theatre in

Lincoln's Inn Fields, with instructions that in future women and not boys should play female roles. At the same time, a Royal Society was founded for scientists and philosophers, its first tract by the diarist John Evelyn being 'A Discourse on Forest-Trees and the Propagation of Timber'. Its leading lights were Oxford's liberal empiricist John Locke, the physicist Isaac Newton, the chemist Robert Boyle and the scientist and architect Robert Hooke. The king built them a laboratory in Whitehall. Another founder member was the young Christopher Wren. Wren had received the sort of polymath upbringing that so often holds the key to great achievement. He studied classics, mathematics and science at Oxford, and was a professor of astronomy at twenty-nine, reading the Royal Society papers on cosmology, mechanics, optics, surveying, medicine and meteorology.

The advent of the London square

Whatever might be the ambitions of the monarch, they were equalled by those of London's aristocracy, owners of mansions across the West End, most with extensive gardens. There was now a popular king, a burgeoning court and a need of that court for somewhere to live, somewhere commensurate with the dignity of its members. The equivalent in Paris was the *hôtel particulier*, with a front courtyard and high walls protecting it from surrounding streets. London's aristocrats simply wanted a grand pied-à-terre for the 'season', and the West End boasted a number of such mansions, notably along Piccadilly and around Green Park and Hyde Park. But there were not enough.

The concept of the 'square', also borrowed from Paris, had been initiated before the Civil War in the Earl of Bedford's Covent Garden, but here the individual house was subordinated to an aesthetic whole, a unified architectural composition. At Lincoln's Inn Fields and later squares, the pretence was of a private palace, complete with pediment, pilasters and rustication, sandwiched between party walls, yet looking out as if over its own parterre.

Residents would arrive by carriage at their front door within view of their distinguished (they hoped) neighbours. Meanwhile, the noise and nuisance of servants, ostlers, tradesmen, carts, carriages and horses were consigned to the rear, as would be the case in a palace. Here was a pandemonium of lanes, alleys and mews, all with rear access to the grand houses fronting the main thoroughfare. Round the square would be a right-angled grid of lesser streets, with a clutter of church, market, shops, ale houses and tenements.

Such was the layout of almost every inner London estate over the next two centuries, even in the poorer east and south of the city. It became the signature of London planning. Its *rus in urbe* ('country in town') was enhanced by trees, initially formal but left over time to grow wild. The 1930s Danish urbanist Steen Eiler Rasmussen regarded the square – though only Soho Square is truly square – as embodying London's mystique. He recalled that in a summer fog, 'the London square appears to be at the bottom of the sea, under branches whose indistinct outlines form a pattern like the seaweed floating overhead'. They are the same today, though the trees are often even larger, the only sadness being that so many are closed to public access.

These ventures carried a high degree of financial risk. A square was not a terrace, to be extended or curtailed according to market forces. It relied on aristocratic landowners not wanting to dirty their hands with building or even speculation. They preferred to subcontract construction, as well as risk, to builder/developers on long leases, often as long as ninety-nine years. Owners would sacrifice short-term revenue for steady ground rent and long-term reversionary value.

This required scrupulous attention to the social status of a square's occupants, which meant the early squares were often slow to be completed. The reason some London squares – notably the early ones in St James's and Mayfair – have a patchwork appearance compared with those in, for example, Belgravia or Bloomsbury is that houses were often erected only when the 'right' tenant was available. So exclusive a market was always on the brink of saturation.

Immediately after the Restoration in 1660, the Earl of Southampton, Thomas Wriothesley, realized his ambition to develop land in front of his Tudor mansion north of Covent Garden, which took its name from its Norman owner, William de Blemond, hence Bloomsbury. Southampton wanted a new mansion for himself, facing a three-sided square with behind it streets for tradespeople and servants, stables and markets. He won his permission, but Bloomsbury Square took six years to complete.

Not to be outdone, in 1662 Henry Jermyn, Earl of St Albans, applied to build on his portion of the old St James's leper hospital estate. This was more sensitive, being adjacent to the king's St James's Park. Jermyn relied on his reputedly close friendship with the king's mother, Henrietta Maria, when in Paris during the Commonwealth. Permission was granted in 1665 for a square and streets running north to Piccadilly and west to St James's Street. To the east lay Jermyn's market, with cattle and the requisite hay from which the market took its name.

Given its location, St James's Square could hardly fail. It housed six dukes and seven earls. For some, the verticality of a London townhouse was a novelty. Jonathan Swift, on visiting the Duke of Ormonde, found himself conversing with his host below stairs, moving on to the duchess on the ground floor and their daughter Lady Betty on the first. When Swift then suggested Betty's maid might join him in the garret, he recorded that 'she was young and handsome and would not'.

The servicing of these premises needed careful attention. One townhouse might have twenty servants, at least during the spring season, requiring more space than the house could supply. As a result, the hinterland of even the smartest London square became a warren of low-rise cottages, stables, warehouses and workshops. St James's had Ormond Yard and Mason's Yard, Grosvenor had Three Kings Yard and Shepherds Place, a layout replicated round Berkeley, Cavendish, Portman and Belgrave squares. Even lesser squares had their mews, a name derived from the cages of the hawks that used to be kept there. While the squares were subject to strict controls, there was none over their service quarters. As a result, the interstices of the London estates became socially mixed, and were later to embrace some of London's poorest slums. Gentrified and conserved, they today make discreetly compact townhouses.

The arrival of plague

This Westminster revival came to a halt in the fifth year of Charles's reign. Already 1663 had seen a severe epidemic of bubonic plague, but it returned with a vengeance the following year. The City's stifling alleys and open sewers, its ditches and sloughs, were easy hunting ground for rats and their fleas, landing from along London's riverside. The plague appeared to wane in the cold of winter, but by spring 1665 it was rampant. Crosses appeared on doors. 'Bring out your dead!' was the new cry of the streets, accompanied by the rumble of the 'dead carts'. Responsibility for handling this horror fell to the hundred or so local parish authorities, whose self-appointed 'vestrymen' were charged with collecting the victims and digging and filling their plague pits.

Of all those who people London's story, few are more engaging than a young clerk in the navy office at this time named Samuel Pepys. The king in the same year as the plague had resumed

Cromwell's intermittent war with the Dutch over trading rights in the Americas, culminating in 1667 in a Dutch fleet sailing up the Medway and destroying or taking possession of thirteen English ships. Pepys was struggling with others to reform the navy and confronted a humiliation without parallel in Britain's naval history. His diary of the decade from 1660 to 1669 describes in meticulous detail his public and domestic life.

During the plague, Pepys had to stay working at his desk. He sent his wife into the country, revised his will and noticed, 'Lord, how empty the streets are, and melancholy, so many poor sick people in the streets, full of sores, and so many sad stories overheard as I walk, everybody talking of this man dead, that man sick.' The rich had fled. The Royal Exchange emptied. Soon there were not enough people to record, let alone bury, the dead. Pepys deplored how the court had dispersed from 'the place of business, and so all goes to wrack as to public matters, they at this distance not thinking of it'.

The plague affected people in different ways. Pepys's contemporary Daniel Defoe remarked on the 'strange temper of the people of London', who believed themselves deserted by God for their sinfulness, or at least that of their immoral monarch. The streets resounded to the cries of roaming preachers, foretelling doom. Yet Pepys seemed able to capitalize on the distress. He contrived, we know not how, to quadruple his fortune. He even concluded, 'I have never lived so merrily (besides that I never got so much) as I have done this plague time.' By January 1666 the cold weather abated the disease. Carriages returned to town and business resumed. No one was able to assess how many died, but it was probably 100,000, or a fifth of the population.

Pepys was a master diarist, able to marry the horror of public events with his private affairs, dusting formal history with the quotidian joys of humanity. His diary's lasting appeal owes much to his turbulent relationship with his wife, his social and sexual activities, his visit to an execution and his operation for kidney stones. He loved wine, music and women, and is never quite sure how to explain, let alone reform, his behaviour. Caught by his wife in flagrante, he admits, 'I was at a wonderful loss upon it, and the girl also.' He is one of those precious Londoners who contrived, like Chaucer, to open briefly a window on how people behaved and thought in the world of his day.

The Great Fire

The City had had little time to recover when six months later another calamity arrived. On 2 September 1666 a baker's shop in Pudding Lane in the City caught fire. As soon as Pepys heard the news he buried his papers, his wine and his Parmesan cheese and put his household and harpsichord into a boat on the Thames. The bulk of the population fled to Southwark or north to Islington and Highgate. Pepys joined those trying to organize fire breaks. At first the lord mayor dismissed the fire as 'a woman might piss it out', but he was soon desperate as his orders to demolish houses in the fire's path went ignored. Pepys saved the Tower of London by getting sailors to blow up buildings around it. After three days, as the south-east wind turned south-west, he stood across the river and saw 'one entire arch of fire from this side to the other side of the bridge . . . an arch of above a mile long.' It was, he said, 'like a bow of flame'.

Pepys's friend and fellow chronicler of Restoration London, John Evelyn, wrote of countless citizens dazed and frantic, 'nothing heard or seen but crying out and lamentation, and running about like distracted creatures'. When old St Paul's started to explode into flames, he watched as its stones 'flew like grenades, the melting lead flowing down the street in a stream and the very pavements glowing with fiery redness'. All that escaped destruction in this quarter of the City were the Guildhall records, stored deep in the medieval basement. Evelyn also helped demolish buildings to halt the fire at Holborn. Its Staple Inn, much restored, is the best surviving relic of a pre-fire London facade. To Evelyn, 'London was, but is no more.' A resident of distant Kensington wrote of 'my garden covered with the ashes of papers, linens, plasterwork blown hither by the tempest'.

By the week's end, 373 of the old City's 448 acres had been burned, as well as sixty acres in the outer wards of Farringdon. Eighty-seven churches out of 109 were lost. St Paul's and all public buildings were considered unrestorable. It was unquestionably the worst disaster to hit the City since the great fire of 1087, which also destroyed an earlier St Paul's. Some 70,000 of the City's 80,000 residents lost their homes. Meanwhile, desperate refugees gathered in the fields of Islington and Highgate, huddled in tents and primitive shelters as they watched their city burn. No more than a dozen people were recorded as dying in the fire – though an unknown number may have died in Newgate prison, engulfed in flames.

The phoenix rises

Despite accounts of cataclysm, historians have come to doubt how devastating was the actual burning, especially where houses were built of brick and stone. The Museum of London estimates that total devastation affected only about a third of the City's area, and this may explain the speed with which the rest was rebuilt. Within four days, refugees began to move from the northern heights either to less distant villages or to Moorfields and Clerkenwell, to be within reach of their smouldering properties. Many went back to squat, lest they lose land to a neighbour. A new edible brassica known as London rocket was noticed growing vigorously in the ruins – reports claim that it reappeared after the Blitz.

Whatever the returning citizens wanted, enterprising individuals were soon wandering over the smouldering ruins with sketch pads and measuring tape. On 10 September, less than a week after the fire ended, the king received a proposal from Wren for a wholly new city. On the 13th he received another from Evelyn, who wrote that 'Dr Wren got the start of me'. Within a week, plans piled in from Robert Hooke, Valentine Knight and others. As London was to find after the Blitz, there is nothing architects crave more than a chance to redesign a city.

Wren appears to have had the king's ear. He saw 'the great plain of ashes and ruins' as a new London, comparable with the Renaissance jewels of southern Europe. His plan borrowed from the Rome of Pope Sixtus had two great *ronds-points*, one at the Royal Exchange and another almost at the Strand. A grid of streets in between radiated from a new St Paul's. There would be palaces, churches, obelisks, avenues, circuses and wharves along the Thames. Everywhere there would be vistas.

Evelyn was equally visionary. He wanted all 'tiresome trades' moved east and groves of 'fragrant and odoriferous plants' to take their place. His layout was like a great chequerboard. Evelyn was among the first Londoners to worry about its air. It was wrong, he wrote, that a city that 'commands the broad ocean to the Indies' should 'wrap her stately head in clouds of smoke and sulphur'. Londoners, he said, 'breathe nothing but an impure and thick mist, a fuliginous and filthy vapour'. They should burn wood, not coal. The first true London gardener, Evelyn even foresaw a green belt round the suburbs, though in a sense Elizabeth I had proposed the same.

Other ideas included Sir William Petty's for a new 'Greater

London' government, with 5 million inhabitants in garden cities spread over the surrounding country. He was a man before his time. A Colonel Birch proposed the state acquire the entire City by compulsory purchase, and begin afresh. For good measure the Royal Society pitched in with a tract rebutting those blaming the plague and fire on London's sinfulness. It was time to put aside old 'rebellious humours and horrid sacrileges . . . as men begin now everywhere to recover their spirits again, and think of repairing the old and rebuilding a new city'.

The king initially took Wren's advice and sent a letter to the City authorities forbidding any immediate rebuilding of houses, or 'they will be demolished and levelled again'. The king had seen Wren's plan and 'manifested much approbation of it'. Yet within three days, Charles changed his mind. Perhaps realizing the implications of demolishing all that was left of the City and evicting its inhabitants, he was 'concerned and solicitous for the rebuilding of this famous city, with as much expedition as is possible'. It should be of brick and stone, not wood, and permission should be sought before proceeding, but shall 'in a short time receive order and direction'.

Most remarkable, in cases of street widening and other adjustments, officials should inspect the site and refer any dispute to a jury, which could award compensation. Where any development profited an owner, the assessed 'added value' should be paid 'to the community'. Any property not reoccupied within five years would be forfeited to the town. Policy respected private property, yet the City should be helped back to life, regulated and taxed to a wider public good. The Stuart government embraced neighbourhood conservation, building standards, property inspection, jury adjudication and compensation. In my judgement London's urban renewal was never so carefully considered as in the few months after the Great Fire.

A committee of six was set up to oversee the rebuilding, with

Wren as a member, though he was angry at the 'obstinate averseness of a great part of the citizens to alter their old properties', a cry of London's architects down the ages. An Act for Rebuilding the City of London was passed in 1667, laying down the requisite materials, brick, stone and tiles. The dimensions were fixed for four grades of house, to be set back along wider streets within limits delineated with ropes. Anyone moving his property's frontage line would be 'openly whipped near unto the place where the offence shall be committed, till his body be bloody'. Most remarkable, there was a scale of compensation, though hardly generous, for those who lost property through street widening, funded by a tax on coal.

While new facades conformed to the regulations, City dwellers had little time for the visions of grandiose planners. As they trooped back through the ashes, they carried such building materials as they could, to reopen shops and pick up their lives. They had little option. One Elizabeth Peacock was reported to have spent £800 on her house just before the fire, but was offered only £10 compensation afterwards. In reality the restored buildings, says the Museum of London, were various 'forms of Elizabethan and Jacobean houses re-clothed in brick'. However, new sewers and stone pavements were put down, and the streets cambered into gutters. A King Street and a Queen Street were created to give Guildhall a direct pathway to the river. Speed was what dictated the look of the new City, and it was largely rebuilt within four years. It was a phenomenal undertaking.

A once and future City

The fire appears to have caught London's much revered self-government off guard. The recovery and rebuilding were ordained from Westminster. The king himself was everywhere. During the fire he rode through the streets encouraging the fire-fighters. Despite the failure of Wren's plan, Charles showed himself an intelligent administrator. It says much for his authority that Londoners acquiesced in his decisions and those of arbitrators appointed to settle post-fire disputes. This was undoubtedly helped by the pre-fire street plan being adhered to so closely.

In the event, some 9,000 houses replaced 13,200 old ones, the reduction in living space eased by population losses from the plague the previous year. Given the retention of the old streets, layouts remained informal. Houses were often built in gardens, requiring new alleys to reach them. John Ogilby's map of 1677, drawn in part to help plan the new city, shows a configuration little different from a pre-fire version. Map-makers assessed the new City as having 189 streets, 153 lanes, 522 alleys, 458 courts and 210 yards. The old administrative divisions were restored unreformed, comprising twenty-four wards plus Southwark, subdivided into 122 parishes. It was as if everything had changed, and yet nothing.

One opportunity was seized: to regularize open markets on more convenient sites. Most liveried company halls and half the churches were rebuilt. Of the 109 churches lost, 51 were rebuilt (of which 24 survive today). The new ones were all overseen by Wren, and are traditionally attributed to him, but research by Simon Bradley for Pevsner attributes many to his assistant, Robert Hooke. Given that most of the church sites were medieval, and that parish amalgamations meant maximizing space, Wren and Hooke had to show great ingenuity. Plans were variously square, rectangular, oval or irregular. Towers were all different, and interiors, where records survive, different too.

Bradley detects in Wren's work 'the scientist's delight in experimenting. How many types of useful parish church can be developed'. St Stephen Walbrook is thought to be a miniature trial run for St Paul's. The most perfect Wren interior, St Mary-at-Hill on Lovat

Lane near Billingsgate, was regarded by John Betjeman as 'the least spoiled and most gorgeous interior in the City, all the more exciting by being hidden away among cobbled alleys, paved passages, brick walls and overhung by plane trees'. In an enclave redolent of the pre-war City, this church was fire-damaged in 1988 and its seventeenth-century woodwork put in store. The City, for all its wealth, still declines to restore it. It awaits a nobler generation.

As for St Paul's, it had been the City's spiritual heart since the seventh century. The steeple had collapsed in 1561 and Inigo Jones had designed a classical west front in the 1620s. At the time of the fire, Wren was proposing a new crossing dome, and its encasement in wooden scaffolding is thought to have facilitated its conflagration. There was talk of restoring the blackened shell in its original gothic, but Wren was adamant for modern baroque – its beauty derived from geometry. He still hoped that at some future date it might be the focus of a radial street layout.

Battle was then joined over how Wren's plan might be executed. Churchmen are bad compromisers and indecision brought Wren close to despair. His model, built six years after the fire, was cruciform but traditionalists wanted a longer nave and shorter transepts. Eventually the king demanded progress, leaving Wren free to make 'adjustments as from time to time he should see proper'. The cost rose to a staggering £720,000, close to £100 million today, and the cathedral took over thirty years to complete.

St Paul's became the outward expression of London's post-fire revival and was, at least until the 1960s, the visual focus of the metropolis from all angles. Its scholarly classicism was much admired by John Summerson, the leading historian of eighteenth-century London, who wrote, 'that such a monument should rise, not among the new streets and squares of Westminster, but on the barren, unintellectual soil of the mercantile stronghold, is one of the freaks of history'. The elderly Wren was at least able to see it finished, hoisted to its roof in 1711 by his son in a basket.

The City could restore its buildings, but not force anyone to live in them. The reality of the fire was that thousands never returned. Wealthier citizens had taken temporary lodgings to the west, and many decided to stay. Merchants found they could work from Covent Garden as well as from Cheapside, or could walk from the one to the other. The glamour and entertainment of the Stuart court had a magnetism the City could not match. Nor were other suburbs idle, with speculators quick to capitalize on the surge in demand. To the east, short-term leases were available in Hoxton, Shoreditch, Finsbury and Spitalfields. The higher the prices, the straighter the streets, as notably in Spitalfields. Meanwhile, less desirable properties spread along the polluted Thames, from St Katharine's to Wapping and Shadwell. A survey of Shadwell in 1650 had 700 houses, of which almost all were one or two storeys.

The aldermanic council was alarmed. Hundreds of newly built houses lay unoccupied by their absentee owners and awaiting tenants. The 1672 census showed 3,000 houses built since the fire still empty. Aldermen were warned they would lose their privileges if they did not live in their wards – a hopeless requirement then as now. City companies offered open apprenticeships, leading to readily conferred freedoms of the city. The City lobbied desperately against a new bridge proposed upstream at Westminster, afraid that trade from the provinces would bypass London on its way to Kent and the coast. In this it was successful, crippling the growth of south London for yet another century.

Newly arriving craftsmen none the less found they could avoid guild restrictions by settling outside the City's jurisdiction. Jewellers gathered in Hatton Garden, silversmiths in Clerkenwell and tailors north of Covent Garden. The jewellers are there to this day. The City was set on the long road of losing its crafts and manufacturing industry. Its population of 200,000 before the fire fell to 140,000 afterwards. Three-quarters of all Londoners now lived outside the City, which began to head inexorably towards being a 'central business district'.

There were gains as well as losses from the fire. Had Wren or Evelyn been successful and revival been delayed, not only might the City economy have collapsed, but businesses desperate to resume trade might simply have upped sticks and moved to Westminster – as the Anglo-Saxons did to Lundenwic in the fifth century. Old London might have ceded commercial as well as political pre-eminence to its younger sibling, and become a suburban slum.

So the City was right to lobby Charles to let the market take its course, though it was the crown and not the City corporation that laid down the regulation of the rebuilding. There were also gains from retaining the medieval street plan. Had London adopted Wren's geometrical layout, it would have fallen easy prey to twentieth-century redevelopment, the fate of Nash's Regent Street. Even today, the ancient street plan casts a spell over the City's planners, who readily demolish their old buildings but hold Alfred the Great's layout in awe.

Westminster comes of age

The principal beneficiary of the Great Fire was Westminster. The fields round London's western fringe had been mostly grazing land and market gardens. They now disappeared under brickfields, wagon tracks, lime kilns and labourers' encampments. Licences cascaded from the Privy Council, successor to the Star Chamber. Demand was frantic. The story of London's early property speculation reads like the pages of *Debrett's*. Where the Restoration's early grandees, Salisbury, Bedford, Southampton and St Albans, had led the way, others now followed the Great Fire. The Earl of Leicester built round Leicester fields, now a square. Lord Arlington built a house facing Green Park, though he lived in what became Buckingham House down the road. Also facing the park were Lord Berkeley, the Duke of Albemarle and the earl of Cork and Burlington, with mansions and later streets that bear their names. Lesser mortals followed.

When the Earl of Clarendon fell from favour, his Palladian mansion on Piccadilly designed by Roger Pratt was bought and promptly demolished by a developer syndicate headed by Sir Thomas Bond. Lord Gerard, later Earl of Macclesfield, built over part of Soe Hoe fields. A gambler named Colonel Panton acquired Haymarket, with the land to its north falling to Richard Fryth, Francis Compton, Edward Wardour, William Pulteney and Thomas Neale. All left their names on the map of London, memorials more familiar than any stone plaque in Westminster Abbey.

Most assiduous was Nicholas Barbon. He was no aristocrat but son of the Baptist parliamentarian Praise-God Barbon. Born in Holland in 1640 and a physician by training, he settled in Fleet Street in 1664 and became London's first 'professional' developer. All Westminster was his hunting ground. Barbon entertained, bribed and threatened his way across town. If an offer was refused, he might send his henchmen to demolish a property overnight. The historian Christopher Hibbert wrote that, if sued, 'he wearied his opponents with appeals, counter-claims, non-appearances, apologies, withdrawals, specious arguments, disingenuous excuses, lies and incomprehensible speeches'. Like the Elizabethan Gresham, he was a star in London's rogues' gallery.

Barbon was everywhere. On the death of the Earl of Essex, his house off the Strand vanished and Essex and Devereux Streets emerged. The Duke of Buckingham's house at Charing Cross went likewise. The duke pleaded with Barbon at least to preserve his name. The answer was George Street, Villiers Street, Duke Street, Of Alley and Buckingham Street. Only the alley is now 'formerly'. At Red Lion Square, Barbon led two hundred of his workmen into a pitched battle of sticks and stones with protesting lawyers at neighbouring Gray's Inn. He also developed streets for the Temple and Bedford City, the latter north of Holborn. Like many of his breed, he overstretched himself and ran out of money. His defence to his critics was that of every developer – that he was only bowing to demand.

In 1669 Wren was appointed surveyor of the king's works. His awesome task was to carry forward a programme of palaces to match those Charles had admired during his continental exile. First of these were improvements to royal Whitehall. The palace had become a sprawling enclave of courtyards and royal apartments, with favoured courtiers and servants allowed to extend their rooms at will. It was reputedly the largest palace in Europe (though soon to be overtaken by an expanded Versailles), with 1,500 rooms over twenty-three acres. Inigo Jones's earlier plan for a Tuileries-on-Thames for James I had progressed only to its Banqueting House.

Charles first decided to extend the palace grounds westwards towards Hyde Park, employing the French landscape designer André Le Nôtre to redesign a part of the estate of the old St James's leper hospital. He included a canal and an avenue for the current craze for *palla al maglio*, a sort of long-distance croquet, moved from its site on the present Pall Mall. At the west end of the park lay an old mulberry grove, planted by James I to house what proved unproductive silkworms. This later passed to the Earl of Arlington and then the Duke of Buckingham, for what became Buckingham House.

As for Whitehall itself, piecemeal improvements continued, but there was no sign of a Tuileries-on-Thames, nor of Wren's vision of a Versailles on the water. Charles ran out of money. Eventually in

1691, after the king's death and the departure of his brother James, the entire enclave apart from the Banqueting House went up in flames. Future monarchs deserted damp, polluted Westminster, never to return.

Few great houses of this post-fire period in London's history survive. In the City, there is the old Deanery (1672), off St Paul's churchyard, together with the College of Arms nearby and some surviving liveried company halls. Apart from the rebuilt Staple Inn in Holborn, houses in Cloth Fair off Smithfield may pre-date the fire, relics of the mid-seventeenth century City, brick-faced with wide oriel windows, overlooking a maze of alleys and passageways. What did not vanish was the Restoration idiom, that of the four- to five-storey continuous terrace of single houses, each with its own front door, with ground- and first-floor reception rooms, with or without basement, and then bedrooms continuing above. It was present in exaggerated form in the grandest square and, scaled down, in humble back streets. It was not ostentatious or over-spacious, just dignified and smart. Other than in the poorest tenements, the form was the London norm throughout the eighteenth and nineteenth centuries, until the advent of the still-popular apartment block at the end of Victoria's reign.

The London that embarked on the eighteenth century was the most modern city in Europe. Almost all its properties, rich and poor, had been built within the previous century, when other cities were mostly still accretions to a medieval core. One consequence was that, when Europe finally renovated their centres in the nineteenth century, mostly with multi-storey apartment blocks, London was left with streets of townhouses supporting much lower residential densities. This meant that if it were to accommodate an ever rising population, it would need to occupy ever more land. Luckily, of that it had plenty to spare.

8

Dutch Courage
1688–1714

Succession crisis

London at the time of the Restoration was passing through what was later termed the Little Ice Age. It experienced a two-degree fall in average temperature, relieved by importing large quantities of coal. The Thames was wider and slower than today, with old London Bridge forming a virtual dam. The result was it froze regularly. In the winter of 1683–84, the river was solid for six weeks, leading to a celebrated frost fair. A street of temporary shops was erected from the Temple to London Bridge, with coaches plying their trade along its length.

Evelyn recorded a festival atmosphere. There were stallholders with 'booths in which they roasted meat . . . sleds, sliding with skates, a bull-baiting, horse and coach races, puppet plays and interludes, cooks, tippling and other lewd places so that it seemed to be a bacchanalian triumph'. The king and queen tucked into an ox-roast off Whitehall. There was also a downside: 'Many parks of deer were destroyed, and all sorts of fuel so dear that there were great contributions to keep the poor alive . . . London, by reason for the excessive coldness of the air hindering the ascent of the smoke, was so filled with the fuliginous steam of the sea-coal that one could hardly breathe.'

Charles's capital was beginning to lose some of its Restoration shine. The king was increasingly at odds with parliament over the financing of his palatial ventures. Rumours of the king's secret Catholicism were reinforced by the fact that his brother and heir, James, Duke of York, was a practising Catholic. Parliament strongly objected to this, leading in 1682 to an open breach over the succession, with the City mostly siding with parliament. London had been enthusiastic for the Restoration and was averse to any recurrence of the conflicts of the Civil War. None the less its Protestantism was firmly embedded, and it had no wish to return to a Catholic monarchy.

A furious Charles responded with an unprecedented revocation of the City guilds' royal charters, followed by a revocation of that of the City corporation itself. When this decision came to court, loyalist judges sided with the king. The Lord Chief Justice, Judge Jeffreys, pointed out that 'the king of England is likewise king of London'. The capital, he said, was 'no more than a large village'. It was not language that City aldermen had ever heard before.

In 1685 France's Louis XIV revoked his predecessor Henry IV's Edict of Nantes, supposedly tolerant of Protestant worship. This echo of the St Bartholomew's Day massacre drove another mass exodus of Huguenots to London, many crowding into the French enclaves of Soho and Spitalfields, bringing with them horror stories of their persecution. The same year, Charles II died and the Catholic James II (1685–88) succeeded. He did nothing to allay public suspicion of where his sympathies lay. He used his patronage to promote Catholics throughout the government, the army, the civil service and Oxford University. He appeared to be on the side of the French persecution.

Lacking his brother's tact or charisma and now remarried to a Catholic, Mary of Modena, James's position quickly became unstable. Though he could rely on a core of Catholic support in parts of the City, his hold on power was tenuously based on his heir being his daughter, Mary Stuart, a Protestant married to

William of Orange, Protestant hero of the Franco-Dutch wars. This Security ended, however, when in 1688 James's second wife gave birth to a male child, replacing Mary as heir to the throne. The prospect of a Catholic dynasty in alliance with James's French patron, Louis XIV, a king at war with William of Orange, was beyond London's tolerance.

England had been at war with the Dutch in the 1650s and 60s, but it was a war of trade and conducted at sea. Most English people felt an affinity with those who had been fighting militant Catholicism for much of the past century. It was Dutch rather than French taste that had followed the Restoration to London. Kew Palace was known as the Dutch House. London portraiture was dominated by Peter Lely and Godfrey Kneller, while Jan Kip and Leonard Knyff supplied the aristocracy with spectacular panoramas of its rural mansions. England naturally looked across the North Sea, not the Channel, for help in its political turmoil.

Invasion, coup and new regime

William of Orange needed little encouragement. Abetted by his agent in London, Hans Willem Bentinck, a group of Whig conspirators 'invited' him to invade England and seize James's throne. In November 1688 William did so with a naval force twice the size of Philip of Spain's armada of a century before. He sailed west to Brixham in Devon, and marched from there towards London, anticipating a predicted uprising against James. There was no uprising, but the royalist army offered only token opposition, after one of its commanders, John Churchill (later Duke of Marlborough), defected to William's side.

William's arrival in London was the first time since the Norman Conquest that the city had come face to face with a foreign invader.

Extreme caution was shown on both sides. James was still in Whitehall, but with no army at his disposal he was allowed to flee to
France. William distributed a manifesto reasserting parliament's
pre-Civil War Petition of Right and Grand Remonstrance. It professed his 'greatest reluctance and humility' at being obliged to save
England from James's 'evil counsellors'. Locke was summoned to
the cause, writing his *Two Treatises of Government* in 1689 and dedi-
cating them to 'our Great Restorer'. William, he said, had 'saved
the nation when it was on the very brink of slavery and ruin'. It was
masterly spin on what had been the armed toppling of a legitimate
king.

Unlike Charles II on his restoration, William dared not go near
the City, aware that James had supporters there. A welcome was
carefully staged in St James's Park, with much distributing of oranges
and orange ribbons. Dutch troops lined Whitehall, instructed to use
the word liberation rather than conquest. None the less, all English
soldiers were ordered out of the capital and replaced by a Dutch garrison. Evelyn recalled the Civil War and wondered, 'to such a strange
temper and unheard-of in any former age, was this poor nation
reduced, and of which I was an eye-witness'.

William's invasion was presented by its propagandists as a 'Glorious Revolution'. Its outcome was certainly benign and it averted an
imminent clash between parliament and the Stuart monarchy.
Many Tories and Catholics regarded William as a usurper, with
some actively conspiring for James's return, but parliament was
secure in Whig hands, and it passed a series of measures to secure,
once and for all, a Protestant succession under parliamentary
sovereignty. To this the new king William III (1689–1702) assented,
provided only that he and Mary rule jointly, as equal king and
queen, which they did until her death in 1694. In 1690 bills were
passed restoring the City's various charters, ordaining that 'hence-
forward the City's Charter be never forfeited for any cause whatever'.

This emphatic step down the road to democracy was achieved without London's streets seeing a drop of blood – though much was to be shed over coming years in Scotland and Ireland.

The suburb to a suburb

Since Edward the Confessor, the monarchy had ruled England from upstream of its capital, in the Middlesex parish of Westminster. It first occupied Edward's old Palace of Westminster, now housing parliament and the monarch's courts. Then, under the Tudors and Stuarts, the monarch moved, when in London, to the adjacent Palace of Whitehall, crowded with buildings old and new and housing a large retinue of crown servants and officials.

William and Mary disliked Whitehall and were no more enamoured of their lesser residence at St James's. William suffered from asthma and Mary called Whitehall 'nothing but walls and water'. The couple decided to move out of town altogether and bought Nottingham House near the village of Kensington, which they had Wren fit out with palatial apartments. To emphasize the binary nature of their monarchy, the king and queen required individual quarters and personal royal receiving rooms. At Hampton Court they even had separate ceremonial entrances.

The move saw the monarchy virtually detach itself from the metropolis. Neither William and Mary nor their successor, Anne, used the palace at St James's. This evolution in London's political geography matched that of its constitution. The principles in the 1689 Bill of Rights were enshrined by association in the Palace of Westminster, now home to a formally sovereign parliament. As parliament increased in stature, the sovereignty of the monarch seemed to drift westwards, gently dissipating in the glades of Kensington Gardens.

Queen Anne (1702–14) continued her sister's fondness for out-of-town residences. The poet Alexander Pope wrote affectionately of Hampton Court, where 'great Anna, whom three realms obey/ Dost sometime counsel take, and sometimes tea'. The queen's practice of meeting her ministers in her private cabinet gave rise to their adopting it as their collective name. In 1707 the Act of Union made London capital not just of England (and Wales) but also of Scotland. A delighted Anne paraded in the robes of the Order of the Thistle, and declared herself ruler of one nation, with 'hearts disposed to become one people', a fond but faint hope. The act saw the arrival of forty-five Scottish MPs in parliament, reinforcing a Whig ascendancy that was to last, with hiatuses, for half a century.

Money talking

As the population dispersed after the Great Fire, much of the City's traditional manufacturing went with it. Factories closed, craftsmen departed. The remaining workforce was left to concentrate on a refinement of its former mercantile activity, that of dealing in money, or banking. The term was derived from the Italian word for the bench on which loans were laid for all to see. This supplanted the traditional lending of money against the gold and silver reserves of dealers in those commodities. A Bank of England was founded in 1694, initially as a private venture to co-ordinate government debt. This led two years later to 'paper money' in the form of promissory notes drawn on the Bank of England's gold reserves. The growth of government borrowing was facilitated by the East India Company and the South Sea Company, in effect state enterprises in which bankers, ministers and the public were able to purchase large sums of speculative debt.

As in medieval Venice, fortunes turned on ships far from home and events overseas. This in turn placed a high value on contacts and information. The City proved ideally suited to the necessary networking. New banking institutions came to supplant the old liveried companies. Bankers were no longer goldsmiths or mercers, and some did not bother to become freemen and thus participants in the political life of the City. Of the initial twenty-six directors of the Bank of England, six were Huguenots and half were Dissenters from the formal Anglican church. Their business was lubricated not by guild networks, but by intelligence gleaned at the coffee houses of Cornhill and Threadneedle Street. From now on, the London guilds become clubs more than trade cartels.

By 1700 there were over 500 coffee houses in London, many specializing in particular goods and services and charging for entry. Thus Lloyd's house became a centre for insurance, and Jonathan's for livestock. The term stock market is believed to derive from the latter's location near the old punishment stocks. The first list of market prices, the Course of the Exchange, was issued from Jonathan's in 1698, while the first British daily newspaper, the *Daily Courant*, emerged in Fleet Street in 1702.

The roots of London journalism thus lay in finance. The gazettes became the lubricant of an oligopolistic market for money. The rich might flee to the comfort and air of the new suburbs, but nothing could replace the compact intercourse of a coffee house. Information was word of mouth before it became word of print, and it was geographically specific. Propinquity to the docks and the markets was the City's unique asset, at least until the coming of the telegraph.

This City increasingly developed a distinctive outlook on the world, quite separate from that at Westminster. It was divided over England's (now Britain's) involvement in the War of the Spanish Succession (1701–13). It rejoiced in Marlborough's victories, but it sided with the Tories in their eagerness for a peace. This was reflected in the final Treaty of Utrecht in 1714, when Britain's negotiators were instructed to ignore the territorial carve-up of Europe and concentrate on matters of trade. Utrecht awarded Britain Gibraltar, Minorca and Newfoundland, and confirmed it in Jamaica, Bermuda and the American colonies. The treaty also won Britain a lucrative – and increasingly controversial – monopoly over the slave trade between Africa and Spain's American colonies.

The westward drift

Despite a lull in building after the post-fire boom – which left the City with a housing surplus – the zeal to regulate suburban growth did not diminish. In 1703 a visitor, Fletcher of Saltoun, echoed the Tudor John Stow. He said London was 'like the head of a rickety child, which by drawing itself nourishment that should be distributed in due proportion to the rest of the languishing body, becomes so overcharged that frenzy and death unavoidably ensue'. Yet all parliament did was regulate further the actual design of the London house. Statutes in 1707 and 1709 banned any projecting wood as a fire risk, and required windows to be recessed, so flames would not spread up the exterior. Pre-1707 houses can still be seen in the fine door-hoods in the City's Laurence Pountney Hill, in Westminster's Queen Anne's Gate and Smith Square. A remarkable survivor is Schomberg House of c.1695 in Pall Mall, probably the only extant exterior of a grand seventeenth-century mansion in Westminster, built for a Dutch Huguenot and today divided into three.

As for the new suburbs, concern was expressed over their godliness, or at least their lack of churches. Developers had failed to supply them, partly because existing parishes feared the loss of congregations. Many estates, such as Marylebone and Mayfair, had to make do with chapels of ease – 'easing' the distance from a main parish church. The eastern and northern suburbs had few churches of any denomination. In 1710 a commission was duly set up to build fifty new ones, financed by the tax on coal first introduced to pay for rebuilding after the Great Fire.

Initially only twelve so-called 'Queen Anne' churches were built. They were not just in Westminster but also in poorer parishes such as Spitalfields, Stepney, Limehouse, Bermondsey, Greenwich and Deptford. They were to be designed by the finest architects of the day, Wren's successors as masters of English baroque. Nicholas Hawksmoor produced Christ Church Spitalfields, St George's-in-the-East and St Mary Woolnoth in the City, each an eccentric variant on a baroque theme. Thomas Archer's St John's Smith Square church with its four towers was called 'Queen Anne's footstool', allegedly for her kicking over this piece of furniture when asked how she would like it to look. James Gibbs's St Mary-le-Strand remains the jewel of the set, fit for the Rome of Bernini and Borromini. The churches were the finest public patronage of architecture between the ages of Wren and John Nash.

London outside the City was still governed by nothing more substantial than the parish vestries of the counties of Middlesex and Essex, often coterminous with ancient manors. Frequently chaired by the vicar, they were supposedly responsible for law and order, welfare and what passed for public utilities. These authorities were now playing host to thousands of newcomers, many of them provincials working in the building trades and in factories spreading out from the old City. They were soon helplessly out of their depth.

This new London had none of the coherence of the City's wards and guilds. Outside the self-policed boundaries of the new estate developments, Londoners lived in virtual anarchy. There were regular street disturbances, including fights between Irish slum-dwellers and anti-Catholic City mobs. In 1709 a sermon in St Paul's by a high

churchman, Henry Sacheverell, attacking Dissenters and Huguenots led to days of rioting by a mob of 5,000. Such incidents were
sufficiently serious for the passage of the draconian Riot Act of 1714.
Once publicly 'read', this enabled the authorities – in Middlesex the
county magistrates – to ban assemblies of more than a dozen
people, and indemnify any vigilante force assisting their dispersal.

London's population under the Stuarts had risen from 200,000 to
600,000, but from the start of the eighteenth century it began to
slacken. Provincial immigration was no longer replacing a falling
birth rate. Worse, the death rate rose. The chief reason appeared to
be a novel menace. William of Orange had relieved duties on gin to
boost its consumption as an alternative to brandy, to penalize the
hated French. He also ended the distillers' monopoly, allowing gin
to be made without licence, while control continued on the brewing of beer. Brandy sales indeed collapsed and, Defoe reported,
'Distillers have found a new way to hit the palate of the poor, by
their new fashioned compound waters called Geneva.' The impact
of gin on early eighteenth-century London was devastating. Even
Queen Anne became an avid gin drinker.

1. Reconstructed view of Roman London *c.*120.

2. Fragment of Roman wall with medieval additions, Cooper's Row in the City.

3. Norman decorum, chapel in the Tower of London, 1080.

4. The first Westminster Hall, 1098, artist's impression with abbey in background.

5. Dick Whittington (1358?–1423), mercer, lord mayor, City benefactor, depicted with his legendary cat.

6. Tower of London, *c.*1500, with London Bridge beyond.

7. Coronation procession of Edward VI in 1547. Imaginary view showing Tower Hill, Southwark, Cheapside and old St Paul's.

8. Nonsuch House on old London Bridge in 1577. Reassembled from sections made in the Netherlands. Demolished 1757.

9. Staple Inn, Holborn, 1585, restored 1886; rare survivor of pre-fire City building.

10. Cattle still being driven to the slaughter through the streets. Eastcheap meat market, 1598.

11. Sir Thomas Gresham, c.1560–65, first master financier to the Crown and City; presided over London's banking supremacy and founded the Royal Exchange.

12. Globe Theatre in 1616, located outside the City's jurisdiction in Bankside.

13. Westminster across the Thames, 1631, by Claude de Jongh, showing the new Banqueting Hall, Westminster Hall and Abbey.

14. London Bridge and the Tower of London, detail from a 1650 edition of Visscher's panorama.

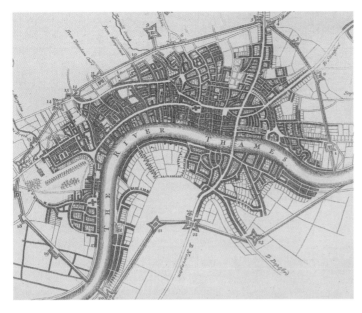

15. London prepared for royalist siege, 1642. Twenty-three forts with eighteen miles of ramparts surrounded the City and Westminster. None was needed.

16. Samuel Pepys by Geoffrey Kneller, c.1689, diarist of London's plague and fire.

17. Great Fire of London. Buildings aflame at Ludgate with citizens escaping across the Fleet.

18. Sir Christopher Wren with his new St Paul's Cathedral in the background.

19/20. Plans for a rebuilt City by Wren and John Evelyn, both drawing on Italian examples and presupposing the elimination of all existing properties and streets. They were not seriously considered.

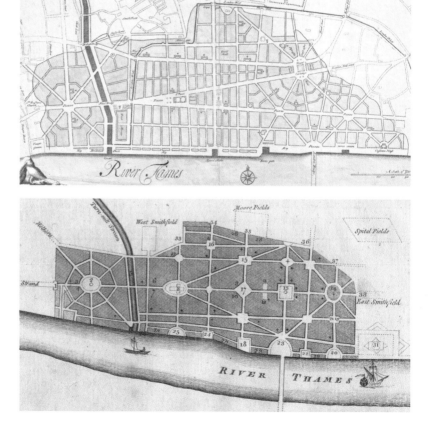

21. Frost fair on the Thames, 1677, with London Bridge and Southwark in the background. London's little ice age saw frequent freezings of the Thames in the seventeenth and eighteenth centuries.

22. Whitehall Palace c.1680, with Charles II and Prince Rupert by Danckerts; Banqueting Hall and Holbein Gate behind.

23. Covent Garden, St Paul's church and piazza. Begun by Inigo Jones in 1631 as London's first residential square.

24. St James's Square, London's most aristocratic speculation, by Henry Jermyn in 1662.

25. Hanover Square, Whig estate planned to welcome George I in 1714, with church named St George's in his honour.

26. Seven Dials, Covent Garden, a rare Georgian hub-and-star layout by developer Thomas Neale, never to achieve its intended fashionability.

27. The Thames as Grand Canal. St Paul's on Lord Mayor's Day by Canaletto in improbably clear light, *c.*1747.

28. The Royal Exchange, 1788. The second of what were to be four exchanges on the site of Gresham's original.

29. Gin Lane by Hogarth, 1751. The depiction of London's St Giles's quarter at the height of the gin craze was influential in securing regulation and reform.

30. William Hogarth, 1735, self-portrait. Hogarth represented the conservative tradition of Wren and Gibbs against the Grand Tour Palladians gathered round Lord Burlington.

31. St Marylebone watch house in the 1800s. London outside the City was still run by the old and corrupt parish vestries under the county of Middlesex.

32. East India Docks, looking towards the Greenwich peninsula with the Isle of Dogs to the right, c.1808 by William Daniell. The mouth of the River Lea is on the left.

33. Beau Brummell, embodiment of West End fashion at the height of the Regency. It was he who initiated the 'dark suit' as appropriate men's wear.

34. John Nash, Prince Regent's architect/
impresario, designer of the Royal Way from
St James's to Regent's Park.

35. Nash's Cumberland Terrace and Chester Terrace, Regent's Park, 1831.

36. *London Going out of Town, or the March of Bricks and Mortar, 1829.* George Cruikshank was satirizing the building boom as it advanced across the fields towards Hampstead.

37. Belgrave Square rising beyond Hyde Park Corner in a 'frenzy of building'.

38. Thomas Cubitt, 1840, master developer of the Grosvenor Estate.

9

Hanoverian Dawn
1714–1763

Whig ascendancy

The arrival of George I (1714–27) was greeted by Londoners with relief rather than enthusiasm. At the age of fifty-four, he was the princeling of a minor German state, who had leap-frogged fifty-five Catholics to gain a throne for which his sole qualification was to be a Protestant. He spoke little English and had visited London only once, recalling that he did not like it. George brought with him two mistresses, known as the elephant and the maypole, with whom he was said to play cards on alternate nights. Seldom did a European nation change dynasty with such banality.

George settled into St James's Palace but soon opted, like Mary and Anne before him, for the cleaner air of west London. Kensington Palace, already rebuilt by Wren, was again reordered by Colen Campbell and William Kent. It became the Hanoverians' principal home until George III moved to Buckingham House in 1760. The new king at first tried to conduct cabinet meetings in French, but gave up and left the business of government to a group of Whig peers. They were led in the commons by a genial but shrewd Norfolk grandee, Sir Robert Walpole, as First Lord of the Treasury. The king's most insistent conflict was with his son, George, the Prince of Wales, whom he evicted from St James's Palace. The heir set up a rival court in Leicester Square, an address that became a refuge for political malcontents, the Islington of its day.

George turned out to be no fool, carefully respecting the settlement of 1688. But just as William of Orange had sought English taxes to fight Dutch wars, so George sought them for German ones. Walpole eventually resigned over the resulting cost, but he returned during the financial crisis of 1720, caused by the 'bubble' and collapse in South Sea Company shares. The scandal, in which many ministers were implicated, was so vicious that the Riot Act was read in parliament. One City gazette demanded that bankers be 'tied up in sacks filled with snakes and tipped into the murky Thames'. It signalled the prominence the banking profession had now achieved – and was a sentiment that did not die with the times.

Walpole now enjoyed twenty years of political supremacy as Britain's first 'prime minister' (1721–42), much aided by the Hanoverians' laissez-faire approach to monarchy. As parliament emerged into the political daylight, so did London's taste for critical journalism. Walpole was lampooned by a galaxy of satirists, by John Gay in his *Beggar's Opera*, by Jonathan Swift, Daniel Defoe, Henry Fielding and Samuel Johnson, for whom he was 'Cock Robin', and soon to be 'killed'. This tradition of political scepticism invigorated and informed London public life, but it also made unthinkable the idea of state censorship customary on the continent. London was to see many a scrap between free speech and the law, but the notion of licensed criticism, like that of 'loyal opposition', was entrenched.

On one matter the prime minister did need his monarch's assistance: where to live when in London. In 1732, George II (1727–60) gave Walpole a modest terrace house, No. 5, in a Whitehall cul-de-sac built as a speculation by a Restoration courtier, Sir George Downing. Walpole turned three houses into one, with rooms redecorated by the ubiquitous Kent and facing Horse Guards Parade. The present street facade of 'No. 10', later rebuilt, was its rear entrance. Though the house was a private gift, Walpole declared it the official home of the prime minister. Until the twentieth century most of his successors used it only as an office.

Development by matrimony

Westminster was by now larger in both area and population than 'the City'. But just as the City lacked buildings distinctive of capitalism, so Westminster lacked buildings worthy of a capital. Whitehall was a ruin, St James's Palace a Tudor warren. Along the Thames were no royal edifices, avenues or impressive vistas, no stately bridges and ceremonial ways, let alone a Tuileries, Kremlin or Escorial. Instead of *grandes places* there were quiet squares, where the rich or less than rich lived cheek by jowl in terraces. London's only truly grand buildings, Westminster Abbey and St Paul's, belonged not to the state but to the church. St Paul's was the focus of almost every topographical painting and print of London, floating above the City like a guardian angel, attended by a host of heavenly steeples. Its celebrated witness was the Venetian, Canaletto, whose Thames was a silvery lake, glistening in improbably clear sunlight.

Westminster's growth had mostly taken the form of neighbourhoods developed round or in place of aristocratic mansions that had been dotted with their grounds across seventeenth-century Mayfair and St James's. It was no longer a London suburb, rather a 'second city' dependent on the industries of government, the professions and leisure. A last statute restraining its growth was passed in 1709, but was withdrawn under a hail of pleas for exemption. From now on there were to be no more prohibitive edicts from the Star Chamber or Privy Council. Instead there was just a queue of wealthy developers at the government's door seeking building permits, with friends in parliament and money for licences. It was significant that the arbiters were central, not local, government. The capital belonged to the nation.

What distinguished these developers from their successors today was that few had any interest in dealing in land. Most aristocratic families held their estates in entail for their heirs, and so could not sell. This meant there was little way in which an owner, however enterprising, could expand into a neighbouring estate, except through the accident – or conspiracy – of matrimony. The result was that London's growth in the eighteenth century was dominated by the market in marriageable heiresses, of whom there were an unusual number.

The first such match was in 1669, between William Russell, heir to the Earls (now Dukes) of Bedford, based in Covent Garden, and Rachel, heiress to Bloomsbury's Earl of Southampton. This united their two estates, bringing Covent Garden piazza and Bloomsbury Square into the same demesne, their surroundings still mostly covered in small tenements and market gardens.

This marriage was followed eight years later by 'the selling of Mary Davies'. Mary was the child heiress of Hugh Audley, a rich Stuart lawyer who had bought Westminster Abbey's former Manor of Eia from the Earl of Middlesex. The manor's extensive fields lay in a swathe across west London, from the Thames at Millbank north to Hyde Park Corner. Another portion lay to the north of Mayfair and south of Tyburn Road (modern Oxford Street). It was separated by the old Hay Hill farm, which had belonged to St James's hospital.

In 1672 Mary's unscrupulous mother 'sold' the seven-year-old Mary for £8,000 (around a million pounds today) to Lord Berkeley as a future wife for his ten-year-old son. Berkeley had a mansion in Piccadilly and the deal would have given him a massive holding across modern Mayfair and Belgravia. But Berkeley failed to find the final payment of £3,000 and Mary's mother aborted the transaction. For five more years the girl was again paraded on Rotten Row in Hyde Park, eventually receiving a bid from a twenty-one-year-old Cheshire grandee, Sir Thomas Grosvenor.

Mary was just twelve when she married Grosvenor at St Clement Danes in the Strand. The rest of her life was a misery of court cases and dementia. The Grosvenors never looked back. Thomas's son, Sir Richard, obtained an act for the development of the Mayfair fields in 1710, though building did not commence until after 1720, and in Belgravia not for another century. It remains among the largest and richest private estates in England.

Estate management, city style

London's growth now settled into a rhythm. Landlords regarded their estates much as they might their country manors, theirs in perpetuity. They left management to their agents, naming streets and squares after family members and rural estate villages. The London historian Donald Olsen wrote of Bloomsbury, 'The whole business of an estate office would be unintelligible without the assumption that the first duty of the ground landlord was to pass on to succeeding generations the value of the property unimpaired, and if possible enhanced.'

Owners mostly played safe. They let properties on lifelong 'repairing' leases, such that a lease carried a growing liability as it neared termination. All involved thus had an interest in ensuring the value of the estate over time. So cautious were the Bedfords about the long-term 'tone' of their area that they refused to allow any shops or pubs to open in Bloomsbury. Consequently, there are virtually none – other than a bookshop – between Euston Square and the British Museum.

The Bedford and Grosvenor 'mergers' stimulated a frenzy of

building elsewhere in the West End. The arrival of the Hanover-ians in 1714 was feted by the Whig Earl of Scarbrough with a strangely funnel-shaped 'square' on his land north of Lord Burling-ton's mansion in Piccadilly. Dutifully named Hanover Square and with a 'St George's' church, its houses were even decorated with 'aprons' beneath their windows, German style. These curiosities can be seen today on the terrace opposite the church.

North of Hanover Square, half of the manor of Marylebone was bought in 1710 by John Holles, Duke of Newcastle and husband of Margaret Cavendish. When he died with no male heir, his daughter Henrietta was snapped up by Edward, son of the leading statesman of the day, Robert Harley, Earl of Oxford and Mortimer. Harley thus acquired not just half of Marylebone but Holles's estates at Welbeck in Nottinghamshire and Wimpole in Cambridgeshire. Marylebone would not be allowed to forget Harley, Cavendish and Holles, and their country estates at Bolsover, Carburton, Clipstone, Mansfield, Mortimer, Welbeck and Wigmore.

The Harleys were intractable Tories, eager to cock a snook at Scarbrough's upstart Whigs to the south. They duly laid out Tory Cavendish Square the same year, 1717, as Whig Hanover. Its tenants were a rollcall of Harley's political allies: Carnarvon, Dartmouth, Chandos, Harcourt and Bathurst. The estate developer John Prince and his (Tory and Catholic) architect, James Gibbs, were the most ambitious builders London had yet seen. The Duke of Chandos offered to build a mansion on the square's north side. A chapel of ease, St Peter's, was built in Vere Street to the south. Though Chan-dos's house was abandoned after the South Sea Bubble, a grid of townhouses soon ran west to Marylebone Lane and east to Lord Berners's estate above Soho. In an effort to emphasize its *rus in urbe*, Prince even put sheep to grazing in Cavendish Square.

Edward and Henrietta Harley were again without a male heir, and their daughter Margaret was talked of as the richest young woman in England. In 1734 she duly married the eligible twenty-four-year-old William Bentinck, grandson of William of Orange's London agent. The events of 1688 had seen his family showered with honours, as Dukes of Portland, Marquesses of Titchfield and Viscounts Woodstock. As if that was not enough, William was known as 'the handsomest man in England'. He duly became Margaret's 'sweet Will' and she his duchess. Her dowry was half of Marylebone, which now became the Portland estate.

Margaret was a remarkable figure. She took after her Harley grandfather, a noted book and manuscript collector, and turned her house at Bulstrode outside London into a zoo and botanical research centre. When the visiting encyclopaedist Jean-Jacques Rousseau declared no woman could be a scientist, she rebutted him so emphatically that he asked if he could work for her. Margaret was an early member of Elizabeth Montagu's Blue Stockings set (see below). After divisions and lateral inheritances, the bulk of the estate went to the Howard de Walden family, in whose custody it remains.

No sooner were Hanover and Cavendish squares under construction than the dilatory Grosvenors came to life. Grosvenor Square was laid out in 1721 to be twice the size of Hanover Square, with fifty houses four storeys high. The plan was for each side to form a coherent classical composition, as Bedford was later to achieve in Bedford Square and Nash round Regent's Park. Colen Campbell even submitted an appropriate design. But by the 1720s the market was weakening and Grosvenor's builders had to erect houses as and when purchasers of suitable status were forthcoming. The patchwork result was dismissed by a contemporary critic as 'a wretched attempt at something extraordinary'. Not until the twentieth century did the Grosvenors impose a frigid classical order on the whole square. To the south, Lord Berkeley, spurned by Mary Davies's mother, was having similar trouble getting Berkeley Square off the ground. It proceeded piecemeal from 1739, though with one superb town-house by Kent surviving at No. 44.

In 1755 a number of these landlords and their agents petitioned for a new road to be built across the north of the manor of Marylebone, to relieve congestion along the Tyburn Road. They argued that it was not conducive to the marketing of their estates to have herds of cattle and sheep driven past their gates. The result was one of inner London's few 'planned' thoroughfares, from Paddington along the present Marylebone and Euston Roads to Pentonville Road and down to the City at Moorgate. It was a toll road and would be the path also of the Metropolitan Line. It is one of the few roads in the capital that today's traffic managers try to keep free-flowing.

Virtually the only eighteenth-century estate to go up for actual sale was that of William Cheyne, whose father had bought the manor of distant Chelsea after the Civil War. He built Cheyne Row in 1709, and retired to Buckinghamshire. In 1712 he sold the manor to Sir Hans Sloane, a doctor, antiquary and founder of the British Museum.

Sloane in turn built Cheyne Walk along the Thames and, in 1753, divided the manor between his two daughters, the western half to Sarah and the eastern half to Elizabeth, who married a descendant of the medieval Welsh warlord Cadwgan ap Elystan. As Lord Cadogan, her husband would later let the architect Henry Holland develop Hans Town in the north of the manor at Knightsbridge, named after his generous father-in-law. Holland also built himself a pavilion, recalled in Pavilion Road. At the end of its leases in the 1880s, Hans Town became the most ruthlessly rebuilt of all estates, in redbrick Victorian neo-Dutch. The Cadogan estate remains active today.

A metropolis of enlightenment

This was the stage on which was enacted London's 'Golden Age', running from the mid-Georgian era to the Napoleonic wars. The stage must often have seemed shambolic. Where once had strolled shepherds and gardeners, the air was filled with clouds of dust and noise. New purchasers complained they had been promised rural bliss. Instead, the houses of Marylebone were 'rising like exhalations'. A scholar in Richard Steele's play *The Lying Lover* said he need hardly have returned from Oxford, since 'had I stayed a year longer . . . they had builded to me'.

Yet London was a city almost without a city. The social historian Raymond Williams saw it as 'being intensely observed as a new kind of landscape, a new kind of society', neither town nor country. The same clash of opposites became a Georgian leitmotif. It was seen politically in the rivalry between Tories and Whigs, between the old 'patriotic' Stuarts and new 'European' Hanoverians, as well as between a latent Catholicism and a dominant Protestantism. It was seen in the flourishing of a sceptical periodicals market, led by Addison and Steele's *Spectator*, precursor of today's newspaper, appearing three times a week from 1711.

The clash was also stylistic, between the English baroque of Wren, Hawksmoor and Gibbs and a revival of Inigo Jones's Palladianism. The latter was spurred by a resumption of the grand tour following the Peace of Utrecht. Wealthy young aristocrats led by Burlington and Leicester returned to London laden with Italian and French paintings, furniture and pattern books of the Roman architect Vitruvius. In 1719 Burlington, together with his friends the architects Campbell and Kent, rebuilt his family mansion in Piccadilly – now housing the Royal Academy – and developed its gardens running up to Hanover Square. The new streets recall Burlington family names at

Cork Street, Clifford Street and Savile Row. The group also built an immaculate Palladian villa and park near the river at Chiswick.

Just as the Burlingtonians saw themselves as the height of fashion, they became the butt of ridicule from the Tory old guard. As they gathered at Chiswick, the 'British bulldog' artist William Hogarth would fume over the wall of his neighbouring country house, satirizing them in his prints *Marriage à la Mode* and *The Rake's Progress*. Pope lauded his patron Burlington, 'You show us, Rome was glorious, not profuse,/ And pompous buildings once were things of use.' This eulogy in turn drove Hogarth to deride them both in his *Man of Taste*, portraying them as whitewashing Burlington's gate while tipping paint over the (Tory) Duke of Chandos riding past.

Hogarth was a one-man critique of the new Whig London, and of what he saw as its effete degeneration. He was a classic lower-middle-class Londoner, son of a Latin teacher imprisoned for debt and trained as a business-card engraver. Self-portrayed with his favourite pug, he was a Tory chauvinist in all things. He characterized the French as cringing, emaciated, superstitious and frog-eating, notably when threatened by John Bull and a British sirloin. But Hogarth did not spare London. His backdrops ranged from the stews of St Giles to the salons of St James's, and he was to become a champion of the fight against gin. Hogarth joins Chaucer and Pepys in my pantheon of London observers. We can still stand in his Chiswick garden and gaze over the wall towards Burlington's palace – excusing the villas in between – and imagine him fulminating.

London's rivalry with Paris was now more than one of upstart versus historic arbiter of European taste. France after Louis XIV's death in 1715 saw an extraordinary intellectual release. The French Enlightenment, led by Diderot, Voltaire, Montesquieu, Rousseau and their encyclopaedia, took European thought into new fields of curiosity and the pursuit of reason. The Enlightenment's one deficiency, its authors acknowledged, was France's intolerance of open debate. It was constantly running the gauntlet of crown and church. London's Royal Society might have been eclipsed for a time, but the baton had passed from science to literature, and the talents of Pope, Swift, Dryden, Gibbon and above all Samuel Johnson, whose pen equalled Hogarth's brush as a window on the Georgian city.

Johnson was, like Hogarth, a Tory. A large, ungainly figure with nervous tics, he suffered from partial blindness and deafness, as well as gout, depression and testicular cancer. He drank wine and tea copiously and conversed with all and sundry into the night, having the good fortune of an admiring scribe, James Boswell, being on hand to record his words. Johnson was critic, essayist, poet and lexicographer, creator of the first dictionary of the English language. His devotion to reason was passionate. 'Every man has a right to utter what he thinks truth,' he declared during a lifetime of epigrams, 'and every other man has a right to knock him down for it.' Above all he personified London. He who tired of it, said Johnson, 'is tired of life, for there is in London all that life can afford. You will find no man, he said, 'that is at all intellectual, who is willing to leave London.' Johnson's house still stands off Fleet Street.

Visitors from the continent agreed. They were astonished at the reckless satires that delighted London's salons and publishing houses – publishers were to be forever 'houses'. When Voltaire arrived in 1726 after his expulsion from Paris, he praised a city where 'men could say what they think'. In Paris, Pascal could 'make jokes only at the expense of Jesuits, while London's Swift entertains and instructs us at the expense of the whole of the human race'. The encyclopaedist Diderot complained that in London 'philosophers rise to public affairs and are buried with kings, whereas in France warrants are issued against them' for their arrest. By the 1750s, 800 houses in Soho were occupied by French refugees. Their appearance and atmosphere is well evoked in Spitalfields' Folgate Street in the Dennis Severs' House, a 'time capsule' recreation of the home of a 1720s Huguenot silk merchant.

Entertainment flourished. The Theatre Royal in Drury Lane was under the actor-manager Colley Cibber, despite Pope attacking his 'miserable mutilation of crucified Molière and hapless Shakespeare'. Nocturnal gamblers flocked to Ranelagh and Vauxhall Gardens. There were open-to-all (but not free for all) dances and masquerades, notably those staged by Casanova's Venetian lover, Teresa Cornelys, in Carlyle House in Soho Square. Most celebrated of all was George I's finest gift to London, his court composer George Frideric Handel.

In 1717 the king's commission of Handel's *Water Music* saw the Thames crowded with flotillas of barges, 'driving with the tide without rowing, as far as Chelsea'. According to the *Daily Courant*, the king liked the music 'so well as he caused it to be played over three times'. Handel's importing of foreign singers was a source of typically London complaint, not for their quality but for the absence of English ones. It was a measure of his popularity that he could pay his top performers £2,000 for a season (£250,000 today). Only in the 1740s did Handel's operatic star begin to wane, whereupon he turned with equal success to oratorios.

One duty the Hanoverians took seriously was their leadership of the Church of England. George I continued with the uncompleted 'Queen Anne' churches. The Catholic Gibbs, architect of St Mary-le-Strand, was chosen for the prominent St Martin-in-the-Fields in 1721. Its unusual steeple rising above a classical portico was to become the prototype for Anglican worship throughout the English-speaking world. Yet despite royal patronage, the Church had grown indolent and corrupt. While rich church-goers monopolized (and paid for) pew seats in parish churches, the poor were forced to stand in the aisles, to be championed by Hogarth in his popular satirical print of *The Sleeping Congregation* (1736).

Such a church was vulnerable, if not to officially outlawed Catholicism, then to the 'methodist' preaching of John Wesley. Wesley's appeal was as basic as that of Wycliffe and Luther, 'preaching inward present salvation as attainable by faith alone'. He always asserted his devout Anglicanism, but he was banned from churches and, much to his advantage, took to preaching in the open air. His London venue was Finsbury's Moorfields, where thousands gathered to hear him. Even Dr Johnson was impressed by Wesley's 'plain and familiar manner', while George III contributed masts from the shipyard at Deptford for the pillars in Wesley's City Road chapel.

Law, order and gin

For the first time, many Londoners were becoming publicly aware that all was not well in much of their city. Conditions in the 'rookeries' along the banks of the Thames had barely improved from Tudor times. Dr Johnson was hyperbolic with horror, at sharing his city with 'people not only without delicacy but without government, a herd of barbarians or a colony of Hottentots'. Johnson was not sparing in his comments on the lower orders, while always identifying himself as poor. The debauchery of street life likewise appalled the novelist Samuel Richardson. He found apprentices given the day off for executions at Tyburn, known as 'Tyburn fairs'. He once encountered what he probably overestimated as 80,000 people heading for the gallows, with the condemned men stopping in pubs to get drunk with friends. They were events, said Richardson, which 'in other nations . . . are said to be little attended by any beside the necessary officers and the mournful friends'. Yet in London it was treated as a festival, the crowd afterwards fighting to sell the corpses to surgeons for dissection. 'The behaviour of my country-men is past my accounting,' said Richardson. In 1783 executions were moved to Newgate to limit the crowds, but they simply followed.

The contrast between the City and beyond was most marked in policing. Within the City, each ward had to parade some form of constabulary, while 'trained bands' of volunteers could be called on in an emergency. In Westminster and elsewhere, order was the responsibility of vestry watch committees, with mostly elderly vol-unteers as constables. Like Shakespeare's versions, they had little reason to do anything but keep out of trouble, or be bribed to ignore it. On a visit to Soho, Casanova was advised always to carry two purses, 'a small one for the robbers and a large one for ourselves'. An attempt by a group of Westminster parishes to establish a per-manent watch in 1720 was opposed by both the church and parliament, it appears for no other reason than that it was new. In 1735, however, the vestries of St James's Piccadilly and St George's Hanover Square did secure a paid night watch, recruiting the first employed constables.

These were reinforced in 1748 when the novelist Henry Fielding was appointed London's first stipendiary magistrate at Bow Street court. His crown salary of £550 a year (£65,000 today) was kept secret for fear of vestry opposition to any centrally appointed police force. Fielding was a remarkable combination of writer and bureau-crat. The historian Dorothy George saw him as viewing 'the terrible state of the poor and the perversities of the laws, with the imaginative sympathy of a great novelist who was also a trained lawyer'. Fielding followed his novel *Tom Jones* in 1751 with an *Enquiry into the Causes of the Late Increase in Robbery*. He was angry that 'the sufferings of the poor are less observed than their mis-deeds'. They 'starve and freeze and rot among themselves, but they beg, steal and rob among their betters'. Fielding founded a Marine

Society for settling vagrant boys on ships, and an Orphan Asylum for Deserted Girls.

By the 1750s London was facing an acknowledged crisis over gin. The availability of cheap liquor had created mass addiction. One in ten central London houses was a 'dram shop'. In Westminster it was one in eight, and in the slum parish of St Giles one in four. Respectable opinion was shocked that a quarter of gin sellers were women. Alcohol had become a plague. It was said 'you could get drunk for a penny, dead drunk for tuppence'. An estimated 100,000 Londoners were now living on gin alone, and 9,000 gin-soaked children died each year.

Fielding declared that should 'this poison be continued at its present height during the next twenty years, there will by that time be very few of the common people left to drink it'. He was unequivocal. Blame lay with legislation and its indulgence of gin purveyors, whom he described as the 'principal officers of the king of terrors, having conveyed more people to the regions of death than the sword or the plague'. In 1739 this produced one spectacular charitable response, when Thomas Coram launched his Foundling Hospital on land east of Bloomsbury for abandoned children, it being in large part a response to the menace of gin. It became a fashionable cause, with dukes and earls on its board, costumes designed by Hogarth and an anthem by Handel. Opening in 1741, it was inundated with babies deposited at its gate. Though the hospital has gone the shelf for abandoned babies can still be seen in its old wall.

Between 1720 and 1750 was the only time London's population growth actually stagnated, as infant mortality rose and gin deaths soared. Hogarth's depiction of Gin Lane, published in 1751, was horrific. It showed emaciated drunkards littering the streets, mothers dropping babies down stairs and inn signs of coffins or pawnbrokers' balls. In the distance, St George's Bloomsbury hovered over the tenements of St Giles, backing onto the most fashionable parts of town. Hogarth contrasted Gin Lane with the benign Beer Street, beer being 'a common necessity which Britons deem to be part of their birth-right'. These widely distributed prints were art at its most political. Hogarth said of their impact on public debate, 'I am more proud of having been their author than I should be of having painted Raphael's cartoons.'

Campaigns by Fielding and Hogarth among others had an effect. They secured an act of 1751 imposing swingeing taxes on gin, and requiring the costly licensing of premises. Within seven years, gin-drinkers were reported to be switching to beer, probably safer than London water, much to the advantage of their health. Eleven million gallons of gin drunk in 1751 fell to 3.6 million in 1767. Infant mortality under five fell from 75 per cent in the 1740s to 31 per cent in the 1770s. Admissions of infants to Coram's hospital also fell dramatically. As a result, London's population returned to growth, to reach a million by the end of the century. The case for curbing such harmful consumption, not by banning but by sensible regulation, was never better demonstrated.

Henry Fielding died in 1754, but his work was continued for another twenty-five years by his equally trenchant brother, the blind magistrate Sir John. Henry had formed a group of detectives known as Mr Fielding's Men, later the Bow Street Runners. John Fielding advertised 'the immediate despatch of a set of brave fellows on trusty steeds . . . always ready to set out to any part of this town or kingdom on quarter of an hour's notice'. Though only eight strong, their reputation, discipline and honesty became celebrated. They drew up records of incidents on the highways round London, in one week noting robberies of travellers near Finchley, Paddington, Gunnersbury, Syon, Turnham Green, Hounslow Heath, Hampstead and Islington. The Fieldings rank among the great reformers in London's history.

Crossing the river

Crime was not the only price paid for London's growth. Congestion was another. The longstanding stranglehold of the City over
aspects of London's government was now absurd. The jams on
London Bridge were a scandal, while the City's lobbyists in parliament were able to block any new bridge over the Thames below
Kingston. The ferry owners too lobbied, including the most potent,
the Archbishop of Canterbury and his Lambeth 'horse-ferry' to
Millbank. As a result, the south bank of the river lay undeveloped,
with silent, open fields just a hundred yards across the water from
the teeming quaysides and massed tenements on the northern side.

In 1722 another bill for a bridge at Westminster was killed by
the City, the corporation declaring it contemptible 'to the birth-
right and privileges of freemen of London'. It would 'take the
meat from [the City's] mouths . . . In short it will make Westminster a fine city and London a desert.' But the City's power was
waning and this was its last throw. Within four years a bill for a
Putney bridge passed through parliament, and finally in 1736 one
for Westminster.

The City was now stung into action to bring itself up to date.
In 1733 the Fleet Ditch had been put in a culvert and covered, and a
market placed on top of it. The corporation's surveyor in 1735–67
was the Palladian architect George Dance, joined by his son, also
George, and by an architect/alderman, Sir Robert Taylor. In 1739
Dance designed a new mayoral residence, the Mansion House, giving the City at last a building worthy of its status.

This was not enough. In 1754 an economist, Joseph Massie,
chided the City for being 'supine and inactive', risking being
rivalled and eclipsed 'by cities both abroad and at home'. He advised
that the still-standing medieval walls and gates be demolished,

streets widened and houses on London Bridge removed to aid traffic. The City should also build its own new bridge, at Blackfriars.

For once the City took this advice. It sought an act from parliament to widen its streets and clear London Bridge of its picturesque but tumbledown houses. This clearance won the 600-year-old structure another sixty years of life. As for the new Westminster Bridge, built by a Swiss, Charles Labelye, and opened in 1750, and a new toll bridge at Blackfriars in 1769, they were exquisite structures, crossing the river in delightful parabolas. London's south bank was at last open for business.

10

A Tarnished Age
1763–1789

New times, new politics

Georgian London was a city ill prepared for the age of industrial revolution and world trade. Its buildings had been renewed and overcrowding relieved by suburban expansion. But its governance was either inert or absent. The fact that the City and the Westminster vestries needed acts of parliament merely for street widening or bridge building showed the immaturity of its leadership. Slum clearance was non-existent, as was proper sewerage, water supply and policing.

Politics was now beating at the city's gates. In 1756 William Pitt had led the country into the Seven Years War (1756–63) and the *annus mirabilis* of 1759, when Britain acquired an empire, said a Victorian historian, 'in a fit of absence of mind'. The capital was already redirecting its commercial attention from the continent to the globe. Its old staples of wool cloth, furs, spices and rare woods had given way to coal, tin, sugar, cotton and shipping. But Britain's industrial focus was shifting to the north, the home of coal and iron and where ports faced the Atlantic. London's business had evolved from handling things to handling money, and that required new forms of consent to government.

In 1761 the new king, the twenty-four-year-old George III (1760–1820), precipitated a political crisis by sacking Pitt and choosing to 'rule' through an aristocratic coalition led by his old tutor, the Earl of Bute. London reverted to being in opposition to Westminster. It faced rising prices, a resumed upward pressure of population in need of food and shelter, and growing industrial unrest. The long compact between the City's employers and their labour, cemented by the guilds, was breaking down. Workers demonstrated against novice apprentices and broke the new mechanical looms, both of which were pushing down wages.

While prosperous newcomers to the Westminster suburbs might remain politically apathetic, the City in the 1760s was turning turbulent. Street disorder became frequent. The ghost of London's past, the mob, was back on the scene. In 1763, seventy-six Huguenot looms in the East End were smashed in one night. Sooner or later, a radical leader of ability was certain to emerge, and that year one did. He was the journalist and MP for Aylesbury, John Wilkes, arrested for libelling Bute.

Wilkes was diminutive, cross-eyed and unprepossessing – declared 'the ugliest man in England' – but he had an extraordinary talent for rousing a crowd. He fled prosecution to France, but returned in 1768, to be followed everywhere by an uncontrollable crowd. During his successful campaign for election as MP for Middlesex that year, a mob smashed every window in the Mansion House, while a riot in St George's Field in Southwark saw half a dozen men shot by the militia. The street cry 'Wilkes and Liberty' was demanded of passers-by on pain of a beating. Wilkes was a menace to public order. Three times denied admission to the commons, his argument that it was for electors, not ministers, to choose their MPs secured widespread sympathy including from Pitt himself.

Wilkes was no ordinary rabble-rouser. He was well off, a member of the Royal Society and the aristocratic Hellfire Club. He had sufficient support to be made a City alderman, eventually winning his way back to parliament in 1774, when he also became Lord

Mayor. In 1776 he introduced the first bill for electoral reform. Wilkes's cause was taken up by enough Whigs to ensure that the franchise remained an issue of public and parliamentary argument for half a century, until reform triumphed in 1832. However violent was Wilkes's mob, it was parliament that kept control of the argument.

The Gordon riots

The mob soon had a more immediate agenda than the franchise. The cause was legislation to emancipate Catholics in Ireland, though the real bone of contention was an inrush of Irish workers into London's fragmenting labour market, coupled with widespread sympathy for the then rebellious American colonists. In 1780 London experienced a sudden outburst of anarchy, led by an anti-Catholic Scot, Lord George Gordon, at the head of some 60,000 apprentices and others. Armed with lists of addresses of magistrates, MPs and anyone who had supported Catholic emancipation, they attacked houses across the capital. In most European cities, the ruling classes lived behind blank walls and heavy gates. In London their houses faced the street, windows and all. These windows became the favoured target of what was dubbed King Mob.

The Gordon rioters confronted the government of Lord North, unprepared either to treat with or to suppress them. Ministers were terrified into inertia. An eye-witness account of the resulting chaos was given by a Londoner, Ignatius Sancho. Born on a slave ship, Sancho was butler to the Duke of Montagu, a friend of the actor David Garrick, painted by Gainsborough and a correspondent of Laurence Sterne. He wrote of the crowd storming past his upstairs window: 'The maddest people that the maddest times were ever plagued with . . . a poor, miserable, ragged rabble from twelve to sixty years of age 'parading the streets' ready for any and every mischief.' Eventually, the militia was mobilized. Estimates disagree but the riots seem to have culminated in over 500 dead and injured, by some counts 850, mostly by military action, lynching, fires and executions. It was the worst outbreak of civil violence in London's modern history.

The North government was at the time enmeshed in a trading dispute with its new colonies, first infuriating and then trying to suppress commercial interests in Boston. From 1775 to 1783 the American states fought back, with considerable and ready help from France. Substantial elements in parliament and the City were openly supportive of the rebels, including Pitt (now the Earl of Chatham), the radical Charles James Fox and the conservative Edmund Burke. Burke was furious at George using 'the hireling swords of German vassals . . . against English flesh and blood'. When eventually the 'jewel in the crown' of the new British empire was lost, George III was humiliated. In desperation, in 1783 he asked Chatham's son, the twenty-four-year-old William Pitt the younger, to head a government.

The City's response to American independence was predictable. Merchants raced to do business with the new United States. London saw its first substantial black immigration as freed slaves who had fought for the crown during the rebellion were given sanctuary. By the end of the century, the number of black people in London was estimated at 5,000 to 10,000, and they were sufficiently familiar to appear in many of Hogarth's London prints. Dr Johnson employed a black servant. Two years later the first American ambassador, John Adams, took up residence in a corner house in Grosvenor Square (still standing). He was warmly greeted by a chastened George, though he suffered ostracism by many Londoners, who dismissed him as from a country not likely to remain independent for long.

The spirit of improvement

The younger Pitt's appointment brought a degree of stability to British government, but the 1780s were not stable times in Europe. Migrants from Louis XVI's France were arriving in London in rising numbers, bringing news of a nation bankrupted by the Bourbons and by the cost of aiding the American revolutionaries. France was on the brink of governmental collapse. London was nervous. It was still recovering from the Wilkes and Gordon riots. Support for reform in parliament and the loss of the American colonies had induced a rare political fragility.

In London, this was reflected in doubts over how ready the metropolis was to accept ever increasing immigration without a violent reaction from existing citizens. A widely noted book by John Gwynn, *London and Westminster Improved* (1766), deplored the lack of planning in an ever more crowded West End. Development might be popular, but Gwynn warned against 'so wretched a use . . . made of so valuable and desirable an opportunity'. The new London was 'inconvenient, inelegant and without the least pretension to magnificence or grandeur'. He reiterated the Stuart call that 'proper bounds may be set to that fury which seems to possess the fraternity of builders, to prevent them from extending the town in the enormous manner they . . . still continue to do'. Another writer, Jonas Hanway, noted that London's once-rural environs were now 'displeasing both to sight and smell, surrounded by a chain of brick-kilns, like the scars of the smallpox'.

Gwynn's words were heard and this time even the indolent Middlesex vestries stirred themselves to life. Over a hundred London 'improvement' acts were passed in the 1760s and 70s, mostly concerning policing, workhouses for the poor and paving commissions. The Westminster Paving Act of 1762 was radical. It made new commissioners responsible for maintaining drains, and for cleaning and lighting all streets west of the City boundary at Temple Bar. There should be stone kerbs to protect pedestrians, and gutters to carry off rainwater. There were even acts against the 'contemptible and forbidding' state of Lincoln's Inn Fields, that 'is become a nursery for beggars and thieves'. That this should require crown intervention showed the impotence of London's local government.

The new Westminster Bridge spurred the local commissioners to extend Whitehall through the old palace gates to what is now Parliament Square. Even today, Whitehall officially stops at Downing Street. A cross street was also created to link the new bridge with St James's Park. Something like a government quarter at the heart of Westminster was beginning to emerge.

The opening of the two new bridges at last stimulated development south of the river. Here the City's surveyor, Robert Mylne, in 1771 planned building in the swampy fields of Lambeth as a spacious contrast to the 'stews and tenements' of old Southwark. His proposal was unprecedented in London – other than by Wren – for a *rond-point* and obelisk at a new St George's Circus. Spokes would radiate from this hub, leading to Westminster, Blackfriars and London bridges. Their lines were straight enough to have gladdened Wren's heart.

As it turned out, London's planners treated Mylne's plan much as Alfred the Great treated Rome's, as a rough first draft. There were ribbons of terrace houses along Mylne's spokes, and there was even a scatter of squares, such as West Square and Trinity Church Square. But south London had been too long postponed. The circus and obelisk survive, but distorted and in a traffic scheme that strips the layout of its intended drama. The south would never compete with north of the river as the heartbeat of the metropolis.

The 1774 Building Act

The most emphatic sign of a new approach to London was the 1774 Building Act, creation of the City's Dance and Taylor. The act updated regulations begun after the Great Fire and revised in 1707 and 1709, and was highly prescriptive. It stipulated four 'rates' of terrace house, with rules for dimensions, party walls, materials and fireproofing. Exposed woodwork was now banned, except around doors. Every street should be uniform, varying only by the 'size' of house, each with an 'area' in front for the storage of coal and the admission of light into the servants' quarters. Behind would be a strip of yard with outhouses. The humblest property should be a miniature version of the grandest, and regulation should apply, in theory, even to the poorest.

Adaptable, extendable, pleasing to the eye, these houses embodied privacy amid good neighbourliness, perfectly suiting the social hierarchy of the new city. However anonymous, a house facing proud onto a street was a Londoner's castle, home to Voltaire's city of free spirits. What is extraordinary is that the resulting houses should be as popular today as when they were built. Even London architects professing the dictates of Corbusian modernism (mostly) prefer to relax after work in a 1774 Act townhouse. London's most expensive offices per square foot are not City towers but Mayfair 'first-raters'.

The act's deficiency was that it could not tackle the poorest and most overcrowded parts of the city. Wapping, Shadwell, Stepney and Southwark were left out of account, and had to wait another century for similar regulation and relief, and then from private philanthropy. Another deficiency, which emerged only over time, was dullness. To Summerson, the act's creations yielded 'the inexpressible monotony of a typical London street, a monotony which must, at one time, have been overpowering'. Benjamin Disraeli would later blame the act for 'those flat, dull spiritless streets all resembling each other, like a large family of plain children'. It was a defect the Victorians were to rectify with a vengeance.

One architect who did contrive to vary the formula was the Scotsman Robert Adam. To him the classicism that had ruled Georgian architecture from Burlington through to George III's surveyor, William Chambers, was 'a Palladian prison of tabernacle frames'. Stimulated by recent excavations at Diocletian's palace in modern-day Croatia, Adam stretched the 1774 Act to the limit. He adorned his London houses with skylights, roundels and plasterwork. Interiors danced with swags, ribbons, masks and pillars, 'light mouldings, gracefully formed, delicately enriched'. They were intensely popular.

Adam's rivalry with Chambers became the talk of the town. Chambers represented the old guard of the Hanoverian establishment. As chief surveyor, in 1775 he began a grand project to give London a 'national building' to house its burgeoning civil service, located on the site of old Somerset House. It became a bureaucratic Valhalla, 'Salt Office, Stamp Office, Tax Office, Navy Office, Victualling Office, Publick Lottery Office, Hawkers and Pedlar Office, Hackney Coach Office'. Chambers led a tour of Inigo Jones's old mansion on the site, pointing out its magnificent features before his men smashed them to the ground.

Next door upriver, Adam set out to show what his new style could offer. The Adelphi, named in honour of himself and his brothers, was a private housing speculation, though it turned out to be a poor one that had to be rescued from bankruptcy by a lottery. The resulting rival palaces were the first attempts to embank the Thames, rather than leave gardens down to the river's edge. They rose, said Summerson 'out of the sodden margins of the river on arcades of Palatine grandeur' – today marooned behind a later Embankment.

Chambers regarded Adam as an upstart and his work as frippery and affectation. He refused him admission to his new Royal Academy, formed in 1768, and opened in Somerset House ten years later. Adam became the darling of fashion, with grand houses across London and beyond, at Osterley, Kenwood and Syon. His work was a supreme moment in London design, exemplified by town-houses in Portman Square, St James's Square and Queen Anne Street (sadly inaccessible). But Chambers had the last laugh. His Somerset House still rides the river bank resplendent, while the centre block of Adam's Adelphi was demolished between the wars. Only its side streets survive.

The great estates return to life

The most spectacular product of the 1774 Act was on the Duke of Bedford's Bloomsbury estate. Instead of the disjointed, piecemeal frontages of Grosvenor, Berkeley and Cavendish squares, Bedford Square was of four coherent facades. They were of first-rate houses, three bays wide, four storeys high and with restrained door cases. Their surrounds displayed the new artificial stone, from the Lambeth factory of Eleanor Coade. This remarkable businesswoman, originally a linen draper and sculptress from Devon, invented a composite form of plaster that could be moulded and hard-fired. It came to adorn houses, churches and public buildings throughout Georgian London. Coade-dressed Bedford Square was, and remains, immaculate.

West of Marylebone Lane – which still follows the curving path of the Tyburn stream – the landowner Henry William Portman began in 1780 to build the square that takes his name. To mark its status, he had Adam design a house in the north-west corner for the daughter of a sugar baron in Jamaica, the Countess of Home. Her raucous parties had her dubbed by hackney cab drivers the Queen of Hell, but Adam's interiors were (and are) among his most exquisite. At the same time, the society hostess Elizabeth Montagu moved ostensibly 'upmarket', from Mayfair's Hill Street into a house in Portman Square next door to the countess, designed by another Scot, James 'Athenian' Stuart. She was the founder of the Blue Stockings Society and a militant campaigner for the abolition of slavery. She and the countess were not good neighbours.

Portman's buildings swiftly extended across west Marylebone. Their names recalled his ancestors, the Seymours, Fitzhardinges and Wyndhams, and his Dorset estates at Blandford, Bryanston, Crawford, Bridport and Durweston. A charming break with tradition was Montagu Square, named not after a duke but as a thank you to Elizabeth Montagu for the party she gave each year for the estate's chimney sweeps, one of whom, David Porter, went on to become the square's developer.

To the east, the Portland estate was now nearing completion. In 1778 it commissioned the Adam brothers to develop the fields north of Foley House, long-leased by Lord Foley on the understanding that his view north would not be impeded. The condition was met in form if not in spirit. The Adam brothers designed a wide avenue, the widest in London, Portland Place. The destruction of its harmony by the Howard de Waldens between the wars was a tragedy, leaving one of London's loveliest townscapes sorely wounded.

Builders now looked further afield. The Fitzroy descendants of the Duke of Grafton, Charles II's illegitimate son, developed their manor of Tottenhall, running north of Oxford Street across the New Road to the border of Lord Camden's estate. Fitzroy Square, designed again by Adam, was begun in 1791 but came to a halt during the slump of the Napoleonic wars, when 'Marylebone bankruptcies' became a catchphrase for builders in the area. Fitzroy Square's eighteenth-century form is still evident. A grander

Euston Square straddled the New Road, named after the Duke of Grafton's house in Suffolk, but later sacrificed to the new station.

Further east, the governors of the Foundling Hospital in 1790 leased Brunswick and Mecklenburgh squares to an enterprising developer, James Burton, who built 600 houses on Coram's land. This was too far out for the smartest tenants, intended for what were called 'the middling classes', of doctors, lawyers and merchants. The sister of the title character in Jane Austen's *Emma* felt obliged to insist that Brunswick Square's qualities were 'so very superior to most others . . . the neighbourhood decidedly the most favourable as to air'.

West End land prices were now soaring. A plot off Piccadilly, bought by a brewer for £30, was sold soon afterwards for £2,500. Another in Mayfair's Hay Hill had, under Queen Anne, been valued at £200 and went in the 1760s for £20,000. Nor was the fever confined to central London. Builders turned to outlying villages within commuting distance. As early as the 1720s Georgian terraces appeared in Stoke Newington, Church Row in Hampstead, Holland Street in Kensington and Maids of Honour Row in Richmond. By the 1770s they were blossoming in Chiswick, Camberwell, Greenwich and wherever there was clean air and a carriage to London.

Such commuting, often in the most primitive of vehicles, soon became a fashion. A writer in 1750 remarked of Turnham Green that 'every little clerk in office must have his villa, and every tradesman his country house', whether for daily or weekend commuting. Horace Walpole, resident in Twickenham, wrote in 1791 that 'there will soon be one street all the way from London to Brentford . . . to every village ten miles round. Lord Camden has just let ground in Kentish Town for building fourteen hundred houses.' Walpole once had to stop his coach in Piccadilly fearing that it was invaded by a mob, but 'it was only passengers' apparently on their way to work.

The changing winds of fashion

As it approached a million residents, London in the 1790s was a different city from a century before. The West End had evolved from an enclave of pieds-à-terre – for those attending parliament and 'the season' – to become a permanent, occupied metropolis. The *Critical Review* reported that 'almost every house has a glass lamp with two wicks . . . Beneath the pavements are vast subterranean sewers arched over to convey away the waste water, which in other cities is so noisome above ground.' Most noticeable was that 'wooden pipes supply every house plentifully with water, conducted by leaden pipes into kitchens or cellars, three times a week for the trifling expense of three shillings per quarter'. There were said to be more lights in Oxford Street than in the whole of Paris. This was so unusual that a prince of Monaco, visiting London, thought the illuminations were staged in his honour.

Not all London was so lucky. Despite attempts at self-improvement, the pleasures of living in the old City were in decline. A lady in George Colman's *The Clandestine Marriage* complained of being stuck in 'the dull districts of Aldersgate, Cheap, Candlewick and Farringdon Without and Within', while she longed to be 'transported to the dear regions of Grosvenor Square'. Even within the West End, there were gradations of status. Lord Chesterfield feared his Piccadilly house was so far out he would require a dog for company.

Dr Johnson's biographer, James Boswell, stressed the delicacy of choosing the 'right end' of Bond Street to rent an apartment. Seeking a lodging, he said, 'was like seeking a wife . . . two guineas a week a rich lady of quality . . . at one guinea, like a knight's daughter'. He could only manage £22 a year (£2,500 today), which he considered 'like the daughter of a good gentleman of moderate fortune'. Byron took chambers in adjacent Albany, where there was 'room for my books and sabres'. London, he said, was 'the only place in the world for fun'. Casanova agreed, describing the brothels as 'a magnificent debauch and only costs six guineas'.

Fun took many forms. Charles Lamb tried to convey to the Wordsworths up in Cumbria what they were missing with all their 'dead nature'. There were the 'lighted shops of the Strand and Fleet Street . . . the bustle and wickedness round about Covent Garden, the very women of the town, the watchmen, drunken scenes, rattles, life awake . . . at all hours of the night, the impossibility of being dull . . . the crowds, the very dirt and mud, the sun shining on pavements . . . the coffee houses, steams of soup from kitchens, the pantomimes'. London, said Lamb, was 'a pantomime and a masquerade'. We do not have Wordsworth's reply, though his sonnet on Westminster Bridge – 'Earth hath not anything to show more fair' – was perhaps agreement enough.

Two London pleasure gardens came to embody both London's vitality and its perceived immorality. Vauxhall Gardens had opened in 1729 and Ranelagh Gardens by Millbank in 1741. For a shilling admission, anyone could attend disguised as they chose, and associate with whoever took their fancy. When the Pantheon, the largest interior space in England, became 'the winter Ranelagh' in Oxford Street in 1772, it attracted 1,700 people to its masquerades, charging six guineas for a season of twelve evenings. Horace Walpole declared himself amazed by 'the most beautiful edifice in England'. Similar events were staged in aristocratic townhouses, often merely to see how many people might come. One such 'rout' at Norfolk House was described by a German visitor as a pointless crush, 'everyone complains of the pressure . . . yet all rejoice at being so divinely squeezed'. Another declared it was, 'no cards, no music, only elbowing'.

Artists came forward to satisfy a booming demand for portraits, the most prominent being Joshua Reynolds and Thomas Gainsborough. The young Mozart performed his first symphony in London in 1765 at the age of nine. In the same year, Johann Christian Bach, the 'London Bach', took up residence and performed in Hanover Square. Joseph Haydn arrived from Austria in 1790. Audiences were noisy and frequently heckled players on the stage. Garrick dominated the theatrical scene from the 1740s to the 1770s, but when he presented a Chinese festival in 1754, rumours of foreign actors in the cast led to a riot and the stage was destroyed. Fires frequently consumed theatres, including ones in the Haymarket, Covent Garden, Drury Lane and Lincoln's Inn Fields.

Shopping boomed as a social activity for women, William Fortnum and Hugh Mason opening their first grocery in 1707, William Hamley his toy shop in 1760, James Christie his auction house in 1766 and John Hatchard his bookshop in 1797. Jane Austen confessed to being a shopping addict at Layton and Shear's in Henrietta Street, Covent Garden. She recorded spending five pounds in a day.

Such activities melted the boundaries of social class, at least among wealthier newcomers. People subject to rigid hierarchy at home in the provinces found London's openness intoxicating. They mixed at pleasure gardens, theatres, concerts and walks in the park. When George II's queen Caroline asked Walpole what it would cost her to remove the public from St James's Park to keep it for her private use, she was told 'three crowns' – those of England, Ireland and Scotland. Foreign visitors noticed how even London's beggars and urchins were lacking in deference, seeing no reason to give way to gentlemen on the pavement. The street was equal to all. This was a new metropolis, exhilarating, uncertain and perhaps unstable.

39. The Palace of Westminster in flames, 1834. Its gothic replacement was to stimulate the 'battle of the styles'.

40. Nash's Buckingham Palace in 1835, with the Marble Arch in its original location in the front courtyard, later obscured by the present facade.

41. Birmingham comes to London – the portal of Robert Stephenson's railway at Primrose Hill, 1838.

NORFOLK SQUARE, HYDE PARK.
NEAR WESTBOURNE TERRACE.
HOUSES TO BE LET OR SOLD, APPLY TO Mr LINDFIELD, AT THE OFFICE.

42. Norfolk Square, let as 'near Hyde Park' but nearer Paddington station. The Italianate London suburb in its prime.

43. Bazalgette's great sewer, the central Octagon of Crossness pumping station on Erith marshes, 1865.

44. Third-class passengers on the first 'underground' at Baker Street, engraving by Doré.

45. Fleet Street in 1897, showing early omnibuses.

46. Elizabeth Garrett Anderson, physician and first woman elected to London office in 1870, topping the poll for the London School Board.

47. Octavia Hill, initiator of the London philanthropic housing movement, by John Singer Sargent, 1898.

48. Arnold Circus, Boundary estate, Bethnal Green, the LCC's first tentative venture into public-sector housing.

49. East Ham Town Hall, 1903; for the early boroughs, nothing but the best would do.

50. Early poster for Golders Green underground service – clear air, trees and fields for all.

51. First map of the London 'Tube', showing its heavy bias to points west and north.

52. Providence Place, Stepney, 1909, as slum clearance gets under way.

53/54. Webb Street School, Bermondsey, illustrating the transformation in living conditions for London's poor between the 1890s and 1930s.

55. Office workers enjoy a rooftop lunch overlooking the Pool of London in 1934. The Great War and the growth of clerical employment transformed opportunities for women.

56. Official vandalism. Herbert Morrison begins the demolition of Rennie's Waterloo Bridge.

57. Blitz London: bomb damage in Battersea, 1943; the power station is in the background.

58. Londoners sheltering in the Tube, defying a government ban on doing so.

59. Pea-souper smog, Piccadilly Circus, 1952.

60. Colour amid the gloom: the Festival of Britain, 1951.

61. Post-war master planner: Sir Patrick Abercrombie.

62. Boom-time impresario: Richard Seifert and the NatWest Tower.

63. A London fit for the car: Fitzrovia according to Buchanan, 1963.

64. Victorian Cricklewood awaits gentrification.

65. First steps to hipsterdom: advert by Roy Brooks, *Observer*, 1967.

DESPERATE ENGLISHMAN & FRENCH GIRL WOULD CONSIDER ANYTHING SORDID – they missed house we sold in Lilyville Rd. 3 months ago. FULHAM or similar. It really *is* urgent, please respond.
15th January 1967

66. Carnaby Street swings, by Malcolm English.

67. Abercrombie's London: Jamaica Street, Stepney Green, 1961.

68. Template for a vertical city: the Barbican sends pedestrians aloft.

69. Winter of discontent: rubbish in Leicester Square, 1979.

70. London isn't working: Ken Livingstone, County Hall, 1982.

71. Biking mayor: Boris Johnson on display, 2010.

72. A city born anew: Canary Wharf from Mudchute, Isle of Dogs, 2012.

73. King's Cross, Coal Drops Yard redevelopment, 2019.

74. A mayoral skyline: the City from Waterloo Bridge, 2019.

75. Cosmopolis: Notting Hill carnival, 2016.

II

Regency: The Dawn of Nash
1789–1825

Revolution and Napoleon

The French revolution of 1789 greatly excited London. Its citizens had long regarded Bourbon Paris as a rival if not an enemy. They had offered asylum to its refugees over centuries, priding themselves as a liberal oasis in a desert of European autocracy – even if they abused 'aliens' when it took their fancy. As news filtered through of an uprising in Paris, the consensus was with the young Wordsworth, that 'Bliss was it in that dawn to be alive . . . to happiness un-thought of.' The radical Whig Charles James Fox declared the storming of the Bastille the most important event in world history. The younger Pitt, in a rare misjudgement, declared in parliament that the event presaged fifteen years of alliance with a new France. Only Edmund Burke struck a sceptical note, predicting that the revolution would descend into anarchy, followed by 'some popular general [who] will establish military dictatorship'.

Pitt's government held fast to Britain's traditional aloofness, and did not join Europe's fellow monarchies in taking up arms against the new republic. But events in Paris worried the London government. In 1792 French offers of support to all anti-monarchists led Pitt to issue a proclamation against sedition, and to arrest revolutionary sympathizers. One such, Tom Paine, fled to Paris in 1792. By 1795 the prospect of war with France had spawned new laws on treason, censorship and political assembly. London's much-vaunted light of liberty dimmed. Radicals and conservatives alike were confused. Did Paris point to the urgency of reform, or the necessity of repression?

When Napoleon vindicated Burke's prediction and staged his 1799 coup, he confronted London with the prospect of hostile invasion. The French emperor detested Britain's sense of superiority, as well as his portrayal as a diminutive madman by the cartoonist James Gillray. He was sure Britons longed to be liberated from the Hanoverian yoke, and in 1805 mustered a vast 200,000-strong invasion force in Boulogne. Had Napoleon managed to cross the Channel, there was little chance of impeding his march on London. As it was, the Battle of Trafalgar denied him any hope of a safe passage. Shakespeare's moat served its purpose. London celebrated Trafalgar extravagantly, in the names of squares, streets, pubs and, thirty years later, a column to its victor, Nelson. The custom was repeated after the Battle of Waterloo in 1815, with a bridge and later a station.

A war economy

The chief impact of the French war on London was an interruption to trade. The French taunt that Britain was a nation of 'shopkeepers' was a mistranslation of 'merchants', but the reality was the same. The City worried chiefly over the security of Britain's recently acquired colonies, threatened by Napoleon's expansionism. In 1806, British participation in the slave trade came to an end, though not the practice of slavery itself, nor the sale of sugar and cotton harvested on its back. The biggest threat to the City was Napoleon's attempt to block the sea lanes used by the British merchant fleet to transport goods to and from the Baltic States and Russia. This led in 1807 to the Royal Navy destroying a possible blockade fleet in Copenhagen harbour.

London was quick to capitalize on Europe's troubles. The commercial markets had emerged from their coffee houses to become specialized exchanges, Lloyd's insurance exchange even retaining its old name. The Baltic Exchange merged with the South Sea Company to become the international market for merchant shipping. Other exchanges dealt in wool, metal, hops, corn and coal. But business supremacy was for the first time being challenged by geography. As imperial trade tripled between 1720 and 1800, it began to pass through Bristol, Liverpool and Glasgow. London docks were ill sited and outdated. Each wharf had its monopolies and restrictive practices, and goods might spend days waiting to be unloaded, and then weeks in warehouses.

In 1793 parliament licensed the City to buy land and construct new harbours further east. The West India Dock on the Isle of Dogs was begun in 1800, and two years later the magnificent London Dock in Wapping was built, with its Piranesian colonnades. These were followed by Surrey Docks, Blackwall Docks and, in the shadow of the Tower, Thomas Telford's St Katharine's Dock, wiping out a slum settlement of some 1,300 houses. All were enclosed by tidal gates. Cheap housing swarmed after these new centres of employment, down Cable Street, the Highway and Narrow Street to reach Limehouse and the old village of Poplar. Over the next century, the East End was to become the greatest working-class city in England, largely unknown to the remainder of London.

The arrival of Nash

In 1811 George III was suffering from mental illness and his son, George Prince of Wales, was declared regent. He was a gross figure, his liberal outlook and dilettante taste overwhelmed by his debauchery. He was fascinated by Napoleon, even as the latter approached defeat, following his every move and ordering the emperor's coronation robes to be copied for his own. Most of all, the Prince Regent felt, like Charles II before him, that Britain deserved a capital that was more of a match for Napoleonic Paris.

Curiously, the prince was drawn not to the architectural grandeur familiar in the capitals of Europe, but to a concept long favoured by London's bourgeoisie, an ever finer suburb. North of the New Road beyond Marylebone lay an opportunity in the former royal hunting fields leased to the Duke of Portland, their lease falling due in 1811. The Prince conceived of a boulevard, a Champs-Élysées, from his new palace on the Mall, Carlton House, to an estate of villas set in a new park. He had allies in parliament and, for the time being, access to funds. He needed only a plan.

John Nash was of Welsh parentage, brought up in Lambeth and articled to the City architect Sir Robert Taylor. He was thus schooled in Taylor's Palladianism rather than the decorative innovations of Robert Adam. Nash had gone bankrupt in 1783 and retired to Wales to build gentry houses, forming an alliance with the landscape designer Humphry Repton. He supplied buildings to order, classical, Italianate, gothic or castellated, with an eye for landscape acquired from his partner.

In 1798 Nash's career took an abrupt and unexplained upturn. He was forty-eight, a widower, unusually short and 'with a face like a monkey's but civil and good-humoured to the greatest degree'. How he met the attractive twenty-five-year-old Mary Anne Bradley is a mystery. She was 'bringing up' five children, surnamed Pennethorne, on the Isle of Wight, rumoured to have been fathered by the Prince Regent. Nash's biographers cannot establish whether he was 'making an honest woman' of Anne as a favour to the prince, or if the prince took Nash's wife as his mistress. We also know that Nash was a close friend of his own lawyer, John Edwards, twenty years his junior, and left his estate to his protégé's son, who was called Nash in his honour. The two men were inseparable, and their families shared Nash's London mansion in Waterloo Place.

For whatever reason, in 1806 an otherwise jobbing architect suddenly became virtual head of the Commission of Woods and Forests, the present Crown Estate. He acquired mansions in London and on the Isle of Wight, and resources to invest in his own projects. More significant, Nash became the prince's muse. An earlier plan to extend built-up Marylebone north across what is now Regent's Park was abandoned, and Nash adopted the prince's vision of a 'royal way', from Carlton House north across the West End to a newly laid-out grand estate.

The royal way

Nash's task was both aesthetic and practical. He had to fuse a princely dream to the realities of the London property market, to subject the romance of the picturesque to commercial necessity. Nash's layout, published in 1812, was the urban application of the new informal landscape, as espoused by Capability Brown and Repton. It was *rus in urbe* on a spectacular scale, more dramatic than anything seen in London since Wren's abortive plan for the post-fire City.

The route began in front of Carlton House. It ploughed north through Jermyn's St James's estate, demolishing its old market and rising to a circus at Piccadilly. It then demolished the old Swallow Street, curving round a quadrant and up the east side of Mayfair. Nash's intention was explicit. He promised 'a complete separation between the streets and squares occupied by the Nobility and Gentry, and the narrower streets and meaner houses occupied by mechanics and the trading part of the community'. Until the later building of

Shaftesbury Avenue, there were only narrow service lanes from Regent Street into the old slums of Soho.

A slight kink to the street was needed to get to Oxford Circus and avoid intruding on the Portland estate's Cavendish Square. The route then swung left and right to incorporate Portland Place, and on across the New Road. Here Nash came into his own, proposing a circus in the style of Bath, followed by a Reptonian park of fifty villas set amid trees. The intention was that 'no villa should see another, but each should appear to possess the whole of the park'. A serpentine lake and a landscaped Regent's Canal would thread through the greenery. To the east round Cumberland market Nash also designed an extensive working-class neighbourhood to service the development. It was demolished in the twentieth century.

Since much of this land belonged to the crown, and its repurposing would require public permits and possibly public funds, the Prince Regent's relations with parliament were crucial. But by the 1820s the Treasury was no longer bankrolling the venture – its chancellor still angry at having to pay for the rebuilding of Carlton House. In the event, the prince obtained his permissions, but not his money. Unlike Sixtus in Rome or, later, Haussmann in Paris, Nash could neither expropriate property nor command money. This meant the entire scheme would need to rely, as did all London development, on speculative cash. From the start it was a risky venture.

Given the spasmodic nature of London's growth, Nash's plan might well have gone the way of Wren's. In the event it was completed, albeit not wholly as intended. The circus, began in 1812, became a semi-circus plus a square, and just eight of the park villas were built. More problematic was the new Regent Street. Planned for shops with flats over them, it had to be built in one sweep or no one would want to buy a building site. Nash's showpiece, the colonnaded quadrant to Piccadilly Circus, was initially a disaster. As each builder/tenant demanded something distinctive, Nash would negotiate a seemly variant, a church, an assembly room, a hotel, desperate to retain aesthetic coherence. Where Regent Street turned into Portland Place, Nash himself designed All Souls' Church in Langham Place to face both angles, as it does today.

In other words, the scheme became Nash's project. He had to put his own money at risk and bring in a fellow developer, James Burton, already active on the Foundling and Bedford estates. Nash employed Burton's architect son, Decimus, who designed some of the park villas. These proved hard to sell, and Decimus also took over Nash's replacement concept, to surround the entire development with terraces, designed to look like palaces but concealing townhouses, each just one house deep. The park became the venue for horse shows, a botanical garden and the popular London Zoo, carefully designated a 'zoological garden' so as not to offend the rurality of its setting.

The terraces, born of financial necessity, and built from 1820, were to prove the sensational climax of the entire development. Chester Terrace was adorned with Roman triumphal arches, Cumberland Terrace with continuous porticos, Sussex Terrace with domed roofs and wings curving to octagons, Indian and classical styles in one. It was St Petersburg without the water, and as far from the austerity of the 1774 Act as could be imagined. London might not have the grandeur of the banks of the Seine, but it was running them close.

Anyone proposing such structures today would be dismissed as a Disneyland freak. In the 1940s, the fogeyish Summerson called the terraces 'careless and clumsy . . . sham, flagrant and absurd . . . an architectural frolic'. But even he could not deny their irresistibility, seen through 'the mists of time' as 'dream palaces, full of grandiose romantic ideas . . . which make Greenwich tame and Hampton Court provincial'. I lived as a child in Nash's Park Village East behind Albany Street, and it was the sight of this stucco fantasy, dazzling in sun filtered through trees, that first made me wonder at London's townscape. In 1945 there was a move by the St Marylebone Council to demolish the terraces, given their then derelict state. It took a determined campaign by the Royal Fine Art Commission to save them, though not all were safe until the 1960s.

Mammon and God

A feature of the Georgian era was the decline in supremacy of the Church of England. The City still had some one hundred places of worship, most of them dating from Wren. Otherwise, apart from two dozen Queen Anne churches, there were none that were new. For almost the entire eighteenth century, the only church building in London was to expand those in villages swallowed by the city's growth, such as Hackney, Islington, Hampstead, Paddington and Battersea. London was severely 'under-churched'.

This lack was filled by the onward advance of Nonconformity. As with the Jews, exclusion from much of public life ensured a collective cohesion. Quakers, Presbyterians, Baptists and Moravians joined with now burgeoning Methodists in establishing what amounted to an alternative Christian London. While Anglican church membership declined between 1720 and 1800, Nonconformist membership doubled. In some places, religious dissent became political dissent at prayer. The free-churchman Richard Price of Newington Green, who championed both the American and French revolutions, gave Islington a radical reputation it continues to hold. The Anglican evangelical Clapham sect bred early opponents of slavery around William Wilberforce and John Thornton.

Eventually even the bishops were stirred to action. Under a repeat of the Queen Anne Churches Act of 1712, the 1818 Church Building Act set aside £1 million for what were dubbed, with yet more patriotic fervour, 'Waterloo churches'. Thirty were built in the 1820s and a hundred and fifty by the 1850s. They were spread equally from the west London estates to the slums east and south of the City. As under Queen Anne, they were designed by the leading architects of the day. Thomas Hardwick produced St Marylebone on the New Road, John Soane designed Holy Trinity in Great Portland Street, and Smirke produced churches in Wandsworth and Hackney and on the Portman estate at Wyndham Place. Churches also sprouted opposite Waterloo Bridge and in Eaton Square, Chelsea, as well as in the poor districts of Bermondsey and Bethnal Green. Many were designed for 2,000 worshippers, posing an impossible challenge to less populated modern parishes.

These buildings opened a new chapter in the story of London taste. Those designed under the 1818 act were almost all Greek classical. St Pancras New Church was entered through a portico, while its transept exterior was graced with a facsimile of the Erechtheum in Athens. Its lonely caryatids gaze out today over the pandemonium of Euston Road. The churches were not universally popular. To Summerson, the buildings showed the last gasp of the classical revival, 'an institutional character' quite different from the friendly domesticity of those of Queen Anne. Not long after, the young Augustus Pugin was more outspoken: the Waterloo churches were 'a disgrace to the age . . . A more meagre, miserable display was never made, nor more impropriety and absurdity committed, than in the mass of paltry churches.' Each generation scorns the work of its predecessor.

In the West End, the City's coffee houses morphed into gentlemen's clubs. White's in St James's Street was founded as White's Chocolate House in 1693, but soon acquired an upmarket clientele, to be imitated by Boodle's and Brooks's. A different tradition was initiated by Lord Castlereagh during the Napoleonic wars, with the Travellers' Club, a retreat for those prevented from going to Europe, and with a rash of rival service clubs. In 1827 Nash designed the

United Service Club in Waterloo Place – London could not stop bashing the French – in the 'Roman' style. A year later his assistant and later rival, Decimus Burton, answered with the 'Greek' Athenaeum. Today the two buildings glare at each other across the road, their entrances deliberately facing in different directions.

Public London diversified and privatized. Social groups began to retreat into neighbourhoods and clubs. Masquerades and routs were no longer open to all. Almack's in St James's admitted only those with 'vouchers of approval' from the committee, and only lemonade and tea were served. That said, a visiting Prince Pückler-Muskau found himself lionized on the strength of his title alone, with 'five or six invitations' on his table 'for each day'.

A symbol of a more formal age was Beau Brummell, the original St James's 'dandy' and the embodiment of fashion snobbery. He was appalled once to be seen 'as far east' as the Strand, and protested he was lost. Yet he became the arbiter of male style. He spent five hours each day dressing, and championed the 'new man', dedicated to personal hygiene and sober dress. Every gentleman, he said, should wear clothes such that he would 'not be noticed'. Proper dress was a clean white shirt, dark tight-fitting trousers and a dark jacket, with a high collar and cravat. Such was Brummell's influence that his personal bootmaker, George Hoby, had to employ 300 workmen to meet demand.

The new style was the epitome of male restraint, after the effusive embroidered coats and pantaloons of the Regency. It was soon imitated not just in London's West End, but by middle-class males across the nation and eventually abroad. I not long ago noticed that all the men in the United Nations assembly, apart from some Arabs, were dressed in dark suit, white shirt, collar and tie. Brummell would have cheered, quietly. He died of syphilis, exiled to France by his gambling debts. But his statue, surely to the world's most influential dictator of taste, stands in Jermyn Street.

12

Cubittopolis
1825–1832

Cubitt and Belgravia

While Nash was pursuing his speculations for the Prince Regent, the post-war recovery saw more cautious developers enter the market. In the 1820s the Duke of Bedford decided to build over his land north of Bloomsbury Square, turning to an enterprising young builder, Thomas Cubitt, as developer of Russell Square, Tavistock Square and Gordon Square. Russell Square was landscaped by no less a figure than Repton.

The self-made son of a Norfolk carpenter, Cubitt would be to London's middle class what Nash had been to its flamboyant Prince Regent. He had worked in India and set up as a builder in Gray's Inn Road, employing his own workmen, as opposed to Nash's practice of subcontracting. Where Nash's builders were slapdash, Cubitt's were thorough and immaculate. Queen Victoria, for whom Cubitt built Osborne on the Isle of Wight, later said of him that 'a better, kinder-hearted or more simple, unassuming man never breathed'.

Yet Cubitt's ambition knew few boundaries. He was soon drawn to richer pickings than Bloomsbury, to the tide of prospective demand rolling enticingly westwards of the emerging Buckingham Palace. Here lay the Grosvenors' southern manor of Ebury, a place of grazing land and market gardening. There was already some building round Trevor and Montpelier squares, beyond the 'knights' bridge' over the Westbourne stream. Holland's Hans Town was already installed on the Cadogan estate. But between this and Hyde Park Corner lay a swamp fed by the Westbourne.

In 1825 Cubitt acquired a lease from the Grosvenor estate on nineteen acres between Hyde Park and the King's Road. Two years later, he also leased land from the Lowndes family, straddling the Westbourne. He then rebuilt the old Ranelagh sewer, and stabilized the marshy ground with soil from the excavated St Katharine's Dock by the Tower. There followed two of London's grandest and most daring speculations: Belgravia, named after a Grosvenor village in Leicestershire, and Pimlico, named after the owner of an ale-house in Hoxton (no one knows why). They rank with Regent's Park as the handsomest urban developments in London's history.

Cubitt's builders descended on Belgravia in their hundreds. *The Times* remarked in 1825 that 'the rage for building continues unabated . . . the market gardeners [of Pimlico and Chelsea] have perceived notice to quit'. As the market approached saturation, two of Cubitt's Grosvenor developers, Seth Smith in Wilton Crescent and Joseph Cundy in Chester Square, went into debt. The latter's plight is reflected in the cramped layout of Chester Square and surrounding streets. Cubitt was adamant he would not desert his initial plan, if necessary refinancing himself in the City. He was developer, financier and builder in one. To Cubitt, design was all. When in 1838 he began to build Pimlico, he experimented with a grid of squares criss-crossed by diagonal avenues. It was – and is – as confusing as Washington DC.

The houses were advanced in every way. They were supplied with running water and gas, with airy basements and efficient sewers. The roads were ballasted and cobblestoned. While Nash's terraces soon began to crumble, Cubitt's remained rock solid. Mayfair, Marylebone, Bayswater and Bloomsbury went on to be bashed, abused and dismembered, but Belgravia and Pimlico have survived virtually intact, their great creamy cliffs of stucco coming to symbolize upmarket living to rich expatriates the world over. Cubitt's biographer Hermione Hobhouse quotes an ode sent him by an admiring resident, 'A fairer wreath than Wren's should crown thy brow/ He raised a dome – a town unrivalled thou!' Few modern tenants address their landlord in such terms.

A field too far

Cubitt was not alone. The Bishop of London's fields in Paddington and Bayswater also came forward for development soon after Waterloo, and were put in the hands of the bishop's surveyor, Samuel Pepys Cockerell. They were laid out with similar panache to Belgravia, notably round Leinster and Porchester terraces and Lancaster Gate. Here were squares, crescents and terraces, again in Italianate stucco, some with the added luxury of trees lining the streets. Bayswater never achieved the eminence of Belgravia – it was too far off centre – and when the leases fell due a century later, the church put its bulldozers to work, replacing Regency dignity with modern houses and flats.

By now, no point in the compass was safe from the surveyor's rod. Scaffolding was the emblem of the new London. In 1829 George Cruikshank published what became a much-reproduced cartoon of London as an army on the warpath out of town. His *March of Bricks and Mortar* was stimulated by new building along the Finchley Road towards Hampstead. Soldiers in the form of picks, shovels and chimney pots are drawn up as regiments of terraces. They advance across Middlesex, firing fusillades of bricks at petrified villagers, cows and sheep.

The most ambitious, indeed reckless, project was far to the west beyond Notting Hill. Here the Ladbroke family was bitten by the speculative bug as early as 1821. They granted leases on a plan laid out by the architect Thomas Allason, grander than anything risked by Nash or Cubitt. It comprised a circus a mile in circumference dominating Notting Hill, on a sloping site overlooking Notting Dale. The estate was to be studded with villas, each one set in five acres of private garden.

For this there proved to be no market. In 1837 the hilltop briefly became a racecourse, the Hippodrome, intended to rival Ascot. But its clay soil and proximity to the brickfields and potteries of north Kensington attracted a crowd far less salubrious than its Berkshire model. Indeed, in the opinion of *The Times*, 'a more filthy and disgusting crew we have seldom had the misfortune to encounter'. The racecourse, like the villas, was a failure. By 1841 Allason's villas had been replaced, like Nash's at Regent's Park, with terraces. Trapped by its leases in a downward spiral, Notting Hill was to become the South Sea Bubble of London's estate development. Thousands lost their savings.

Points north and east

More success attended the Eyre estate north of Regent's Park. An auction plan as early as 1794 indicated a development of villas, detached and 'semi-detached', on land round Thomas Lord's first cricket ground. Though the Eyre did not materialize until the 1820s boom, it acquired a reputation as a place where gentlemen 'settled' their mistresses. Holman Hunt was to use St John's Wood as the setting for his Tate Gallery painting *The Awakening Conscience* (1853), depicting a mistress in the act of detaching herself from her lover.

The adjacent slopes of Primrose Hill resisted development by Eton College on its Belsize estate until the end of the nineteenth century, but on the Fitzroy family's Chalcot estate modest terraces blossomed. The fields acquired by Lord Somers in the eighteenth century saw Somers Town arise, with Agar Town continuing beyond round St Pancras. The appellation 'town' for an estate was intended to assist marketing, but while Lord Camden's town prospered, those of both Somers and Agar fell victim to a down-market slide and eventual railway assault.

Beyond the Foundling estate, on the hillside overlooking King's Cross and the old valley of the Fleet, Henry Penton created Pentonville – preferring a classy French word for town. The fields next door, belonging to William Baker and his wife, Mary Lloyd, were laid out in the decorous terraces of today's Lloyd Baker estate. Its quiet stucco villas on curving streets make it one of central London's most charming neighbourhoods. As a result of these developments, the parish of Islington's population went from 37,000 in 1831 to 155,000 just thirty years later.

The manors of Clerkenwell and Canonbury were no less enticing. They were owned by a City grandee, Sir John Spencer, known as 'Rich Spencer', whose daughter eloped with a Northamptonshire nobleman, Lord Compton, smuggled out of her father's house in a basket. In true estate style, she acquired his title and he acquired London's most lucrative property holding outside the West End. Building began in the 1800s with Northampton Square, Compton and Spencer streets, and Canonbury Square to the north.

The land east of the City may have been less spectacular, and less profitable, but the market was no less active. The manor of Stepney, much of it owned by the Mercers Company, was developed in the 1830s and 40s. Lord Tredegar built a square in his name in Mile End, in hopeful imitation of Kensington. To the north, Hackney, Clapton and Victoria Park blossomed with middle-class dwellings. South of the river, creeping to life thanks to the new bridges, estates were developing on Dulwich College land in Camberwell and round Clapham Common's old Town. Summerson's catalogue of the metropolis at the end of the Georgian era shows it extending from Hampstead in the north, west to Hammersmith, south to Lewisham and east to Poplar.

While many of these suburbs developed their own industries, most Londoners still worked in the City and Westminster. Their commutes were dire, mostly on foot along miles of streets crowded with pedestrians, tradesmen and animals, with only the rich able to afford private carriages. Not until 1829 did George Shillibeer introduce his omnibus, ferrying eighteen passengers in a covered coach drawn by three horses abreast, a vehicle he had first pioneered in Paris. His 'bus' ran along the New Road from Paddington to the Bank of England and his advertising promised that 'a person of great respectability attended his vehicle as conductor'. It proved immediately popular and cornered the public transport market until the arrival of its mighty competitor, the railway.

Regency epilogue

Upon the death of his father, George III, the Prince Regent succeeded to the throne as George IV (1820–30) and moved from Carlton House to Buckingham House, soon to be termed a palace, which he commissioned Nash to rebuild in regal splendour. The building had been Goring House in the 1630s, then Arlington House, and had been bought by George III for his queen in 1761. Meanwhile, the uncompleted Regent Street degenerated into a frantic search for tenants amid a mile of scaffolding and mud. Nash never gave up, tackling each crisis with ingenuity and compromise. Fighting with parliament to fund Buckingham Palace, he demolished Carlton House, barely thirty years old, and replaced it with two enormous speculative terraces overlooking St James's Park, reputedly modelled on the Place de la Concorde. He also redesigned Le Nôtre's park as a counterpart to Regent's Park. The canal was turned into a serpentine lake, and further terraces were planned, but not built, on the south side.

The project staggered on into the 1830s, rescued by a last surge in the West End property market before the coming of the railways. Nash had by now splashed a river of creamy stucco across the soot-blackened grid of west London. He brought some of the fantasy of a royal city to the taste of Georgian London, raising its temperature and giving it flair. The royal way was never Napoleonic. There was no grand parade ground or sweeping vista, just an inspired twist to the story of the capital's development. For the next thirty years, no builder dared omit stucco from his facades. The new London went from black to white.

As the West End shuddered under Nash's pyrotechnics, Regency London finally grew up. The shortage of Thames crossings was met with new bridges at Southwark, Vauxhall and Hungerford Market below the Strand. All were private, toll-paying ventures, promoted after 1809 when war on the continent was still raging. The Strand bridge, later named after Waterloo, was designed by the engineer John Rennie, and cost over £1 million (well over £100 million today). The Italian sculptor Canova called it 'the noblest bridge in the world'. It met a tragic end, like so many of London's glories, in the 1930s.

London now acquired some of the public buildings expected of a capital. In Bloomsbury, a new British Museum was begun in 1823 by Robert Smirke, intended initially to house the royal library, bought from the now penniless George IV. Smirke's stone columns had a frigid monumentality that made Nash's terraces look positively friendly. Smirke also rescued Millbank prison, begun in 1813 on Jeremy Bentham's progressive layout but, by 1816, costing more even than Buckingham Palace. At the same time, the innovative architect John Soane was completing law courts in the old Palace of

Westminster, and a new Bank of England in the City, both buildings now vanished.

As for Buckingham Palace, what should have been the crowning glory of George's London descended into fiasco. Nash designed it with a marble arch guarding its entrance courtyard, but the project ran to double its £250,000 budget and parliament launched an inquiry into its cost. In 1828, with the king an ailing recluse at Windsor, Nash had to face charges of gross deception in extracting public funds. He was accused as 'the minion who poured poison into the ear of the sovereign'. Such extravagance with public money nowadays earns architects knighthoods. Nash was cruelly denied one, and sacked from the Office of Works in 1830. The arch was removed to Tyburn, where it stands today, to be replaced in 1847 with a frontage by Edward Blore for Queen Victoria, itself later refaced.

Nash's final, astonishing London venture was for a second 'royal mile', from Whitehall north to the British Museum. In 1820, he had moved the Royal Mews from facing St Martin-in-the-Fields to the back of Buckingham Palace, and cleared the site for a new Royal Academy, later the National Gallery. The project never progressed. Nash died in 1835 leaving only the 'West Strand Improvements' with its 'pepper-pot' turrets opposite Charing Cross station, a ghost of his second vision.

The eventual National Gallery, designed by William Wilkins, was everything the British Museum was not, quirky, domestic and undramatic. Charles Barry's final execution of Nash's Trafalgar Square had been intended as the architectural climax to an avenue up Whitehall, but as usual London's informality had the last word. The square became lopsided and ungainly, while Wilkins's gallery served no higher purpose than to fill space. Not until 1839 did London finally crown its Trafalgar celebration with Nelson's Column. Edwin Landseer's four lions were added in 1867, modelled on a corpse sent to his studio from London Zoo. Its paws were by then so decomposed that those on the plinth had to be modelled from Landseer's cat.

Nash's Regent Street development was, in his stated terms, ultimately successful. It isolated St James's and Mayfair as upmarket enclaves, protecting their properties from the westward drift of slumdom from Covent Garden and Soho. St James's Palace was occupied by lesser royalty, while flanking it was a protected aristocratic quarter, in the form of Marlborough House, Clarence House and Stafford (later Lancaster) House. Overlooking Green Park was a sequence including Cleveland (later Bridgewater) House, Spencer House, Devonshire House, Bath House, Egremont House (later the In and Out Club) and Wellington's mansion of Apsley House, known at least to taxi drivers as 'No. 1, London'.

Westminster had now completed its evolution from suburb to a city in its own right – indeed, of London's two cities the larger in population and area. When town gas had arrived in 1813 the first place to be illuminated was not the City or London Bridge, but Westminster Bridge on New Year's Eve. The gas, made from coal imported from the north, was initially confined to street lighting, first along Pall Mall, and was the responsibility of the vestry beadle or constable. Demand was instantly intense. Within two years there were 4,000 street lamps and by 1822 London boasted seven gas companies. Seven years later there were two hundred, an early example of municipal enterprise at neighbourhood level.

Who is in charge?

Still there was no sign of any over-arching authority for the capital. Movements for municipal reform in the 1820s and 30s were largely driven from the provinces, from Manchester, Birmingham, Nottingham and elsewhere. While London's workers were quick to organize in defence of pay and conditions, they were harder to galvanize for political causes. The City continued to enjoy a close-knit, partly democratic participation of its own, rooted in its crafts and guilds, in their misteries and aldermen. Change of any sort was anathema. Westminster was the converse. It had no local politics at all. Ruled by a dozen or more parish vestries, its population was a changing cast of migratory tenants, eager only for space to lay their heads and an opportunity either to make money or have a good time.

The result was a city little interested in the state of the country of which it was capital, or even the region of which it was hub. Throughout history it had supported or rejected monarchs and political movements as circumstance required. Each was judged against the notional interest of the metropolis itself. One thing London did know – it was no friend of central government in Westminster. Since the Conquest, protocol ordained that the monarch did not cross the City boundary without formal permission and escort. This is why later royal trains to Sandringham had to take a circuitous route from King's Cross, rather than sensibly starting from Liverpool Street in the City.

Eventually this central–local malfunction came to a head over London's policing. Local 'watches' were beyond inefficient. In 1829 a reforming home secretary, Robert Peel, secured a Metropolitan Police Act. This established a uniformed and salaried force, to replace the now discredited vestry beadles, and the understaffed Bow Street Runners. Soon dubbed 'bobbies' or 'peelers' after their progenitor, the new force was a success. There were 2,000 applications to join, mostly from the existing watch staff. Vestries naturally protested at having to levy an extra rate to pay for them. But 'the Met' had arrived.

Reform comes to town

Sooner or later even London could not ignore the tide of political dissent that had been rising, albeit tentatively, since the French Revolution. There was no defending a parliament in which Birmingham, Manchester, Sheffield and Leeds had no representatives, while the six south-western counties had 168. London had just ten, when seventy would have been a fairer distribution. Reform consumed public debate, and was accepted as unavoidable by leading Whigs and even by a large number of Tories.

At the 1830 election caused by the death of George IV, reform of both the franchise and the distribution of constituencies led the agenda. The Tory prime minister, the veteran Duke of Wellington, declared that 'as long as I hold any station . . . I shall always feel it my duty to resist' any change. It was the spark that lit the flame. In reaction to Wellington, the London mob returned to the streets in strength. Wellington resigned, handing the ministry to the Whigs under Earl Grey and Lord John Russell. Their reform bill was passed by the commons, but was defeated by the lords. A second election in 1831 returned another pro-reform commons, but Russell's bill was again defeated by the lords, its hereditary majority apparently intent on institutional suicide.

Britain in 1832 was nearer than at any time to a revolutionary crisis. The radical leader Francis Place wrote as soberly as he could to warn the Whig leaders that protest riots would become uncontrollable. Wellington's house at Hyde Park Corner was besieged by the mob. He was to be known as the iron duke, not for his military command, but for the bars with which he had to protect his shutters. The government had no standing army remotely able to defend the capital.

The echo of France in 1789 finally struck home. The crisis was resolved through a demand that the new king, William IV (1830–37), create enough pro-reform peers to end the deadlock. Wellington and the lords capitulated. The Great Reform Act of 1832 increased the franchise by just 60 per cent, much to the dismay of the reform-ers. It was singularly unkind to London, raising its total of MPs to just twenty-two. But a dam had been breached. A torrent of reform ensued.

13

The Age of Reform
1832–1848

An English revolution

The new MPs elected in 1833 did as reformers hoped and conservatives feared. Legislation was passed regulating factories, abolishing child labour, legalizing unions, banning slavery throughout the empire and forcing road vehicles to drive on the left. In 1835, parliament honoured its urbanized membership by replacing the unelected borough aldermen in the provinces with elected corporations. It did not, however, extend this reform to London. The City and the Westminster 'county' vestries fought to be left alone, and they were successful. London outside the City was treated not as if it were a municipal borough but as if it were a collection of rural villages.

One reform that did apply to London was the 1834 Poor Law. Local welfare had long been hit and miss. Some vestries built poorhouses, others did little or nothing. Among the worst was the weavers' community of Bethnal Green, where one local clergyman described a poorhouse inhabited by 1,100 unemployed people, six to a bed, with another 6,000 in receipt of parochial relief. The vestry was hopelessly in debt with every day 'adding to the number of paupers', and diminishing 'that of ratepayers . . . principally small shopkeepers, who are beggared by the rates. The district is in a complete state of insolvency and hopeless poverty.'

Under the new law, welfare was removed from vestries and put under thirty Poor Law Unions with elected 'guardians'. Their sole job was to aid the poor and homeless. Guardians were to establish workhouses, supposedly as temporary shelters for the out-of-work fit. In reality they continued the old poorhouses, though extending them to places that had none before. They were not popular, seen as spending ratepayers' money on that dread of middle-class London, the 'undeserving' poor. As a result the guardians were reluctant to make workhouses anything more than penalties for poverty, with any comfort viewed as simply a reward for idleness.

Westminster in flames

Soon parliament had housing problems closer to home. In October 1834, a clerk disposing of a hoard of old tally sticks set the Palace of Westminster on fire. An enclave of buildings occupied since before the Conquest by monarchs, courts of justice, peers, MPs, civil servants and eight centuries of state clutter went up in flames. Only the stone-built medieval Westminster Hall survived. It was as if the nation's collective memory was erased. The event was depicted in a majestic painting by Turner as a cleansing of the past. The replacement would be symbolic of a new age and a new order.

But what should it look like? London in the 1830s was gripped by what came to be called the battle of the styles. As we have seen, the city's architecture under the Georgians had been classical, Greek, Roman or a hybrid Italianate. A few buildings, such as Horace Walpole's Strawberry Hill, were in a 'gothick' style, sometimes called picturesque. But churches, museums, banks and clubs saw a contest only between Greeks and Romans. Cubitt's domestic architecture was Italianate throughout.

By the 1830s, this convention was under attack from a number of quarters. Classical was seen as the style of the French revolution and of American republicanism, having been chosen for Paris's

Panthéon and Washington's Capitol. To high-church Anglicans it evoked a pagan, pre-Christian past, inappropriate for a place of prayer. As he watched the old Palace of Westminster burn, the twenty-one-year-old Augustus Welby Pugin rejoiced at the sight of its medieval walls standing firm as modern buildings 'fell faster than a pack of cards'. The old verities, godly and gothic, held true. To Pugin the gothic was 'two hands in prayer ascending up to God', and to Coleridge it was 'infinity made imaginable'. In an overwhelmingly classical city, this was a revolution in earnest.

Already by the dawn of the 1830s taste was changing. It began with churches. The Waterloo church of St Peter's Eaton Square was classical, but St Paul's Wilton Place and St Michael's Chester Square, just twelve years later, were gothic. By the 1840s, all Belgravia and Pimlico churches were in brown Kentish ragstone, known as Cundy churches after the Grosvenor estate's surveyor. Their gaunt steeples can be seen soaring skywards above fields of sunny stucco.

Even so, the commissioners for the new Palace of Westminster caused a sensation by declaring in 1836 that the style for competition entries should be gothic or 'Elizabethan', explicitly to be in keeping with Henry VII's chapel of Westminster Abbey next door. The competition was won by the classicist Charles Barry, but only when he met the brief by calling in Pugin to contribute drawings 'in the gothic style'. The site was duly cleared, the river embanked and foundations laid in 1840.

Barry supplied what was essentially a classical layout for the new buildings, and declined to acknowledge Pugin's role. He did not summon the young man for four years, ostensibly just for decorative cladding and interiors. Pugin returned the compliment, calling the palace 'All Grecian, sir, Tudor details on a classic body.' But the palace became a showcase for the new style, with Pugin supplying panelling, glass, tiles, fittings, fabrics, carpets, even a new royal throne. He worked in a frenzy.

The building had been promised by Barry as a six-year project, at a cost of £750,000, little short of £120 million today. It took thirty years and cost three times that sum, and was to be regarded as Pugin's masterpiece, not Barry's. The clock tower, popularly known as Big Ben (originally the name of its bell), was not completed until 1858, six years after Pugin's death. With its sonorous E-natural chime, it became London's signature and the symbol of Britishness throughout the empire. An attempt to rename it the Elizabeth Tower on the Queen's jubilee in 2012 failed to catch on.

A cleaner London

By the time of the Westminster fire, a new plague, cholera, was becoming virulent, an outbreak in 1832 causing 5,000 deaths in the capital alone. An intense debate ensued about the cause, whether it lay in London's water supply, or in the air, the fog or human transmission. Constant inquiries and commissions had demanded improvements to sanitation, water supply and sewerage. All went unanswered. The campaign for reform was then taken up by a forceful Mancunian, Edwin Chadwick, who had served on the 1834 Poor Law Commission, and now turned his attention to London's sewers.

Efforts to counter cholera by flushing sewers faster into the Thames only made matters worse, by draining cesspits straight into the river. The introduction of flush toilets in place of earth ones had the same dire effect. The capital's supposed sanitation authorities, the nine commissions of sewers, were immune to complaint. Such sewers as existed were cracked and outdated, largely dependent on private owners for their repair. With a wealth of statistical and scientific research, Chadwick in 1842 produced a report on the Sanitary Condition of the Labouring Population of Great Britain.

Chadwick was no politician, but a reformer of belligerence and egotism. His promotion of his work became the stuff of tabloid sensation. He wrote of raw filth, offal-filled ditches, pavements overflowing into basements and water courses jammed with faeces. 'Not one half of the entire filth produced by the metropolis finds itself into the sewers,' he wrote, 'but is retained in the cesspools and drains in and about the houses ... how the poor miserable inhabitants live in such places it is hard to tell.' Chadwick's language was alarmist and colourful, describing a city unimagined by most of his readers. For good measure he added that future epidemics would strike rich and poor alike. All would die. His reports were instant best-sellers.

Parliament was sympathetic but found itself fighting, as so often before, against a reluctant City and reactionary vestries, fearful of any change that might involve increasing their rates. The City had London's highest cholera death rate, yet declared its sanitation 'perfect'. There were now some 300 local government bodies in the metropolis, guided by 250 acts of parliament, each able to pass the blame to another. One street, the Strand, had seven different paving boards. London's government was chaotic, yet the innovations of 1832 had passed it by. The result was that, for all Chadwick's lobbying, nothing happened. The cholera crisis seemed to pass, for a while.

The rage of the train

We are fortunate to have a precise and precious record of the appearance of the metropolis on Victoria's accession in 1837. The following year a London printer, John Tallis, produced engravings of every main thoroughfare in the capital, eighty-eight in all, with a directory of each shop or business premises (it was reprinted in 1969). The impression is of a city of extraordinary uniformity, almost entirely of three- or four-storey buildings, interspersed with Palladian churches and business premises. Tallis's London – he scrupulously avoided Chadwick's pestilential courts and alleys – is handsome, decorous and more than a little dull.

These streets had been supplied since Roman times by human power and horsepower. Roads had improved. Rolled grit and stone chippings were introduced to Belgravia by Cubitt, and swiftly extended across the city. But streets were heavily congested, with traffic frequently coming to a complete halt. Horses could only go so fast, and they deposited thousands of tons of dung on pavements each day, fouling men's shoes and ladies' skirts alike. A modern city required ever more efficient means of getting about, and was crippled by the difficulty of communication.

In 1830 George Stephenson had opened his Liverpool and Manchester railway, to instant success. London was not far behind. A year later a group of investors proposed a railway from Greenwich to London Bridge, to run on a viaduct to avoid costly land purchase. Parliament granted permission, and the first service ran into Deptford station in December 1836. A local journal reported that, 'a band of music having taken up position on the roof of the carriage, the official bugler blew the signal for the start and the train steamed off amidst the firing of cannon and the ringing of church bells'. Residents ran to their roofs to watch. Little did they realize the noise, soot and disruption that was soon to descend on their lives.

By then the first railway 'mania' had seized the reform parliament, with London the centre of attention. Plans were brought forward for lines from Birmingham to the Marylebone boundary at the New Road, and from Southampton to Nine Elms (later extended to Waterloo). In June 1837, as the new queen was taking the throne, Robert Stephenson's first 'inter-city' train from Birmingham emerged from a tunnel through Primrose Hill to Camden Town. From there its carriages were drawn on ropes down to a terminus at Euston Square. Tourists flocked to see the apparition, reputedly capable of terrifying speeds of up to fifty miles per hour.

The railway's intrusion into the geography of the metropolis was unplanned, uncontrolled and frenetic. Parliament might have favoured social reform, but it greeted railway capitalism with frenzied enthusiasm. So potent was the railway's parliamentary lobby that Britain's most sacred liberty, private property, was casually swept aside. Private parliamentary acts permitted compulsory purchase for railways, with property owners – not to mention their tenants – defenceless unless they could mobilize political opposition.

The impact on London was drastic. Charles Dickens in *Dombey and Son* recorded Stephenson's Camden Town excavations:

> Houses knocked down, streets broken through and stopped; here a chaos of carts, overthrown and jumbled together, lay topsy-turvy at the bottom of a steep unnatural hill; there lay confused treasures of iron, soaked and rusted in something that had accidentally become a pond. Everywhere were bridges that led nowhere, thoroughfares that were impassable, Babel towers of chimneys, wanting half their height, carcasses of ragged tenements and fragments of unfinished walls.

The most noted feature of the new railway was its profitability. At a time when savings would commonly realize 3 to 5 per cent interest, the railway companies were declaring dividends of 10–12 per cent. The result was a second mania in 1843–45, far more intense than the first. It gripped the stock market and parliament as recklessly as had the South Sea Bubble of 1720. The atmosphere was akin to the contemporary Californian gold rush, that of the "forty-niners'.

The mania marked the end of the piecemeal expansion that had characterized Stuart and Georgian London. Unlike the arrival of the railway in most European cities – under the authority of civic or national government – in London there seemed no question of curbing competition or planning the impact on the urban fabric. Summerson remarked on the change in official attitudes to such planning. The sense of responsibility for the public realm that had lasted, however tenuously, since the seventeenth century, 'was shaken out of the aristocracy, without being shaken into the bourgeoisie'. London's land was up for grabs, and the devil would take the hindmost.

The opening of the 1845 parliamentary session listed 1,300 railway bills. A contemporary historian, John Francis, reported 'the cry at every dinner, uttered by solemn, solid men, upon the glories of rail; they read of princes mounting tenders, of peers as provision committeemen, of marquises trundling wheelbarrows and of privy councillors cutting turf on correct geometrical principles. Their clerks left them to become railway jobbers. Their domestic servants studied railway journals.'

The bubble burst in 1847, by when 4,000 miles of track had been built across the land, laid by hand, without a steam shovel or bulldozer in sight. The result was a crazy tangle of routes, which parliament showed no interest in regulating. The waste was enormous, as were the fortunes lost with the crash. A cartoon showed Queen Victoria pleading with a weeping Albert, 'Tell me, oh tell me, dearest Albert, have you any railway shares?'

14

The Birth of a New Metropolis
1848–1860

London's other face

The metropolis on which the railway was unleashed was experiencing a new sort of self-consciousness. The living conditions of large numbers of its citizens had been the source of occasional concern, as during the gin plague and the activities of the Fielding brothers. But the division into rich and poor and the extent of the city occupied by the latter gradually attracted attention, even if it was largely due to the consequent threat to London's health.

In the first place, it was no one's job to ascertain the nature and extent of the poverty. The London of the 1774 Act was not exclusively for the rich and middling rich. The act's fourth-rate housing was for those with settled jobs but no servants. They were skilled craftsmen, shopkeepers and clerks in City and government offices. This distinction, between what was later termed 'deserving' and 'undeserving' poor, permeated debate on how to reform the Victorian city.

An early commentator was the social reformer and co-founder of the magazine *Punch*, Henry Mayhew, whose researches in the 1840s led to his *London Labour and the London Poor*, published in 1851. Mayhew sought to categorize and identify gradations of poverty, notably the gulf between London's artisans and its labourers, as displayed in their dwellings. He noted that, 'In the one you occasionally find small statues of Shakespeare beneath glass shades; in the other is all dirt and foetor.' In one zone, wrote Mayhew, are intelligent artisans, 'while the slopworkers are generally almost brutified with their incessant toil, miserable food, and filthy homes . . . In passing from the skilled worker of the west-end to the unskilled workman of the eastern quarter of London, the moral and intellectual change is so great that it seems we are in a new land, among another race.'

Mayhew estimated that roughly a quarter of London's population were 'degenerates'. They inhabited a nether world, crammed into every spare foot of space. They lived in the interstices of other people's lives, along sewage-clogged watercourses or on platforms over Thames-side creeks. They occupied wooden shacks, where floor was piled on floor, and courtyards filled with the homeless or 'half-homed'. Many were the flotsam of the city, the comers and goers, seasonal migrants moving between the winter's London gasworks and the summer hop fields of Kent.

The master biographer of this emergent London was Charles Dickens. Born in Portsmouth the son of an impecunious naval clerk and raised in Kent, he moved to Camden at the age of ten. There he experienced the insecurity and poverty of a father imprisoned in the Marshalsea jail for debt. Dickens's novels are filled with the characters, sights, sounds and even smells of London streets in mid-century, to such an extent that the Victorian metropolis is often just 'Dickens's London'. For all the gloom that surrounds many of his stories, they are softened by the city's kindness and its capacity for redemption.

Dickens elevated to grace the outcasts, the small people, the eccentrics. It is hard to imagine him using Mayhew's 'undeserving' of Jo in *Bleak House*, or Lizzie in *Our Mutual Friend* or Scrooge's clerk Bob Cratchit. Dickens became, above all, the scourge of the 1834 Poor Law and what he saw as its institutionalizing and imprisoning of the destitute. To him the menace supposedly represented to respectable opinion by the urban poor was a 'dragon . . . in a very weak and impotent condition; toothless, fangless, drawing his breath heavily enough, and hardly worth chaining up'. The workhouse stood alongside the prison as the embodiment of state cruelty. That said, not all workhouses were as Dickens depicted them, and they were a step towards state responsibility for the victims of London's turbulent growth.

For all his anger, Dickens never lost sight of London's humour. He revelled in the language of the street, such as the Cockney of Mr Pickwick's Sam Weller. Cockney was originally a term of provincial abuse for effete Londoners (from the artificiality of a 'cock's egg'). It mutated into a term for all true East Enders, supposedly those born within the hearing of Cheapside's Bow bells. The dialect was later noted for its rhyming slang – porkies for lies (pork pies) and bread for money (bread and honey) – though rhyming is not found in Dickens.

Starting with drains

The debate in the capital between social reformers and those more concerned to advance the cause of reforming parliamentary government ground slowly over the middle years of Victoria's reign. A year after the queen's coronation, a group of radical MPs and others, mostly based in Birmingham, Glasgow and the North of England, drew up a charter demanding universal (male) suffrage, secret ballots and paid MPs. So-called Chartist clubs, societies and 'conventions' were formed to press the cause. Conventional politics took note. The Tory leader, Robert Peel, elected to government in 1841, warned his party that it had to 'reform to survive . . . to review all institutions, civil and ecclesiastical'. He marked his party's conversion to free trade by repealing the Corn Laws and reducing the price of bread.

Over the course of the 1840s, a series of Chartist demonstrations culminated in 1848 in a rally on Kennington Common which, though peaceful, unnerved the authorities. A small army of some 80,000 special constables was recruited to police it and defend the capital. The Bank of England and the Thames bridges were fortified and the queen was sent to Osborne on the Isle of Wight. The rally was a fiasco. It was pouring with rain and the organizers agreed with the police to send their petition to parliament in two hackney carriages. The argument for reform stalled. Compared with the revolutionary movements storming through other European capitals that same year, Kennington was a pathetic affair.

What did move forward on a quite separate track was Chadwick's campaign to improve the state of urban sanitation. In Britain, it was said, revolution starts with drains. Ten years of relentless campaigning saw Chadwick triumph in 1848 with the government setting up a General Board of Health and a Metropolitan Commission of Sewers, both under his control. Every city was charged with ensuring houses were supplied with fresh water and adequate sewerage, though furious arguments, not helped by Chadwick's tactless belligerence, saw many delays in implementation.

Reform's chief ally was not reason but the return in 1849 of cholera, reinforced by typhus. The City, long inert, appointed as its medical officer of health a young surgeon named John Simon, who proved to be for the City what Chadwick was for the nation as a whole. He too deployed reform's most potent weapon, shame, forcing the corporation to take direct control of its water supply, sewerage, rubbish collection and 'nuisance removal'.

Simon closed half the City's 155 slaughterhouses, ending the tipping of entrails, excrement and blood down open gutters from Smithfield into the Fleet ditch. The use of Smithfield for livestock trading ended, with slaughtering moved to Copenhagen fields in Islington. The City did, however, retain its wholesale food markets, Smithfield for (dead) meat, Billingsgate for fish, Leadenhall for poultry and Spitalfields for fruit and vegetables. So powerful were the City's ancient monopolies that these markets remained in being into the 1970s, with Smithfield still operating in the twenty-first century.

London still lacked the means of fully enforcing Chadwick's reforms, and, for the time being, cholera and typhus retained their grip. In 1854 a doctor in Soho, John Snow, noted that incidence was highest among users of a certain pump in Broad Street (now Broadwick), clearly contaminated by a local cesspit. Yet incidence was low among those drinking from fresh-water conduits. Disease was also rampant among those in Southwark drinking water from the polluted Thames. Cholera was unquestionably linked with water. The science of epidemiology was born.

In 1855 parliament finally set up a new Metropolitan Board of Works (MBW), making it formally responsible for all sewers and other infrastructure throughout the capital. A concession to the backwoodsmen was to omit the word London from the title and to employ the word 'works', to indicate that the new body should steer clear of social policy. Parliament also legislated for the direct election of vestry boards, and merged the small outer vestries into fifteen 'district boards'.

The new MBW was composed of City representatives and vestry members, and was thus distantly accountable to ratepayers. Like them it was obsessed with parsimony, but it was a template for a future metropolitan government. Nor could it ignore any longer the state of the capital's sewers. The Victorian wit Sydney Smith wrote that 'he who drinks a tumbler of London water has in his stomach more animated beings than there are men, women and children on the face of the globe'. Just crossing Waterloo Bridge, wrote Dickens, produced 'a whiff of the most head-and-stomach distending nature'.

It still took the Great Stink of 1858 to force the MBW to specific action. In that year a freak of meteorology led the Thames to emit a miasma that penetrated the new Palace of Westminster and forced its evacuation. Since, despite Snow's research, cholera was widely thought to be odour-borne, the miasma led to panic. Disraeli was seen rushing from a committee room, 'his pocket handkerchief . . . applied closely to his nose, with body half bent, hastened in dismay'. Gladstone did likewise. Investigators were despatched and found excrement on the adjacent Thames bank six feet thick. *The Times* declared the stink should prove 'the best of all sanitary reformers'.

The MBW was ordered to borrow £3 million (£250 million today) and get to work at once. London's taxes were not an issue when MPs had been so inconvenienced and their lives endangered. The outcome was the greatest burst of construction seen in London since Nash. The board's engineer, Sir Joseph Bazalgette, was a match for Chadwick in determination and energy. He proposed two outflow sewers north and south of the Thames, eighty-two miles long. Two more sewers, from Hampstead and Balham, were gravity driven to the Essex and Kent marshes. Two more from Putney and Kensal Green had to be pumped when they got to the east end. The pumping stations still exist, at Abbey Mills in Bow and at Crossness on the Erith Marshes. They rank among the wonders of the industrial world.

Bazalgette's great project, involving 1,300 miles of tunnels, was completed by 1885 at a cost of what at the time was an astronomical £4.6 million. His embankment drastically narrowed – and therefore speeded – the flow of the Thames, turning it at full tide into a torrent and dangerously scouring the footings of the Georgian bridges. By then, London's nine private water companies were already supplying most of the city with piped and reasonably clean water. Belatedly, London's most essential item of modern infrastructure was in place. For the most part it is still in working order today.

The settling of the railway

The railway mania of the 1840s, largely completed in the 1850s, left London with a portfolio of termini – north, south, east and west – in the most unsatisfactory places. It was noticeable that in the west, landlords had proved powerful enough in parliament to fight off intrusion on their estates. Isambard Kingdom Brunel's Great Western Railway was stopped by the church from moving from Paddington into Bayswater. The London and Birmingham could not cross the New Road south of Euston, nor could the Northern get beyond King's Cross into the City. The Great Eastern, at least initially, could not penetrate beyond Shoreditch.

The southern routes were easier, as south London's landowners had less influence and land was cheaper, but the Thames offered an almost insuperable barrier. A spaghetti-tangle of tracks appeared between London Bridge and Waterloo, as companies zig-zagged to get across the water. Some reached the north bank but no further, hence the stations at Cannon Street, Blackfriars and Charing Cross. In 1874 only the London, Chatham and Dover did penetrate 200 yards north of Blackfriars to Holborn, casually throwing a bridge over Ludgate Hill (since removed) and obscuring the famous view of St Paul's.

The one route to pierce the West End was the most bitterly fought, from the south-east. By the early 1850s, four separate companies were seeking to cross the Grosvenor estate from Battersea into Pimlico and central Westminster. It took ten years of pressure for them to reach the doorstep of Buckingham Palace in 1860, and then largely by pleading the convenience of the Queen for her journey to Osborne. The price demanded by Grosvenor was extraordinary, that the track be placed in a cutting down a steep incline from the bridge, as it is today. It then had to be roofed to keep soot off Pimlico washing lines, track had to be silenced on rubberized sleepers and no whistles were to be blown anywhere north of the river. The Queen was supplied with a private entrance and a suite of rooms. They remain on Hudson's Place, as does another suite at Paddington for Victoria's journey to Windsor – neither any longer in use.

The clearing of neighbourhoods for railways was more disruptive of London property than anything since the Great Fire. Unscrupulous companies, their boards packed with MPs, would plead the social benefit of 'slum clearance', with no thought of those who inhabited the slums. Companies would bribe ground landlords to clear sites in advance of their applying for a bill, and then claim to be displacing nobody. Families would be evicted in a matter of days, with a guinea in their pocket, only to be crammed ever tighter into adjacent courtyards and tenements. There they had to fight for space with thousands of construction workers, attracted by the building of the lines that had evicted them.

The Great Eastern's route to Shoreditch displaced an official estimate of 4,645 people, probably far more. The track between Lambeth and London Bridge evicted 4,580, again with just a guinea compensation. The South-Western's path to Waterloo demolished 700 houses in Nine Elms alone. Thousands more made way for Liverpool Street, Blackfriars and Charing Cross. Even as Chadwick was campaigning against the evils of overcrowding for the city's health, parliament was passing railway bills adding to it. Sooner or later this social upheaval became too much even for parliament. In 1853 a philanthropic peer, Lord Shaftesbury, demanded that railway companies stipulate the scale of their clearances, and the possible impact they might have on poverty. He could at least deploy shame. But as so often in London's history, money talked louder than shame, and the railway lobby retorted that for all the misery at least it got things done. Within twenty years of the railway mania, London's surface rail network was largely completed. It was an astonishing if brutal chapter in London's history.

Going underground

London was now ringed by termini, of which those in the north and west were two to three miles from where most of their passengers worked. The City's surveyor at the time, Charles Pearson, saw this as potentially disastrous for business. The City's population was plummeting, from 130,000 in 1800 to half that by mid-century. Its post-fire houses were being replaced by banks and commercial offices. New streets to carry commuter omnibuses and hackney carriages had been pushed through, such as King William Street and Queen Victoria Street, linking the Bank to London Bridge and Blackfriars. But it was from the termini along the New Road north of Marylebone (now Euston Road) that horse-drawn omnibuses were causing the most serious congestion.

Pearson's dream was to build a railway linking Paddington, Euston and King's Cross to the heart of the City. But this would involve buying and demolishing newly completed estates across Marylebone and Bloomsbury. Of this there was no hope. The alternative was to go underground. In 1853 Pearson duly formed what became the Metropolitan Railway Company, to run from Paddington along the course of the New Road and down to Farringdon. The construction method, devised by another pioneer of the railway age, Sir John Fowler, was 'cut-and-cover'. This meant excavating the length of the New Road, laying track in the ditch and roofing it over. It also meant ten years of traffic chaos.

Pearson's line never properly married with the termini, so that surface trains were never able to run through to the City at Farringdon. All passengers had to change from surface to underground, still a maddening inconvenience. The Birmingham railway at Euston refused even to engineer an interchange, forcing passengers to walk 200 yards to 'Euston Square' to reach Pearson's line (now the Metropolitan and Circle). None the less, the world's first underground train ran in 1863, with Gladstone on board. It was declared a 'descent into Hades' as its passengers endured smoke and fumes in a hell of noise and darkness. Yet from its opening day the line was a phenomenon. It carried 30,000 delighted soot-covered passengers into the City and back. The company declared a first-year dividend of 6.5 per cent.

The result was a third railway mania in the 1860s, this time an underground one. Investors rushed to build tunnels. The railway historian John Kellett calculated that if all the railways proposed in 1863 had been built, they would have consumed a quarter of the land area of the City. Parliament at last saw sense and called a halt. It told the proposed District Railway, pushing eastwards towards the City from Kensington, that it had to link with the Metropolitan to form a Circle Line. Along the Thames Embankment, it should also share excavation with Bazalgette's new sewer, then under construction.

The MBW not only insisted the District Line go alongside the sewer, it also laid out a road and gardens on top of it, relieving the Strand. Bazalgette's Embankment was thus a rare London project to see a semblance of co-ordination. Even so, the District had to fight its way across west London. At Sloane Square, the old Westbourne stream had to be carried in a pipe over the platform, where it can be heard there bubbling after heavy rain. The Circle Line was not completed until 1884 (and sadly discontinued as a full circuit in 2009).

In 1861 parliament made a radical requirement, that a condition of any new railway was the provision of workmen's trains priced at a penny a mile. This was notionally to enable those being evicted by the companies to live further out and commute to their place of work. The companies did everything to obstruct this edict. They had no interest in carrying low-revenue passengers to what would become low-value suburban estates. The only workmen's trains on the Metropolitan arrived at Paddington at 5.30 and 5.40 in the morning. That said, the new railways did liberate tens of thousands of London workers from the slums. They speeded the out-migration of working-class as well as middle-class commuters. Nothing like this diaspora was seen anywhere else in Europe at the time.

Booming and busting

London's development was now set on a cyclical basis. Building surged on an upturn in the market, leading to oversupply and a classic hog cycle of boom and bust. In the late 1840s, the railway mania led to mile upon mile of often oversized houses, eventually bereft of buyers – typified by the relentless Italianate streets and squares of Kensington. By the 1840s, not even Cubitt could find takers for his developments. In her biography of him, Hermione Hobhouse reported that the Grosvenor estate received less in Pimlico ground rents than it had from the previous market gardens. Cubitt had been already defaulting on his rents in 1838, leaving Grosvenor no alternative but to forgive him.

Tales multiplied of bankruptcy and disaster. The Crown Estate's most ambitious venture was in the garden of Kensington Palace. Building there, first planned in 1838, was strongly opposed by local residents. One of them, the landscape architect J. C. Loudon, suggested linking Kensington Gardens with Lord Holland's grounds at Holland House, thus creating a 'green corridor' from Trafalgar Square almost to Shepherd's Bush. The crown was unmoved. Yet few of its new plots were taken. In 1844 they passed to a builder named Blashford, but he went bankrupt. The estate went ahead spasmodically through the 1850s, such that a walk down Kensington Palace Gardens today is through a catalogue of Victorian styles, from Italianate to oriental to Tudor to Queen Anne revival.

The ill-starred Ladbroke estate to the north fared even worse. *Building News* in the 1860s noted 'the melancholy vestiges of the wreck are not yet wholly cleared away. The naked carcasses, crumbling decorations, fractured walls and slimy cement work, upon which the summer's heat and winter's rain have left their damaging mark, may still be seen . . . The opprobrious epithet of "coffin-row" was fixed upon the dead street.' With such a sales pitch, lots were sold in desperation, as speculators' savings vanished in the Notting Hill mud. A rare success was a builder named Blake, who acquired plots along the hilltop ridge. His flamboyant architect, Thomas Allom, brought a spark of Belgravian grandeur to Kensington Park Gardens and Stanley Crescent.

Back in South Kensington, the market was firmer. In 1851 the Prince Consort sought to emulate the French industrial exhibition of 1844 in a Great Exhibition in Hyde Park. A palace of glass was designed by the Duke of Devonshire's gardener, Joseph Paxton, which drew 6 million visitors to a bravura display of British – and some foreign – production and design. It also included the largest pearl ever found, as well as India's Koh-i-Noor diamond. Queen Victoria visited forty-two times.

The Great Exhibition cleared a handsome profit, which was put in the charge of commissioners for charitable purposes. Paxton's palace was dismantled and re-erected as Crystal Palace in Sydenham in south London. It burned down in 1936. In adjacent Kensington, the commissioners under Albert's leadership planned a museum quarter stretching from Hyde Park south to Cromwell Road, embracing the Albert Hall and museums of craft and design, geology, science, natural history and the empire. A Royal College of Science later amalgamated with other colleges to become Imperial College. The enclave was a rare London gesture of state-sponsored culture.

The exhibition initiated a building surge across South Kensington. Here land had been given by Cromwell to his secretary, John Thurloe, whose descendant John Alexander developed Thurloe and Alexander squares. They were linked by a thoroughfare named in their benefactor's honour, Cromwell Road. A neighbouring estate, stretching down to Chelsea, was left by Alderman Henry Smith 'for the relief and ransom of poor captives, being slaves under Turkish pirates', then a notorious source of horror. No slaves, if there were any, were celebrated in the resulting streets. But Smith's trustees made sure their own names were remembered: Onslow, Sydney, Sumner, Egerton and Pelham.

When in the early 1850s, Mayhew looked down on London from a balloon, he was amazed by 'the Leviathan metropolis, with a dense canopy of smoke hanging over it'. He could see west to Hammersmith and Fulham, north to Hampstead and Islington, east to Victoria Park and Bow, and south to Dulwich, Sydenham and Camberwell. But while William Cobbett had deplored the 'great wen', Mayhew delighted in 'that strange conglomeration of vice, avarice . . . of noble aspiration and human heroism . . . more virtue and more iniquity, more wealth and more want, brought together into one dense focus than in any other part of the earth'.

Refuge to a continent

Ever since Europe's 1848 turmoil, refugee migration to London had turned from a trickle to a flood. Karl Marx had already settled in

Kentish Town and was working at the British Museum, publishing his *Communist Manifesto* also in 1848. It passed unnoticed at the time, perhaps because it was published only in the original German. At the same time London was playing host to Napoleon's nephew, Louis Bonaparte, who returned to Paris and seized power as Napoleon III. Asylum was then offered to the man he deposed, Louis Philippe, albeit as plain Mr Smith. The metropolis also welcomed Austria's Metternich, Hungary's Kossuth and Italy's Mazzini and Garibaldi. It housed fugitive Russians and Poles without number.

French nobility took a liking to the villas of Twickenham, recalled today in Orleans House. Many others were near destitute, gathering in basements and cafes, gloomily drinking, plotting and writing. The better-off took to Bloomsbury and St John's Wood, the poorer continuing to occupy Soho, a neighbourhood later described by Galsworthy as 'untidy, full of Greeks, Ishmaelites, cats, Italians, tomatoes, restaurants, organs, coloured stuffs, queer names, people looking out of upstairs windows'. I can remember it as much the same.

For many of these newcomers, London was a place of disappointment. Their compatriots at home had by definition failed to answer their regular calls to rebellion. As Adam Zamoyski says in his account of refugee London, 'They had been rejected by the very people they had set out to help. A great vision, born in the 1860s, was seeping away in the London fog . . . they became like a clock that was not wound.'

The reality was that Europe had taken refuge in a city whose strength was built on a steadfast aloofness. Detachment from continental politics had been the policy, explicit or implicit, of every British leader since Elizabeth. London was the ideal place to seek safety and comfort in distress, but not to seek allies in a foreign feud. Its meekness was its strength.

15

The Maturing of Victorian London
1860–1875

London, Paris, Vienna

London in the 1840s finally overtook Peking as the biggest city in the world. By 1860 it had reached 2.8 million inhabitants, while Paris and Vienna were barely half that size. But unlike London both cities were aware of their deficiencies. Napoleon III's Paris housed some of the worst slums in Europe. Wealthy residents retreated behind the walls of their 'hotels'. Even the widest streets could be a mere five metres across, and the narrowest less than a metre. The houses were as crammed as the worst prisons. Four out of seven babies died in their first year.

In 1854 Napoleon ordered his Seine prefect, Baron Haussmann, to do to Paris what Wren had tried and failed to do to London. The prefect proposed a geometrical 'star burst' of *ronds-points* and boulevards, driven through what he called 'the swamp of humanity'. He constructed eighty kilometres of avenues in just seventeen years, alongside a completely new water supply and sewerage system. His building contractors behaved like an invading army, sweeping a third of a million inhabitants into side alleys or the fields outside the walls. London's railways and its Metropolitan Board of Works, set up at the same time, were modest in comparison.

Haussmann's motive was as much political as architectural. It was 'to rip open the belly of Paris, the neighbourhoods of revolt and barricades', and create 'a city as strategically ordered as any battlefield'. He created four parks, two grand rail termini, a public hospital and the biggest opera house in the world. He lined his boulevards with apartment blocks to finance his work, all of them looking the same. This baffled Victor Hugo, who complained he could never tell where in the city he was – a familiar problem today. None the less, Paris became overnight the exemplar of a high-density urban design, regarded as a defining new city and imitated from Bucharest to Buenos Aires.

I have puzzled over what it was that Haussmann understood about human habitation that eluded the slash-and-burn developers of the twentieth century, why the bleak acres of Moscow, Brasilia and Beijing so lack Paris's charm. The answer must be that Haussmann's builders understood how people would respond to materials, decoration, paving, greenery and street furniture. Their warm stone seemed comforting, compared with today's concrete, glass and steel. Paris boulevards could seem tedious, as did much of Georgian London, but both were fluent in the language of a compatible urban architecture.

Not to be outdone by Paris, Vienna followed suit. In 1857 the emperor Franz Joseph ordered the demolition of its old defensive glacis and fortifications. They were replaced by a 'Ring' of palaces and civic buildings of imperial magnificence. These included a parliament, a town hall, a university, a museum, an art gallery and acres of parkland. A new opera house opened in 1869 with a performance of Mozart's *Don Giovanni*. These institutions outclassed anything London had to offer. In the provision of open spaces, the divergence between London and other cities was now glaring. Even robber-baron New York in 1858 set aside 700 acres of Manhattan for a Central Park, twice the size of Hyde Park and designed by the London-born Calvert Vaux.

Recession and the vote

London's 1850s upturn in confidence came to an abrupt end in 1866. The leading City discount house, Overend and Gurney, went bankrupt. The stock market plummeted and unemployment rose. Panic subsided only when the Bank of England confirmed its status as lender of last resort to banks in distress. The crash was felt most acutely in London's East End, where the second biggest industry after the docks was shipbuilding. Iron-clad warships and recently Brunel's *Great Eastern* had slid into the water from the Isle of Dogs, Deptford and Woolwich. At the time, the industry employed 27,000 people, and produced a third of Britain's shipping. By the close of 1866 virtually all these workers were unemployed. Most of their work had moved to the north of England and the Clyde, closer to the sources of iron and coal. It would be only a few generations before the docks themselves, so long the foundation of the London economy, followed suit. A metropolis that had lived on the market economy was becoming its victim.

At the same time, pressure for franchise reform recovered its activism, with London this time in the vanguard. A revival of Chartism at the time of Overend and Gurney and the East End crash saw rallies summoned by a new Reform League. The veteran Liberal Lord John Russell introduced a reform bill in 1866 but, as in 1832, it failed to pass parliament and the government resigned. Tension rose in the streets. In May that year a crowd of some 100,000, awesome in its sheer size, broke down barriers and surged across Hyde Park. When another did the same the following spring, it faced some 10,000 police and troops. This time the government gave way, and Disraeli passed Russell's bill. Street action had unquestionably delivered a political outcome. London might not have Haussmann's boulevards or Vienna's Ringstrasse, but as

Paris and Vienna veered towards military defeat at the hands of Bismarck's Prussia, Britain's capital found a different source of stability. Virtually all adult working males now had the vote.

Of all periods in London's history, Gladstone's first ministry of 1868–74 must have been exhilarating to live through. He called it, with typical modesty, 'the finest instrument of government that ever was constructed'. London was emerging from the 1866 crash. Bazalgette's sewers and embankments were under construction. Streets were cleaned and well lit. Infant mortality under five had fallen to one in three from twice that in the 1750s. The last cholera epidemic was in 1866. London might have a grandeur deficiency, but it had overground and underground railways, and a new parliament building rising over the Thames. Gilbert Scott's Foreign Office was complete, as was his St Pancras station hotel.

Above all, London was seeing a demographic upheaval. The doubling of its population was due almost entirely to the railways and their stimulus to expansion. The companies had been ruthless in wiping out the housing of the poor. But they were stimulating more acres of housing in the suburbs than they destroyed in the city, and those houses were considerably more hygienic and spacious. This both reflected and facilitated a shift in the working population, from so-called blue-collar to white-collar jobs, from manufacturing to services and, above all, finance.

Gladstone's parliament responded to these changes. The worst aspect of the 1834 Poor Law had become the care of the destitute sick. An act now set up a Metropolitan Asylums Board, with power to build hospitals and asylums, initially for the workhouses. The impact was remarkable. By 1900 London would have seventy-four Poor Law hospitals open to all, with only the medieval foundations of Guy's, Bart's and St Thomas' remaining private. In one respect at least, London's welfare was leading the country.

In 1870 came the Forster Education Act, setting up school boards where the church's monopoly on education had left gaps in provision. Given the wider 1867 franchise, the act was dubbed as 'educating our masters'. The London board was composed of forty-nine elected members, with women able to vote and stand for election. Top of the poll was London's first woman doctor, Elizabeth Garrett Anderson, followed by the radical socialist Annie Besant. *The Times* declared that 'no equally powerful body will exist in England outside parliament, if power be measured by influence for good or evil over masses of human beings'. The board pushed London to the forefront of social reform, making school compulsory and free for those who could not afford it.

Such reform to health and education was only modestly paralleled in transport. The rise in commuting led to ever more acute congestion as thousands of horse-drawn buses conveyed passengers from the termini not served by the Underground to their place of work. One horse collapsing at a junction could gridlock a neighbourhood for an hour. After its Embankment success, the MBW moved to create new thoroughfares in the West End. Victoria station was linked to Westminster Abbey by Victoria Street. Shaftesbury Avenue and Charing Cross Road were driven through the slums of St Giles. Northumberland Avenue connected Trafalgar Square to the Embankment, destroying the last of the old riverside palaces, Northumberland House, in the process.

Along the Embankment itself, new buildings arrived to accompany Somerset House, such as the City of London School, the Cecil and Savoy hotels and the National Liberal Club. The Temple's lawyers protested the extension of Bazalgette's Embankment across its gardens, claiming a longstanding right to 'stroll at twilight to the riverside'. They were overruled. However, the new road came to an abrupt stop, when it reached the City boundary at Blackfriars. The stately warehouses of Upper Thames Street withstood the road builders until the 1970s.

A change in taste

These new London buildings displayed a size and ostentation that were wholly novel in the still largely Georgian streetscape on which they were imposed. They came in a bewildering variety of styles. Each generation may rebel against the taste of its forerunner, but never so drastically as in Victorian architecture. The Georgian and Regency metropolis had been a celebration of classicism. By the 1860s, its yellow/black brick terraces and stucco squares were seen as boring and unimaginative. John Ruskin, champion of the Pre-Raphaelite movement, dismissed the Bedford estate's Gower Street in Bloomsbury as the 'nec plus ultra of ugliness in British architecture'. The historian Donald Olsen wrote: 'If the Regency prized smooth stucco, the Victorians produced the roughest stone possible. If the Georgians preferred unobtrusive grey bricks, the Victorians produced the brightest red bricks they could manage, if the Georgians sought restrained, uniform, monochrome facades, the Victorians revelled in glazed polychrome tiles . . . jagged skylines . . . variety.'

Gothic continued to find favour with churchmen and parliamentarians, but the domestic market rejected it almost completely. London's housing estates as late as the 1850s were still decked in the stucco pilasters and enriched architraves of the Italianate. When fashion began to shift in the 1860s it was not to gothic but to Flemish, Elizabethan and Queen Anne, anything that was redbrick, terracotta or sandstone. When, in 1871, the architect E. R. Robson was hired by the London School Board to design what became almost 300 new schools, they looked as if they had been shipped from the canals of Amsterdam. They rose in scrolled and gabled seriousness, frowning down on mile upon mile of London terraces like so many disciplining ushers. A spread of them can still be seen over Wandsworth from a train out of Victoria.

Barely a decade separated the ascetic yellow brick of King's Cross station of 1853 from the fantasy palace of St Pancras next door, begun in 1865. The historian of St Pancras, Simon Bradley, has detected in the latter's facade 'echoes of Bruges, Salisbury, Caernarvon, Amiens and Verona'. South Kensington's avenues, almost before they were built, discarded white stucco for redbrick neo-Dutch. An upmarket artists' colony developed on the Holland Park estate at Melbury Road, west London, culminating in Lord Leighton's exotic Leighton House (now a museum). The Harrington estate off Gloucester Road erupted in extraordinarily eclectic Dutch architecture – unlike anything I have seen in Holland. At Bedford Park in the borough of Ealing, an entire neighbourhood was designed by Norman Shaw in 1877 in quaint redbrick with Pre-Raphaelite decoration. Maida Vale's mile-long Elgin Avenue is a cornucopia of every period of Victorian taste.

For landowners facing the renewal of long leases on Georgian estates, decisions on style were a headache. In Knightsbridge, Hans Town and Cadogan Square were demolished and replaced in overpoweringly brick-coloured 'Pont Street Dutch'. To the south in Chelsea, less valuable Georgian squares and terraces were left in stuccoed peace. The Portland estate's Marylebone was confused. Terraces were undisturbed but their corners were emphasized by gabled and turreted citadels. In Russell Square, the hard-pressed Bedford estate merely 'updated' their doors and windows by giving them ungainly terracotta surrounds.

No innovation was as dramatic as the City's answer to Westminster's Big Ben. In 1877 a committee met to decide on a new river crossing downstream from London Bridge, requiring a retractable deck to permit ships to enter the Pool of London. The style ordained for Tower Bridge from the City engineer, Sir Horace Jones, was to echo the adjacent Tower of London, as Big Ben had echoed Westminster Abbey. These two monuments, both explicitly respectful of context, became instant icons of the new London. No such respect for Tower Bridge was shown when a large brutalist hotel was made its neighbour in 1973.

The metropolis at leisure

The renewals acknowledged that residents of inner London still wanted individual houses with front doors giving onto streets. This had an inevitable impact on social behaviour. Haussmann's Paris of apartments drove its inhabitants outdoors, to congregate in cafes and restaurants and use collective bakeries and kitchens. London had its pubs, but most were in mews or poorer streets, for the refreshment of servants. There were few cafeterias. Londoners relaxed and socialized in the privacy of their homes. The concept of public space depicted in Verdi's *La traviata* or Puccini's *La bohème* did not take hold in Victorian London. Scenes in Dickens, Trollope and Galsworthy rarely occur in public places (Mr Pickwick excepted). The Pallisers and Forsytes were introverted families, as were George Grossmith's Pooters.

Where the middle classes did congregate was in professional or intellectual groups. The affinity might be politics, the army, medicine, the law or scholarship, but the focus was the club. There were a hundred named London clubs by the end of the nineteenth century, including eight for army and navy officers, five for Oxbridge graduates and nine for women. Another shared realm for women was the department store. Oxford Street and Regent Street inspired partnerships familiar to Londoners well into the 1960s, Swears & Wells, Swan & Edgar, Marshall & Snelgrove, Dickins & Jones, Debenham & Freebody, each with its subtly different clientele.

The new stores – never vulgar 'shops' – spread ever outwards. The first was suburban colonizer William Whiteley's 'universal provider' in 1863, aiming to make Westbourne Grove 'the Bond Street of Bayswater'. Whiteley offered not just clothes and food but hairdressing, house-buying, undertaking and the new 'nettoyage à sec' (dry cleaning). Charles Digby Harrod arrived in Knightsbridge after the Great Exhibition, with his telegraphic address 'Everything London', though the store did not achieve its terracotta magnificence until 1901. Harvey Nichols followed close by, as did Barker's in Kensington, Peter Jones in Chelsea, John Barnes in West Hampstead and Arding & Hobbs in Battersea. Most bizarre was Wickhams in the Mile End Road, its imperious facade interrupted by tiny Spiegelhalter, a jeweller, who refused to sell his shop in the middle of the site. Both have now gone but the tiny Spiegelhalter building survives, a work of pure London eccentricity.

A wider society patronized the realm of entertainment. Taverns, pleasure gardens, theatres and music halls offered a tapestry of urban life. The London theatre had been a royal monopoly, supposedly (though not in practice) confined to Covent Garden and Drury Lane, until licensing was liberalized in 1843. Theatres proliferated, principally in the Strand, St Martin's Lane and the Haymarket. Islington's Sadler's Wells revived a stage that had been popular in various guises since the seventeenth century. The Royal Coburg in Lambeth won royal patronage, but changed its name to the Old Vic. Every suburban high street soon had its music hall. Tickets in the galleries could be had for a few pence.

Audiences were often raucous, that at Sadler's Wells reported as 'resounding with foul language, oaths, catcalls, shrieks, yells, blasphemy, obscenity – a truly diabolical clamour'. Dickens described playgoers at Hoxton as 'dirty boys, low copying clerks in attorneys' offices, capacious-headed youths with City counting houses . . . a choice miscellany of vagabonds'. *Punch's* comic hero, Lupin Pooter, appalled his father with his 'fast' habits and addiction to music halls. Yet through all the noise, Londoners also heard the operas of Offenbach, Léhar and Gilbert and Sullivan, the plays of Wilde, Pinero and Ibsen and, at the Lyceum, the Shakespearean partnership of Henry Irving and Ellen Terry.

Open spaces on the march

More ominous was the fate of such patches of open space as survived amid the market gardens and brickfields that lay in the path of London's outward march. As recreational land shrank, a series of commissions called for what survived to be protected, if only to wean the poor from 'low and debasing pleasures . . . drinking houses, dog fights, boxing matches'. Argument tended to focus on remaining common land, privately owned by manorial lords but, by traditional right, publicly accessible.

The most conspicuous example was Hampstead Heath, owned by the Maryon Wilson family. By the mid-nineteenth century, the heights of Islington and Highgate had largely disappeared under bricks and mortar, as had much of Greenwich to the east and Sydenham to the south. Hampstead had offered recreation to Londoners of all classes since earliest times. The arrival of the railway and of bank holidays (in 1871) turned recreation into a torrent. Posters of the Heath show scenes akin to Brighton beach, including policemen chasing thieves among the crowds.

Since the 1820s, the Maryon Wilsons had been applying for legislation to enclose land round the summit of the Heath, as with other suburban manors. In Hampstead they met opposition of a wholly different order and it rose in unison. The Heath was sacred ground. Dickens's Pickwickians 'traced to their sources the mighty ponds of Hampstead'. Keats wrote of the Heath, 'To one who has been long in city pent/ 'Tis very sweet to look into the fair/ And open face of Heaven.' Constable called the view over London from

Hampstead 'unsurpassed in all Europe'. London's classiest protest campaign was joined by Shelley, Byron, Lamb, Hazlitt and the radical Leigh Hunt, imprisoned for attacking the Prince Regent. Hunt sent a sonnet from his cell, celebrating 'nature's own ground . . . its cottaged vales with billowy fields beyond/ And clumps of darkening pines and prospects blue/ And that clear path through all, where daily meet/ Cool cheeks and brilliant eyes and morn-elastic feet.'

As if this was not enough, the current Maryon Wilson, Sir Thomas, faced the fact that Hampstead was home to London's wealthiest weekenders. Having already staked their claim to its hilltop delights, bankers, lawyers and peers were reluctant to share them with others. In 1871 a compromise was reached, with Maryon Wilson allowed to develop what became Fitzjohn's Avenue for villas, while a wide sweep to the north and east of the village was acquired by the MBW as open space. The trenchant campaigner Octavia Hill failed to save the fields round Swiss Cottage, but ten years later Parliament Hill Fields on the borders of Highgate was added to the Heath. A reluctant MBW refused to fund a planned layout of ornamental gardens across the Heath, telling its keepers just to 'wander round spreading gorse seed'. The resulting wildness is Hampstead's magic.

While the battle of Hampstead rolled across the northern heights, other struggles ensued. By the early 1860s a Society for the Preservation of the Commons in the Neighbourhood of London had been formed, and a law passed in 1866 banning further manorial enclosures. Pressure on the MBW led to the acquisition of Victoria Park in 1845 and of Battersea Fields in 1858. These were followed by parks at Blackheath, Hackney Downs, Clapham Common, Tooting Bec and Epping Forest. Still London lagged behind other cities of comparable size, but then many if not most of its inhabitants had their own back gardens. And the London street could be a recreation space in itself.

The relentlessness of poverty

For all this progress, London still contained areas of extreme poverty and overcrowding. Visiting in 1862, Dostoevsky was shocked by London's contrasts. He was entranced by the gas lighting, jostling crowds and easy communion between rich and poor. But he was appalled by the beggars on the streets, and especially by the West End prostitutes. These included girls brought to the Haymarket by their mothers, 'aged about twelve, who seize you by the arm and beg you to come with them'. Another was 'not older than six all in rags, dirty bare-foot and hollow-cheeked . . . covered with bruises'. There were an estimated 20,000 prostitutes in London at this time. Their plight appalled the austere Gladstone, who took to the streets at night trying to find them accommodation.

The doyen of Victorian social reformers was the early sociologist Charles Booth, whose team of assistants, including the socialist Beatrice Webb and the economist and champion of women's employment Clara Collet, combed the city for data. They mapped its social classifications by street location and revealed the destitution that lurked just a few yards beyond the perimeters of the great estates. Booth's initial work, *Life and Labour of the People* (1889), established that a chief cause of poverty was the casual nature of London's work. While he was a meticulous recorder, he was also a savage commentator. An imperial nation, he wrote, should be aware that the English slum resembled the African jungle in 'its dwarfish dehumanized inhabitants, the slavery to which they are subjected'. A third of Londoners were living in poverty, though he did admit that his lowest category, that of 'outcast London . . . lowest, vicious, semi-criminal', probably amounted to no more than 2 per cent of the population of East London.

To the end of his career in the 1860s, Dickens also publicized not just the slums of the West End, but also the rarely noted rookeries east of the City along the Thames. Fagin's Jacob's Island in *Oliver Twist* was a real address in Bermondsey, described as with 'crazy wooden galleries common to the backs of half a dozen houses, with holes from which to look upon the slime beneath . . . rooms so small, so filthy, so confined, that the air would seem to be too tainted even for the dirt and squalor which they shelter'. Here, wrote Dickens, lay 'every repulsive lineament of poverty, every loathsome indication of filth, rot, and garbage'.

When I first tracked down the site of Jacob's Island at the mouth of the Shad Thames inlet, I shuddered even at the derelict warehouse that had replaced it. The warehouse is now converted into flats. London's tenements and rookeries have long gone. But some examples of what were the humblest dwellings have survived the slum-clearance bulldozers. They sit carefully preserved in such originally working-class enclaves as Hillgate village in Notting Hill and back lanes in Stepney, Bethnal Green, Southwark and Lambeth. The best preserved is probably the Duchy of Cornwall's estate round Whittlesey Street behind the Old Vic. Its terrace cottages are so diminutive they might be a film set – as they often are.

In all this, there was something ghoulish in the Victorians' fascination with the squalor and promiscuity of their newly revealed city. They were intrigued as much as appalled by the sailors, thieves, prostitutes, alcoholics and opium dens that filled the pages of Dickens and others. Dickens admitted to sensing 'the attraction of repulsion'. In 1888 London feasted on the unsolved Whitechapel murders of five prostitutes by Jack the Ripper, since then the subject of around 150 catalogued books.

16

Philanthropy Versus the State
1875–1900

Octavia Hill

Late-Victorian London had become a metropolis gorged on growth. It could hardly move, at least in the city centre. Though its water was refreshed, its air was polluted. It was not particularly handsome or even loveable. Foreigners commented constantly on the damp, the fog, the winter darkness and gloomy crowds. John Ruskin declared London 'a ghastly heap of fermenting brickwork, pouring out poison at every pore'. Though observers from Dickens and Conan Doyle to Monet and Whistler had used London's defects to imaginative effect, even an admirer, Henry James, called it 'dreary, heavy, stupid, dull, inhuman, vulgar at heart and tiresome in form'. But he did conclude that it was 'on the whole the most *possible* form of life . . . the biggest aggregation – the most complete compendium'.

What was now changing was London's conscience, reflected in both a rising tide of philanthropy and ever more insistent demands for governmental reform. The first was embodied in the remarkable Octavia Hill, already a veteran of the campaign for London's open spaces. A tiny woman of poor parents but with an icy determination, she had in 1865 persuaded Ruskin to buy her a Marylebone property in which to house families from among the 'deserving poor', financed by commercial investors on commercial terms. Hill was soon buying end-of-lease properties and restoring and reletting rather than demolishing them. She was meticulous in caring for her tenants, provided only that they paid their rent. She used female inspectors and rent collectors and helped 'responsible' tenants when they were in trouble. This distinction – shared with Mayhew and Booth – between moral and immoral poverty was ingrained in the Victorian psyche.

The maxims Hill issued to her staff became a byword for early social housing: 'Repairs promptly and efficiently attended to, over-crowding put an end to, the blessing of ready money payments enforced, accounts strictly kept and, above all, tenants so sorted as to be helpful to one another.' By 1874 Hill had fifteen schemes and 3,000 tenants, all managed by her assistants and delivering her investors a 5 per cent return. The Church of England, widely accused of slum landlordism in Southwark and Paddington, asked Hill to take on the management of many of its estates, thus adding another 5,000 tenants to her care. Others followed suit, including Dickens's friend Angela Burdett-Coutts and the American tycoon George Peabody. They were joined by organizations such as the Improved Industrial Dwellings Company and the Society for Improving the Condition of the Labouring Classes. All stressed that good management made estates financially sound, that philanthropy was a good investment. It was never 'not for profit', just for profit that was modest and secure.

The old established estates soon realized that slums on their doorsteps were bad for lease renewals, with a large number of ninety-nine-year leases falling due in the 1870s and 80s. A report on working-class housing in 1884 found that Grosvenor, Northampton and the church were all offering reduced ground rents to charitable companies to replace slums on their perimeters. There was hardly an estate in London without a Peabody or Improved Dwellings block on its fringe. A number of such estates sprang up north of Grosvenor Square and either side of Oxford Street and survived to recent times. I used to ferry tenants from buildings opposite Selfridge's to Christmas lunches in the 1970s, meeting former flower girls and prostitutes hilariously recalling the 'good old Mayfair days'. Most of these buildings are now private flats.

In 1875 the Cross Act laid down new standards for so-called 'byelaw' housing, similar to the 1774 Act's fourth-grade properties, requiring all houses to have modern plumbing. By then philanthropy had rehoused 27,000 people in what were called 'model dwellings'. A survey counted no fewer than 640 charities, dealing with everything from housing distressed needlewomen to distributing Bibles to the poor. Their combined income was £2.4 million, a sizeable 'tax' on the generous, if not the rich. But all the charity in the world could not meet need in a booming metropolis. At night at this time, some 400 people were counted sleeping rough in Trafalgar Square alone.

Government strikes back, just

What should have been sobering for Londoners – did they care to notice – was that other British cities were racing ahead of them. While they had boards for schools and asylums, they had no overall democratic authority. Manchester, Leeds, Birmingham and elsewhere were showing both civic leadership and social enterprise. They oversaw the building of roads, schools and public utilities. Their town halls were magnificent. Birmingham's was already open in 1834, in a Greek style. Leeds came later in 1853 Italianate, while Manchester's civic palace by Alfred Waterhouse was in 1870s gothic.

The ancient City of London, which in the Middle Ages had enjoyed probably the most representative local democracy in the country, did so no more. To the radical philosopher John Stuart Mill, London's Guildhall was a 'union of modern jobbery and antiquated foppery'. Even that was a paragon compared with the rest of the metropolis. Its archaic vestries, Poor Law guardians and

unelected MBW continued to enjoy the protection of their aristocratic lobbyists in Westminster.

By the 1880s the vestries were sensing their days were numbered,
and many did make an effort to rebut accusations of 'not governing
but guzzling'. Between them they opened thirty-one public libraries
and created 200 small parks. The public washhouse movement had
begun in the 1840s with an 'experiment' at East Smithfield near London docks, welcoming 35,000 bathers in its first year. *The Times*
expressed surprise that 'the very lowest poor, those who have for
years been habituated by hard necessity to the endurance of personal
filth', now when offered a bath 'eagerly avail themselves of any facilities afforded to them for attaining personal cleanliness'. By the 1870s,
providing baths was regarded as a leading vestry function. The
resulting redbrick and terracotta buildings came to rival libraries in
vestry pride – most now reborn as chic restaurants or coffee shops.

For the MBW it was too late. A series of contract scandals
shocked even an unshockable parliament. In 1884 120,000 people
gathered in Hyde Park with a hitherto unprecedented demand for
a new government for London, stirred by what was a strengthen-
ing trade union movement. London was seeing belated signs of
industrial unrest. The dockers' leader Ben Tillett headed a successful campaign for 'the docker's tanner', a wage of 6d an hour. In 1888
700 'match girls' at the Bryant & May factory in Bow went on strike
for better conditions. So too did the gas workers. This time the
broken windows were not those of the Duke of Wellington but of
Marshall & Snelgrove department store.

A central weakness of London's local government was that,
unlike the provincial municipalities, it lacked any single authority
with powers to redistribute taxes from rich to poor areas of the
city. As a result, the vestry of St George's-in-the-East had to levy a
crippling property rate of 3/9d in the pound, while wealthy St
George's Hanover Square levied a mere 6d. Without cross-subsidy,

serious efforts to relieve poverty were impossible. The liberal leader of Birmingham, Joseph Chamberlain, thundered that cities should accept 'new conceptions of public duty, new developments of social enterprise, new estimates of the natural obligations of the community to one another'. Birmingham was pointing an accusing finger at London.

A London county is born

Parliament finally cracked. In 1888 a local government act was passed by Lord Salisbury's Tories, replacing the unlamented MBW with a London County Council (LCC), paralleling similar reforms to provincial county administration. But Salisbury was still adamantly against a unitary authority for the capital. Such a body, he said, would be too big and thus too powerful. Salisbury duly left unreformed the City Corporation, the poor law guardians and, astonishingly, the unelected vestries. He saw them as conservative bulwarks against the possibly spendthrift radicalism of a large and alarmingly democratic LCC.

As a result, the new county authority enjoyed few powers not already possessed by the MBW. The LCC ran a fire brigade, the Thames bridges, the sewers and such council houses as it could afford to build, but it was not permitted to run schools, health or welfare. There was one glimmer of sanity: though there was no move to redistribute vestry rates, a common poor law fund was established, to equalize the burden on the Poor Law guardians between rich and poor areas. This was a major breakthrough.

Despite its limited powers, the new LCC gave London politics a shot in the arm. Two councillors came from each parliamentary constituency. They embraced the old estates, such as those of Lords Onslow, Compton and Norfolk, and radicals from the Fabian fringe such as Sidney Webb and John Burns as well as the Liberal Charles Dilke. George Bernard Shaw railed from his column in a radical newspaper, the *Star*. The council's chairman was the Liberal grandee Lord Rosebery.

Women now had the vote in all county elections. Since holding property was the voting qualification, it was clearly unfair to exclude women property owners. They had already been admitted to the school boards and as Poor Law guardians. Two women were elected to the LCC, for Bow and Brixton, despite determined attempts to eject them (including on grounds that their property really belonged to their husbands). By the 1900s, an estimated 120,000 women were voting in London. Local democracy was far ahead of the national version.

The LCC's radical members did exactly as Salisbury had feared. Webb launched a Fabian manifesto alerting London to 'a sullen discontent among its toiling millions' and demanding action against the 'speculators, vestry jobbers, house farmers, water sharks, market monopolists, ground landlords and other social parasites'. He saw London as a prospective 'self-governing commune' echoing that of Paris in 1871. Webb wanted the 'municipalisation' of water, gas, the trams, the docks and the hospitals. The council's first clerk and later its historian, Laurence Gomme, wrote eloquently of reviving 'the democratic spirit of the medieval charters, and traditions of citizenship as ancient as the Saxon and Roman origins of the city'.

The second LCC election in 1892 saw the council's membership cohere round two groups, the liberal Progressives and the conservative Moderates, with the Progressives initially in a majority. The 1894 Liberal government rectified one failing of Salisbury's reform. It passed a full rate equalization act, taxing rich vestries on a formula in favour of poor ones. Together with the already equalized Poor Law fund, this produced a dramatic shift in resources across the metropolis. The vestries staggered on another decade, until in 1899 even Salisbury, returning to power, finally accepted they should go. They became twenty-eight elected metropolitan boroughs. However, the separately elected Poor Law guardians and the London School Board were left in place, for the time being. Salisbury hoped the new boroughs would be as strongly Tory as he assumed had been the vestries.

After a millennium of London outside the City having no constitutional status, the capital as a whole had at last achieved a degree of accountable self-government. For the first time, the word London was officially applied to a wider area than just the old City. Even so, the new boroughs were ridiculed by G. K. Chesterton in his satire *The Napoleon of Notting Hill*, in which he predicted war would break out between them in 1984 – a date later borrowed by George Orwell for his less humorous dystopia. Chesterton's final, bloody battle took place between a victorious (fictional) borough of Notting Hill and the forces of South Kensington on the slopes of Campden Hill. Come the real 1984, I was sorry the burghers of Notting Hill did not commemorate this glorious moment in their past. In the event, the boroughs were to prove a more robust and successful feature of London's political scene than the LCC and its successors.

This dilatory reform illustrated a recurrent feature of London's political ecology. A Leeds newspaper during the Chartist period had complained, 'Why is London always the last to stir?' During the labour disturbances of the 1880s, the newsagent MP W. H. Smith protested in parliament that 'for at least an hour the most frequented streets of the West End of London should be entirely at the mercy of the mob'. He was outraged that they had broken the windows of the Carlton Club. He seemed unaware that, nine years previously, 10,000 people had died in similar upheavals on the streets of Paris. London was in a world of its own.

Karl Marx had attributed London's relative passivity to its dispersed workforce and lack of large factories, where workers could better be organized. The radical Francis Place likewise complained of workers living at 'considerable distances, many seven miles apart' from their place of work. Ever since the decay of the City's guilds and 'closed shops', London's working class had been local, casual and rootless. Outside the remaining docks and utilities, it had resisted unionization, and was constantly diluted by immigrants, provincial more than foreign.

Though London had been active in disturbances in 1832, 1867 and 1888, the social historian Roy Porter wondered why, even then, 'overall, threats to public order remained remarkably slight'. He attributed it to 'the sheer size of Victorian London and the internal differentiation of its labouring classes'. The city was too big to be coherently agitated. Its workers were in 'little "islands", localized and fragmented'. In other words, the best route to studying London's history remained through its geography. A growing city may explode unless something is present to relieve the pressure. In London there was always space.

Transports of delight

Space needed transport, and this was one area in which London was no longer dilatory, though it was no thanks to its government, new or old. Within the orbit of the 'cut-and-cover' Circle Line lay a no-man's-land where Londoners still had to move on foot or at the speed of a (very slow) horse and carriage. This state of affairs was potentially transformed in 1879 by the invention in Berlin of electric transmission along a metal wire or track. London's railway entrepreneurs saw the opportunity. After various false starts, a City and South London Railway (CSLR) began deep-tunnelling from King William Street near the Monument, under the Thames and out through Southwark to Kennington and Stockwell. It opened for business in 1890, the first underground electric train in the world. Its success was phenomenal. In the first full year, a million passengers used what later became the eastern limb of the Northern Line.

London's thick clay was considered ideal for deep tunnels, using Brunel's moving shield excavator. These lines came to be known as 'tubes', while the cut-and-cover Metropolitan, District and Circle lines were strictly 'undergrounds'. Next into service was the above-ground London and South-Western Railway, whose terminus at Waterloo had long felt painfully without access to the City. The company now dug what was nicknamed the Drain, running from Waterloo to Bank and opening in 1898. At the same time an American consortium began a much grander venture, a long tunnel from Shepherd's Bush under Notting Hill and Bayswater and on beneath Oxford Street to St Paul's. The platforms on what was called the Central Line were reached by lifts, and the train seats were upholstered and comfortable. This luxury was little short of sensational. The line became the aristocrat of the Tube, its fixed fare dubbing it the Twopenny Tube.

If the future of transport in the metropolis lay underground, there was a last sad epitaph on the age of the surface railway. An act of capitalist bravado saw the arrival in the city in 1899 of the Great Central. It was the brainchild, bordering on obsession, of the tycoon Sir Edward Watkin, who dreamed of a luxury service linking the north of England into London's Metropolitan Line, of which he was also chairman. He envisaged his trains running direct from Manchester into Baker Street, then across central London to Kent and on to a Channel tunnel and Paris. His workers even started the undersea excavation. As it was, his railway ended at the Marylebone Road, being forced to excavate Lord's cricket ground over a winter for a tunnel. Watkin's plausible dream remains unrealized.

In May 1900, the Boer War in South Africa reached a climax in the siege of Mafeking. Details of the siege had been minutely followed at home, largely thanks to four British journalists trapped in the town being able to smuggle out their despatches. When news of the city's relief arrived at 9.30 in the evening, London went berserk. Within five minutes of the Mansion House posting the news, 20,000 people had gathered in the streets. At Covent Garden, Wagner's *Lohengrin* was interrupted by a shout from the gallery, whereupon the cast and audience stood to sing patriotic songs – not by Wagner. The Prince of Wales beat time in his box. The hysteria was later given its own verb, to go 'mafficking'. Though the war was a wretched, unresolved affair, its reception in London was that of an imperial capital believing itself at its indestructible peak.

17

Edwardian Apotheosis
1900–1914

Remembering Victoria

In January 1901, the death of Queen Victoria stimulated a national debate on how her long reign should be celebrated. Now surely London could honour its imperial status. It housed, employed and fed 6 million people and had doubled in size in just forty years. After the troubles of the 1880s, the metropolis showed few signs of self-doubt and felt it might boast, if only just a little. As Pevsner put it, 'As the penny-pinching Victorian spirit abated, the desire was commonly voiced that Westminster should become a capital worthy of the British Empire and comparable in splendour to Paris, Vienna or Berlin.' It was decided that the place for this was the royal enclave of St James's, still a rather scruffy jumble of townhouses and a square, overlooking Nash's attempt at a pocket Regent's Park.

The winning proposal came from the architect Sir Aston Webb, for a mall running through St James's Park from Trafalgar Square to Buckingham Palace. The route would lead under a triumphal arch, named after the Admiralty, down an avenue to a statue of Victoria surrounded by emblems of empire. Buckingham Palace would be refaced in an appropriately imperial style. The latter was done in just three summer months in 1913 when the king was away, in a staid classicism that looks much better when lit at night.

London now had space for at least modest state ceremonial, though it required a dog-legged diversion from what might have been the shortest route between the palace and Parliament Square along Birdcage Walk. The Mall also proved an uncomfortable insertion into Nash's carefully informal landscape. Among other things it dared not disturb the private and royal gardens from Marlborough House to Lancaster House past St James's Palace. To this day they turn their backs on passing parades, as if with more important business to attend to.

The other London memorial came close to farce. It was to revive a plan, long in abeyance, to clear the slums of Clare Market round the Aldwych and replace them with a Parisian boulevard north to Holborn. Three thousand people were evicted from the only surviving neighbourhood of pre-fire London, which could and should have been retained and restored. Just one old building, the Old Curiosity Shop, remains on the market's fringe near Lincoln's Inn Fields. This was the inspiration for the novel of that name by Dickens, who called it 'one of those receptacles for old and curious things which seem to crouch in odd corners of this town and hide their musty treasures from the public eye'. It is now owned by the London School of Economics, which seems at a loss as to what to do with it.

The new Kingsway was a commercial failure. It could not penetrate Somerset House to reach the Embankment, and only a tram tunnel (now a road) linked it with the river. When in 1905 the new king, Edward VII, came to open it, he found it strewn with rubble and hoardings. Photographs show him on horseback in what looks like a war zone. The new Aldwych, ghost of ancient Lundenwic, was not completed until the 1930s, while Kingsway turned for tenants to that lifeboat for distressed London developers, government offices. It was no Champs-Élysées, and was to be the last wholly new central London road until the Hyde Park underpass of 1962. Holborn was always 'midtown', a place lost between London's two cities.

New century, new style

Elsewhere London entered into the spirit of Edwardian pomp by continuing the renewal of its Georgian fabric begun by the late Victorians. It did so ruthlessly. There was, as yet, no thought given to respecting, let alone conserving, anything of the past. A campaign of widespread demolition was to continue for half a century. Even places of worship were not sacred. In the City, seventeen of Wren's churches were demolished, to make way mostly for banks. Only the tradition-soaked liveried guilds saved their ancient halls. Elsewhere, as estate leases fell due, owners destroyed with abandon. London's main thoroughfares were almost entirely rebuilt in the boom years from 1890 to 1910.

In the matter of style, there was an eagerness to move on from the domestic 'sweetness and light' of the Dutch and Queen Anne revival. It seemed too meek an architectural language for a great empire. But where to go was unclear. The architect John Brydon called for a patriotic reversion to Hogarth's favourites, Wren and Vanbrugh, whose English baroque had been 'fairly established as the national style, the vernacular of the country'. Brydon even declared baroque to be 'the style of the future', represented by his imposing government office building overlooking Parliament Square.

In the outturn it was a case of anything goes. Andrew Saint's study of London at the turn of the century offers a wealth of promiscuous eclecticism. He lists churches still in formal gothic, such as Holy Trinity Sloane Street, rich in Arts and Crafts fittings (built in 1888). He moves on through the French renaissance Ritz Hotel (1903), the Byzantine Westminster Cathedral (1895), the American neo-classical Selfridge's (1908), the Flemish Middlesex Guildhall in Parliament Square (1913) and the Scots baronial New Scotland Yard (1887).

London's first large blocks of flats, built in 1880 by Norman Shaw, towered over both the Royal Albert Hall and his own Lowther Lodge next door. Similar cliffs rose Haussmann-like along Victoria Street, Buckingham Palace Road, Knightsbridge, Marylebone Road, Maida Vale and St John's Wood. Tenants of this new urbanism were desperate not to be seen as second best. One critic stressed that living in flats per se 'does not stamp them as failures', while 'no one who looks at them from outside should be able to guess that the rents are low'.

By now London's main streets were losing the visual coherence recorded by Tallis in the 1830s. Indeed, the street as the defining element in London's landscape was now replaced by individual buildings. As these buildings tended to be commissioned by users rather than landlords, they inevitably took on a self-regarding rather than a neighbourly personality. Most of London's signature buildings from this period are in some version Brydon's approved baroque: the Old Bailey (1903), the Port of London Authority (1909), the War Office in Whitehall (1906), County Hall (1909), the Methodist Central Hall (1905) and the Victoria and Albert Museum (1899–1909). When plans were drawn up for the demolition of Nash's Regent Street, baroque was prescribed for its replacement, as demonstrated in Norman Shaw's Piccadilly Hotel, linking Regent Street with Piccadilly (see below).

The most satisfying examples of this baroque revival occur not in public buildings but in piecemeal replacements of Georgian terrace houses, such as on the Portland and Grosvenor estates, in Marylebone's Welbeck Street and Mayfair's Park Street. Curving rooflines, pedimented windows, ornate eaves and doorways and even an occasional statue all struggle to give a facade a peculiar personality. If we lift our eyes above street level, we see in the commercial architecture of Edwardian Bond Street, Albemarle Street and Piccadilly facades of astonishing variety, the last era in which revivalism was regarded as a sign of inspiration rather than defeat. They are the true antidote to Georgian monotony.

The West End theatre followed suit. Its genius was Frank Matcham, mostly working for the Stoll-Moss empire. His fantastical auditoriums staged Gilbert and Sullivan, Wilde and Shaw amid a riot of rococo ceilings, velvet drapes and plaster cherubs. Matcham's masterpiece was the Coliseum in St Martin's Lane, while the Hippodrome, Palladium and Victoria Palace pushed the old Covent Garden and Drury Lane into the shade. Matcham saw himself as complementing the playwright in audience escapism, delighted to hear that crowds flocked to see his 'palaces of pleasures' as much to admire them as what was on stage.

Luxury hotels had so far been largely the preserve of the railway companies, though Brown's Hotel dated from the Napoleonic era and Claridge's from the 1850s. In 1889 the profits on the Savoy operas were used by the D'Oyly Carte family to build a new Savoy Hotel, importing César Ritz and Escoffier from Paris as chefs. Ritz's later eponymous hotel on Piccadilly, opened in 1906, was the first steel-framed building in London, its street front modelled on the Rue de Rivoli in Paris. Restaurants now became more than chophouses. Baedeker in 1898 listed sixty good ones in the West End. For the impecunious, there were 'milk and bun' shops, ABC teashops and Joe Lyons's Corner Houses.

Harrod's in Knightsbridge rebuilt itself in 1901, boasting London's first 'moving staircase'. It came complete with a free glass of brandy for terrified customers who made it to the top. Its rival, Selfridge's, arrived in Oxford Street in 1909, with a bombastic classical design by Daniel Burnham of Chicago but much altered. Harry Selfridge's motto, 'The customer is always right', embodied the idea of shopping as an experience rather than a mere purchase. To celebrate the opening, it exhibited the plane in which a Frenchman, Louis Blériot, had just flown across the Channel.

The ascendancy of localism

London's new government entered into the confident Edwardian spirit. Now it was the metropolitan boroughs, intended by Salisbury to check a spendthrift LCC, which proved the most active. No sooner were they elected than the burghers of Woolwich, Wandsworth, Deptford, Chelsea and Lambeth built town halls worthy of renaissance princes. The poorer authorities, liberated by rate equalization, pioneered sanitary inspection of slums, free libraries and public baths (including the Turkish variety). By 1902 Camberwell alone had six public libraries and an art gallery. Fifteen boroughs generated their own electricity for street lighting.

East Ham, an all-purpose borough over the London border in the county of Essex, built itself a town hall described by Pevsner as the 'supreme London example of the power and confidence of the Edwardian local authority'. Within ten years, East Hammers were supplied with a new assembly room, police station, courtrooms, library, health centre, fire station, swimming pool, technical college and tram depot. In contrast, the money-conscious borough of Kensington remained in its old vestry buildings, huddled round St Mary Abbots churchyard. These included the vestry office, primary school, meeting hall, almshouses and watch house. A similar reminder of London's former 'one-stop' vestry government survives in Walthamstow. The Edwardian years were a high water of London local government independence that was to prove all too brief.

At the county level, the LCC's Progressive majority presided over the first seventeen years of city-wide government, from 1889 to 1907. In 1904 it took over the London School Board, meaning that, coupled with technical colleges and buoyed by revenue from local rates and alcohol duties, the council controlled every tier of education in the capital. It owned 940 schools and employed 17,000 teachers, introducing free school meals and virtually ending serious child malnutrition in the capital.

The LCC's other field of enterprise, slum clearance, was more modestly realized. All councils were empowered to clear and rebuild housing on site, and this led to the first two pioneer LCC estates, one at Boundary Street in Bethnal Green and another at Millbank behind the Tate Gallery. They stand today, remarkably handsome in a gabled Queen Anne style. Set in tree-lined streets, they could be smart private apartments, as some now are. Soon there were twelve such estates.

These early toes dipped into the water of municipal development needed both resources and political will. This came at a price. Councils sent uncapped property rates soaring, with equalization meaning they fell hardest on the richer boroughs. The result was a fierce ratepayer backlash. At the 1907 elections, twenty-two of twenty-eight London boroughs went Moderate (Conservative), despite a Liberal landslide at the general election that year. Aversion to high local taxes drove the Progressives from power so emphatically that the Moderates, renamed Municipal Reformers (and later Tories), ruled the LCC for the next twenty-three years.

Yerkes and the wild west

Meanwhile, the London Underground was advancing with the same fervour that the overground had done in the 1840s. Unlike the New York subway or the Paris Métro, there was no move by government to plan or co-ordinate tunnelling under the capital, despite its critical role in the city's infrastructure. What the free market ordained, a British government dared not second-guess. It was therefore ideal territory for the last of the 'wildcats' who created Britain's railways. In 1900 a sixty-three-year-old American, Charles

Tyson Yerkes, ran out of steam as entrepreneur, playboy and finally prisoner for fraud in Philadelphia and Chicago. Stifled by the eagerness of American cities to organize their own subway systems, he learned that London had no truck with such meddling in private enterprise.

Yerkes came to London and immediately bought control of a proposed north–south line from Hampstead to Charing Cross. He then acquired the old west–east District Line, desperate to convert to electricity, and created a Metropolitan District Railway Traction Company to pioneer what were to become the Piccadilly and Bakerloo lines. By the time this empire, as yet unbuilt, had been amassed, the prospective London Tube network was half-owned by Yerkes and fellow American speculators.

The result was a bubble not unlike the railway mania of the 1840s. In 1901, thirty-two tunnelling proposals came before parliament for approval, almost all of which failed. The LCC Progressives began to demand control, and a London traffic board was even suggested by a royal commission in 1905. This lapsed on the Progressives' defeat in the 1907 elections. Yerkes pressed ahead with his three new lines, blocking all rivals by means of parliamentary lobbying.

Progress was not easy. Hampstead had saved its heath from buildings, and it now wanted no trains full of Londoners teeming over, or rather under, its delicate contours. When Yerkes promised his tunnel would be the deepest on the network, far below the Heath, residents complained that he would drain it of water and create a desert. Earthquakes would also ruin Hampstead's trees. Yerkes simply went ahead, setting his northern depot at a crossroads by a field called Golders Green. A new power station to generate the line's electricity was built on the Thames at Lots Road in Chelsea. The enraged local artist James McNeill Whistler demanded Yerkes be 'drawn and quartered'. The station is now a listed building.

Before Lots Road began generating, indeed before any of the new underground trains took to the rails, Yerkes died on a trip home to America in 1905. His lines were built none the less. The rail historian Christian Wolmar has calculated that, in just four years from 1903 to 1907, sixty miles of tunnels were completed, a phenomenal achievement. None was a financial success. The Bakerloo Line was soon being described as 'a beautiful failure'. A year after their opening, shares in Yerkes lines were worth just a third of their flotation value. Unlike the earlier Metropolitan and Central lines, they were victims of the imminent arrival of the motorized omnibus.

Though the network was later extended piecemeal into the suburbs – notably the long Metropolitan lines to Uxbridge, Watford and Amersham – it remained in essence as left by Yerkes in his storming five-year campaign across subterranean London. 'With no exaggeration,' concluded Wolmar, without Yerkes, 'many of today's Tube lines would never have been built.' There was no further tunnelling until the Victoria Line in the 1960s, followed by the Jubilee Line and, more recently, Crossrail.

Meanwhile, in the streets above . . .

While Yerkes's navvies were burrowing under the capital, London above was more dilatory. Electric trams were ubiquitous in European and American cities in the 1880s, but the first ones did not arrive in London until 1891. The idea of putting rails down the centre of London's mostly narrow streets had never appealed to business. Not until 1903 was the tram network extensive, and even then it was resisted by conservative boroughs for fear of bringing undesirables into their domains. Hampstead declared it wanted no trams running up Haverstock Hill.

As for horse-drawn omnibuses, they were succumbing to technology. They had been a feature of London's streets since the days of George Shillibeer, evolving their unique double-decker form, first with a 'knifeboard' dividing two benches on top and then with today's 'garden-seat' layout. The first petrol-engined bus was introduced by the London General Omnibus Company in 1907, and within four years almost all horse-drawn buses had vanished. The routes, which received numbers in 1906, stuck to the places of residence of the old drivers, and even the hay depots of their horses. This meant most routes going from suburb to suburb across the congested centre, playing havoc with any idea of schedules. This, I was told, explained the tortuous wanderings of the No. 88. London's chaotic bus routes continue to defy all attempts at rationalization.

Motor taxis soon followed, until by 1914 petrol engines had wiped out all London's horses, except for some commercial vehicles. The impact on street cleanliness was dramatic. As horses disappeared, so mews were converted for use as garages and for housing servants. These picturesque corners of London's topography were much treasured when conservation areas arrived in the 1960s. But there was another price to pay for the 'motors'. In 1906, there were 222 fatalities in London associated with motor vehicles. By 1913 the number had risen to 625, a figure that did not diminish until the widespread introduction of traffic lights in the 1920s (the first were in Parliament Square). By 2016 deaths were down to 116, largely of cyclists.

A newly divided metropolis

New patterns of transport led to further suburban sprawl, and to new metropolitan divisions. The oldest, between the City and the West End, had long been defined and resolved. Another was between London's old industrial areas and new ones. Blue-collar jobs were collapsing, notably in engineering, and those that remained were in more specialized industries, such as printing, tobacco, jewellery, brewing, china, furniture and foodstuffs. The tanneries of Bermondsey began to close. Ready-made clothes, often manufactured by 'sweated' immigrant labour, replaced the old craft tailors of Soho. The factories strewn along the Thames from Barking to Brentford were ill-sited for a modern rail and road network. Better locations were on industrial estates such as Park Royal outside Acton, to become the largest such estate in Europe.

As shipbuilding had disappeared in the 1860s, so the docks now met commercial headwinds. London remained Britain's pre-eminent port, but it was no longer growing. Wharves struggled to retain their specialism and dredging was needed to admit ever larger ships. In 1902 a royal commission advised nationalization, and the Port of London Authority was duly created in 1909. It joined London's trams as an early experiment in public ownership, and gave the docklands another half-century of life.

London's lifeblood was now services. Sixty per cent of jobs were held by the practitioners of finance, the law, public administration, leisure and their ancillary clerks, typists and messengers. Since the sector also included retail and domestic service, London registered a third of its workforce as female. Women were not well-paid, often labouring in crowded workshops, in attics or below ground. But the availability of work for wives and single women brought some relief to the abject poverty of London's working class.

Immigration continued to supply an increasing proportion of this workforce. The old enclaves were dispersing. The French drifted from Soho, which was also a haven for Greeks, Italians, Hungarians and others migrating from continental conflicts. The one-time home of Canaletto, Casanova and Karl Marx gave way to purveyors of sex and food. The Germans drifted from Fitzrovia and

'Charlottenstrasse' (Charlotte Street). The Italians moved from Saffron Hill and Clerkenwell. On the other hand, those arriving in the East End from eastern Europe were beyond reliable counting. By 1900 there were believed to be 40,000 Russians and Poles in Stepney alone.

Most noticeable were Jews fleeing pogroms in Russia's European empire, bringing an estimated 100,000 Jews to Whitechapel. This in turn led to a steady exodus of the more prosperous among them to Highbury, Woodford, Stamford Hill, Hendon and Finchley, a progress dubbed the 'north-west passage' of Jewish upward mobility. Such communities left behind their places of worship and restaurants, to which families would often return at weekends. There is still an Italian church in Clerkenwell, a German church in Fitzrovia and two French churches in Soho. Closed, however, are the exotic resorts of my youth, Schmidt's restaurant in Charlotte Street and Bloom's in Whitechapel.

Further east, Chinese sailors came ashore from the docks in Limehouse and simply disappeared. Secretive, self-contained and off-centre, London's Chinatown survived until driven out by Tower Hamlets council in the late 1960s. In an extraordinary migration, those evicted moved downtown to settle in Soho's Gerrard Street, at the time recently emptied by a ban on street prostitution. I once tried to tell the story of this ethnic 'great trek', but could get no member of the tight-knit Chinese community to talk about it. In Poplar, a local councillor boasted that he had restored 'our schools for our people'. The Chinese had been there since the 1850s.

The saga of Limehouse brought home another feature of London related by the novelist Walter Besant. Writing in 1901, he called the East End London's 'great secret'. Its population of 2 million made it a bigger city than any provincial metropolis. Yet it had 'no gentry, no carriages, no soldiers, no picture-galleries, no theatres, no opera, they have nothing . . . Nobody goes east, no one wants to see the place; no one is curious.' Besant was equally dismissive of London south of the river, another giant city and by the turn of the twentieth century almost entirely working class. Its only civic edifice, a Frenchman once remarked to him with a shrug, 'was a public house called the Elephant and Castle'.

Though the boroughs of east and south London depended on the inner city for much of their employment, they were otherwise self-contained, including from each other. Stories were often told of residents who had never strayed west of Whitechapel or north of the river, as many west Londoners never strayed east of the Tower. A Church of England housing report remarked that the East End was 'as unexplored as Timbuktu'. Charles Booth wrote, 'it is not in country but in town that [the phrase] terra incognita needs to be written'. Compared with the seething cities of England's north, London seemed geographically cantonized. When George Orwell set out from Notting Hill to describe the London poor, he lodged in Limehouse under a pseudonym, writing of it as might a traveller in a foreign land.

The monster ripple

Deep as were these divisions within inner London, another was fast emerging. This was between inner London as a whole and its ever widening 'doughnut'. Besant might note the isolation of the East End, but it was nothing to that of the new suburbs. While their inhabitants would ride trains into the centre, to work and occasionally enjoy themselves, to their inner-London contemporaries they came from an unknown country. Most Londoners had some inkling of Stepney, Rotherhithe and Brixton. Few knew anything of Catford, Tooting or Edmonton.

By the 1900s this London was stretching beyond the boundary of the LCC into Surrey, Kent, Essex and Middlesex. For the most part, new settlements did not grow outward from existing villages, but simply overwhelmed farms and fields in their way. As in previous expansions, the smartest development was to the west, upwind of the metropolis, and the railway companies wanted to keep it that way. A ninety-degree arc north-west of the metropolis was as if reserved for the middle classes, or so it was hoped. The Great Western fought against running workmen's trains, for fear of bringing low-income residents into their market.

There were some attempts at social engineering. The philanthropist Henrietta Barnett in 1909 founded Hampstead Garden Suburb on the fringes of Golders Green, designed by Raymond Unwin and Edwin Lutyens on garden city principles and intended for 'a mixed community'. The estate was luxurious in its use of space, more garden than suburb. It was given two churches and an institute, though it lacked shops or a station. Socially mixed it was not.

Most new houses were rented from developers, but gradually home ownership became popular. As the market began to weaken after 1905, developers encouraged buying rather than renting. An *Evening News* advertisement of 1909 advocated owner-occupation because thus, 'the future respectability and stability of the district is assured. When a district has a majority of individual owners in it, a far greater interest is taken in local government, and needless or reckless expenditure is avoided.' These suburbs, as they cohered and further expanded over the first third of the twentieth century, became a rock-solid belt of middle-class settlement embracing the metropolis.

Similar developments took place east and south of London, but not without controversy. John Kellett reported the reaction of the Great Eastern to the Great Western's exclusion of workmen's trains on its suburban lines. The GE's general manager, William Birt, protested that his own provision of the statutory trains had 'utterly destroyed our neighbourhoods for ordinary passenger traffic'. Why was the Great Western not forced to do likewise? None the less, he proceeded with the same strategy. The GE excluded workmen's trains from its middle-class enclaves around Epping Forest, notably along its treasured Woodford Loop at Chigwell, Chingford, Hainault and Wanstead.

These eastern suburbs are among London's minor delights. Woodford Green is sumptuously neo-Tudor. Wanstead conceals a number of Georgian townhouses. Most astonishing is Gidea Park near Romford. Laid out in 1904 in explicit imitation of Hampstead Garden Suburb, it was to be an exhibition of contemporary housing, allegedly involving a hundred architects. It was of just two grades of house, priced at £375 and £500. They comprise a remarkable exhibition of English domestic revivalism, overlaid by the decorative flair of the Arts and Crafts movement, by Ashbee, Clough Williams Ellis, Baillie Scott, Curtis Green, Tecton and others. Every conceivable talent was summoned to resist the advancing hordes of Walthamstow, Leytonstone and Manor Park.

Similar defensive manoeuvres were seen south of the river. Georgian Greenwich and Blackheath tried to keep New Cross and Lewisham at bay. Dulwich and Camberwell held out against Peckham, Southwark and Walworth. So did elegant Richmond and Wimbledon against the rising tide of Putney and Barnes. Contour was all. Rows of villas were like cavalry units drawn up on the heights to defend their inhabitants from an attacking infantry of semis and terraces. All were at the mercy of the market. London's suburbs were re-enacting the great Westminster colonization of the mid-seventeenth century, but on the grandest scale.

This new outer London showed no respect for community or infrastructure. At first the builders supplied few high streets, schools, churches, shops or clinics. No thought was given to town or village design, certainly none to infrastructure, unless a kindly developer thought a modest shopping arcade might help sales. It was about houses. Developers did not mind how the houses looked. The pattern books offered neo-Georgian, neo-Tudor, neo-Jacobean, or neo-Queen Anne. The key was neatness, with every inch of space allotted as private property and sold as such. There was no need to waste valuable land on the public realm.

The rating of houses by price imitated the grades of the 1774 Building Act. But whereas that act classified housing by individual streets, suburban pricing imposed what amounted to income uniformity across acres of territory. The Georgian suburb required social gradations within each enclave. The Edwardian suburbs had no servants and increasingly needed cars and their associated infrastructure for their survival. There was none of the intimacy of the courtyard, or the neighbourliness of the terrace. Visitors regularly commented on the absence of company. H. G. Wells wrote in his novel *Tono-Bungay*, 'In London there are no neighbours.' Everyone was an island, every family lived in a keep, and 'they did not know the names of people on either side of them'. It was an early version of England's 'new town blues'.

For all that, the suburbs were what it said on the tin, the answer to the cry of London down the ages, for an escape from the filth and fog of the city into the fresh air of the countryside and somewhere to call one's own. This was typified in a best-selling novel of suburban bliss, *The Smiths of Surbiton*, serialized in the *Daily Mail* in 1906. The nearest parallel I can find to such a freedom to escape 'downtown' was America's flight west to the sprawling homesteads of Los Angeles and San Francisco. A doggerel verse quoted by Donald Olsen sums up the satisfaction:

> He leaned upon the narrow wall
> That set the limit to his ground,
> And marveled, thinking of it all,
> That he such happiness had found.

He had no word for it but bliss;
He smoked his pipe; he thanked his stars;
And, what more wonderful than this?
He blessed the groaning, stinking [railway] cars.

By 1910 the latest burst of expansion, which had lasted since the 1870s, had come to an end. The metropolis had again gorged itself on space and relapsed in exhaustion. Transport capacity was in surplus. Houses were proving hard to sell. In 1899, 27,000 houses had been under construction. In 1913 the total was 8,000. Builders were laid off in their thousands. The census authorities concluded that London's expansion had finally peaked, and would probably go no further. Now was the time for the rest of the country to start catching up.

The metropolis that had spread across the Thames basin still displayed much poverty, but most of the poor, if not the destitute, could look forward to Lloyd George's pensions and national insurance, introduced in 1909 and 1911. At almost every level of society, Londoners were enjoying a lifestyle inconceivable a century before. Georgian London had depended on naked flames for its heat and light, on the river for its water and on horses for its transportation. As such it was little different from the Elizabethan or Stuart city.

Twentieth-century Londoners need no longer walk to work, but could travel by Tube or petrol-driven bus, cab or car. Unprecedented numbers had their own front door and a garden, and were served by sewers, mains water and central heating. They had electric light, gas cooking and hot water. Their clothes were machine-stitched, their larders filled with imported food. Offices were served by typewriters and electronic cables. London had more telephone subscribers than the whole of France.

Cultural life was responding to this novelty. America had ceased to be a post-colonial backwater and now exported musicals and movies to an eager London. Ragtime, the one-step and the bunny hug were a craze. Londoners could listen to recorded music on a gramophone and visit a local public library, swimming bath, technical college and cinema. Newspapers brought world news daily to front doors. Over the course of just a quarter-century, a technological revolution without precedent had occurred – as great if not greater than anything before the internet.

Cities tend to be the victims of politics as much as its masters. Londoners, and indeed all Britons of this period, are sometimes written off as smug and naive, enjoying an Indian summer of Edwardian bliss. But they had no reason to expect, and certainly no means of resisting, the double calamity that was to visit them over the next three decades of the twentieth century. The historian Barbara Tuchman wrote that of all the arts there were advanced by the Europeans down the ages, the one that advanced not at all was that of politics. For all its sophistication, Europe could not kick the habit of war. For once, a Britain that had spent a century on good terms with the continent, could not hold itself aloof when the continent was not on good terms with itself. Disaster beckoned.

18

War and Aftermath
1914–1930

Capital in the front line

Cities dislike crises. They breed uncertainty and are usually bad for business. In August 1914, as ultimatums were being issued and armies marshalled across Europe, the City was in a state of ill-concealed panic. An emissary was sent from the Bank of England to see Lloyd George at the Treasury, to tell him that 'the financial and trading interests in the City of London are totally opposed to our intervening in the war'. *The Economist* agreed, referring to the 'quarrel' on the continent as of no more matter to Britain than one between the Argentine Republic and Brazil or Japan and China. Never was British isolationism more on display, although, given the Balkan origins of the conflict, detachment did not seem unreasonable at the time.

Elsewhere in the capital, this particular whiff of war evoked a different response. An extraordinary jingoism in public opinion and the press was to be sustained almost throughout the coming hostilities. Despite the reservations of politicians, it was clear that Britain would soon have to honour, if not its 'entente' with France and thus with Russia, at least its guarantee of Belgian integrity, now infringed by German invasion. Even so, the City was adamant. Asquith remarked that the bankers were 'the greatest ninnies I ever had to tackle . . . [in] a state of funk, like old women chattering over tea-cups in a Cathedral town'.

As preparations gathered pace, the City's outlook changed.

Military mobilization was intense, government spending rose, City bonds had to be raised and profits accrued. War fever was palpable. A recruitment bus toured the East End boasting 'To Berlin and Back, Free'. Any shop or firm with a remotely Teutonic name – even if Belgian or Russian and thus allied – was vulnerable to attack. My grandfather joined an Inns of Court company and drilled each lunchtime in Gray's Inn Square.

The closure of European markets and the Baltic Exchange, now handling a majority of global shipping, and a shortage of imported raw materials, saw employment initially plummet by 13 per cent. This fall was reversed as mobilization gathered pace. London manufactured Enfield rifles and Maxim guns, to which were added ammunition, vehicles, supplies and clothing. Unemployment promptly fell to 1.8 per cent in 1915, with a severe labour shortage that lasted for the duration of the war. Children were released early from school into part-time jobs. Workhouses emptied, vagrants were rounded up and asylums asked to surrender their able-bodied inmates. Trade union membership in relevant industries rose by 80 per cent in four years.

Unprecedented numbers of women were drawn into factories, hospitals and the workforce in general. Most went into clerical work, notably the civil service, but female employment at Woolwich Arsenal rose from 125 to 28,000. The visibility of working women on buses, in shops, in the services and even in the police force was much noted. A newspaper remarked on women 'who walk through the metropolis at midnight, unprotected, unmolested, safe in the new-found confidence that war work has given to their sex . . . Before Armageddon this would have been impossible.'

London clearly benefited from the war. Dockers' wages doubled, and incomes probably increased faster than at any time in history. Homelessness fell as jobs proliferated, and demand rose to fill the oversupply of the 1900s housing boom. There were reports of a shortage of furniture, even of the pianos without which no 'decent' working-class home was considered complete. The historian Jerry White commented on the difference in school photographs. Pre-war pictures of a slum school in Webb Street, Bermondsey, were of 'ragged, crop-haired scowling forebears, bare toes sticking through the gaping uppers . . . and some with no boots at all'. After the war the same school photograph was of sleek youngsters in blazers, shiny shoes and open-neck shirts. Infant mortality in London continued to fall, from 15 per cent in 1901 to just 6 per cent in 1922. An LCC official attributed this both to the fall in malnutrition resulting from the provision of free school meals, and to rising incomes among the poor.

War also induced a curious and irrational obsession in Whitehall with state-imposed puritanism. Pubs had to close early and, in an extreme measure, 'treating' someone else to a drink, even a spouse, became a criminal offence. It was during the Great War that Britain's notorious pub licensing hours were introduced, not to be suspended until 1988. Sports fixtures were curbed, yet theatres and music halls were packed, as were restaurants. London was awash with uniforms, crowding train stations and parading in parks and squares. Dick Sheppard, vicar of St Martin-in-the-Fields, offered an 'ever open door' in his crypt for homeless soldiers, who were often dumped on leave at Charing Cross station with nowhere to go.

By the war's end 124,000 Londoners had died in battle, including roughly 10 per cent of men aged between twenty and thirty. For the city's population, the most traumatic experience was the advent of aerial bombing. This began in May 1915 with a Zeppelin raid over east London, dropping 120 mostly incendiary bombs on Dalston, Hoxton and Stratford. Seven people died. Zeppelins were followed by the biplane Gotha bombers and then larger Giants, which appeared in the autumn of 1917. The chief effect was on morale. The raids caused panic, not least because the city seemed defenceless against them. Beatrice Webb recorded that the raids 'have wrecked the nerves of Londoners, with the result of a good deal of discreditable panic even among the well-to-do and educated'. She recalled taking refuge in a book and a cigarette. Thousands fled their homes, to quarters in Hampstead or Highgate or as far as Brighton. Not until May 1918 was London's anti-aircraft defence a match for the attacks, and the raids ceased. By then some 670 Londoners had been killed. For the first time since the Vikings, the metropolis had found itself in the front line of war.

At the eleventh hour of the eleventh day of the eleventh month of 1918, the armistice was marked by the firing of maroons. Crowds poured onto the streets, in a rerun of the relief of Mafeking. An estimated hundred thousand people gathered outside the Mansion House, still an emotional focus for most Londoners, while others filled the West End. The rejoicing gave rise to rumours of extreme behaviour. The writer Malcolm Muggeridge claimed to have seen couples copulating in the park at night – an anecdote much repeated and much doubted. A more dignified symbol was the silent crowds in St Paul's Cathedral. The mood of Londoners was largely one of relief, of a desire, in H. G. Wells's phrase, to end 'the war that will end war'.

London lurches leftwards

The Great War, as it was called, was the first to be termed total. As such it raised public expectation of what a modern state could do when fully mobilized. Still in charge of that state was David Lloyd George, the prime minister whose term at the Treasury before the war had seen dramatic advances in public welfare. He now presented himself as the head of a national coalition, promising a government to make a 'country fit for heroes to live in'. He did not specify what that meant. The implication was that a state that could defeat Germany could surely and finally defeat poverty.

Lloyd George held an immediate 'khaki' election in December 1918, the first national election in which all men over twenty-one and all women over thirty had the vote. Coalition candidates, mostly Conservative but also some coalition Liberals, won overwhelmingly. But hopes of a new dawn were soured by the government's debt, which had risen from £80 million in 1914 to £590 million in 1920. This meant a swingeing axe (named after its wielder, Sir Eric Geddes) on public spending. Heroes returned not to a booming economy but to fiscal restraint. The years 1920–22 were of recession, pressuring statesmen into an unwise vindictiveness towards Germany's ruined political economy.

The spring of 1919 saw the Conservatives retain control of the LCC, but with a new London Labour Party, grown from two seats to fifteen, taking thousands of votes from the Liberals. Labour's slogan, borrowed from a then turbulent Ireland, was 'Home rule for London'. It called for the municipalization of everything from coal, bread, milk and meat to passenger transport. More significant, Labour took control of twelve of the twenty-eight boroughs. The party's Herbert Morrison became mayor of Hackney, and Clement Attlee MP for Stepney. Its most celebrated personality was the sixty-year-old mayor of Poplar, George Lansbury, devout Christian and editor of the left-wing *Daily Herald*. A pacifist and later champion of Stalin's Soviet Union, Lansbury declared his project to 'establish the Kingdom of Heaven on earth', or at least in Poplar.

Lansbury was first into battle, and on strong ground. In 1920 he increased Poplar's expenditure dramatically, with equal pay for women and a housing programme. As a result he overspent even his rate-equalized budget and nearly doubled his rate demand. He also refused to add the precept levied on borough rates for spending by the LCC, the Asylums Board and the Metropolitan Police.

Since these payments were compulsory, in July 1921 Poplar's councillors marched with their supporters to the law courts, where twenty-five men and five women councillors went to gaol. Council meetings were held in Brixton prison.

After much frantic conciliation, the councillors were freed and a new and more drastic rate equalization was conceded. London's poorest fifteen boroughs saw their rates cut, and those of the richest western boroughs increased. 'Poplarism' had won a victory. But the dispute deeply divided Labour London. Poplar's defiance had been supported only by Bethnal Green and Stepney. Struggles between the party's often pro-Communist left, and Herbert Morrison's moderates, eager for respectability and middle-class votes, continued after the 1920s recession. It saw frequent divisive marches and strikes.

Conflict within Labour and between it and the LCC's Conservative (Municipal Reform) majority continued through Ramsay MacDonald's brief Labour minority government of 1924. The General Strike called by the TUC in 1926 did not originate in London, but the city's dockers and transport workers obeyed the call to stop work in support of the miners. The mobilization of food trucks, buses and army units by the home secretary, Winston Churchill, and his food depot in Hyde Park, attracted publicity and led to intermittent street battles with the police. The conflict was won by the government, aided in London by some 100,000 strike-breakers. As before, the call to direct action had seen a tepid response from the capital.

The death of aristocratic London

The property market in inner London was hit by a novel trend, that of the West End losing much of its glamour. The owners of the great estates and their tenants had, since the 1880s, experienced agricultural depression, rising income tax and severe death duties. The last rose in 1914 to 20 per cent on estates over £1 million, and in 1919 to 40 per cent on those over £2 million. Most families had lost male members in the war, which had also sent wages rising and emptied houses of domestic staff. Advertisements from estate agents such as Knight, Frank and Rutley read like a roll-call from *Debrett's*. There were land sales by the dukes of Westminster, Sutherland and Northumberland, and the lords Aberdeen, Northampton, Petre and Tollemache. It was estimated that a quarter of the land area of England changed hands in four years – mostly to owner-farmers – probably the biggest transfer since the Dissolution of the Monasteries.

In London, as ninety-nine-year leases fell due, sales became ever more frequent. The Duke of Bedford had already sold Covent Garden before the war. He put the money into tsarist bonds and lost the lot. This first of the old London estates was now a run-down area of warehouses round the old market piazza. Next, Lord Berkeley sold most of his Mayfair estate. In 1925 the Howard de Waldens sold Great Portland Street to Sir John Ellerman, who became a rare new freeholder in the hitherto closed shop of great estates.

Aristocratic townhouses used only for the season seemed an unnecessary extravagance, but there were few buyers. The result was distressed sales and demolitions the length of Park Lane and Piccadilly. Fine Georgian and Victorian mansions as yet unprotected by conservation controls vanished for redevelopment. In 1919 the Marquess of Salisbury sold his house in Arlington Street behind the Ritz for redevelopment as a massive block of flats. Park Lane lost Dorchester House, a copy of the Villa Farnesina in Rome, as well as Grosvenor House, Camelford House, Albury House and Chesterfield House. The Duke of Devonshire sold his mansion by William Kent in Piccadilly, with its garden running north to Robert Adam's Lansdowne House on Berkeley Square. Only the facade of the latter survives. Demolished in 1938 was the Duke of Norfolk's gilded mansion on the south-east corner of St James's Square, its music room salvaged for the V&A museum.

Paris at the time was fortunate that its equivalent neighbourhood, Le Marais, was not in the path of urban renewal. Its degeneration into slumdom preserved it long enough to see its later rebirth. Outside the St James's enclave, scarcely any of London's eighteenth-century mansions survived. Hermione Hobhouse's *Lost London* makes miserable reading. Of the great Piccadilly houses, only Apsley and the old In and Out club remain in anything like their original form. Had the rest held on for a couple more generations, their glories would have been better guarded.

Apart from the great houses, there were other losses. The Cecil Hotel on the Embankment was demolished for the Orwellian mass of Shellmex House (80 Strand, where this book's publisher is located). In 1937 Robert Adam's Adelphi development, neighbour of Somerset House, saw its central block torn down and replaced by a curious Art Deco pastiche. The hard-to-let Aldwych finally passed to an American speculator, Irving T. Bush, his name briefly globalized when the BBC used Bush House for its World Service. The most senseless demolition was of Soane's neo-classical Bank of England. Its loss was widely seen as the greatest vandalism in the City of London of the period – an award for which there was much competition. The bank said it needed more accommodation, which it later obtained by simply expanding elsewhere.

Nothing more symbolized the passing of old London than the loss of Nash's Regent Street. Its premises still operated to Nash's strict leasehold conditions, facades having to be restuccoed every four years and washed annually. In the 1920s the owners of the Piccadilly Hotel, running from Piccadilly to Regent Street, said they needed a bigger rear to their building. The Crown Estate, with no Nash to protest, let Norman Shaw build a neo-baroque frontage, towering absurdly over its neighbours. To Norman Shaw, said the Danish urbanist Rasmussen, 'stucco front . . . could be described as an abusive term'. For a while the hotel sat on the quadrant like an elephant lost in a field of lilies, a typical London planning fiasco. Its Portland stone immediately turned black.

The Crown Estate was clearly eager to rid itself of Nash's masterpiece, and the destruction was eventually complete. Down came the architect's mansion in Waterloo Place, as did entire facades north to Piccadilly Circus and up Regent Street to Langham Place, where the BBC's Broadcasting House was soon to rise. Replacements all took their cue from Shaw's heavy baroque, with facades of stone not stucco. War veterans compared the demolition site to the battlefields of Flanders. The new Regent Street embodied the twentieth-century's baroque revival – heavy, tedious but not without character. Only at Liberty's was there flair. The store's Arts and Crafts owners erected a baroque front to Regent Street, but behind built a neo-Elizabethan elevation, crafted with wood from two old warships, held together with pegs not nails. It connoted, according to Pevsner, 'nostalgia for an older, cosier world that overtook Britain after the First World War'.

'Homes for heroes'

In one area, Lloyd George's government was determined not to be outbid by the left. It had promised homes fit for heroes, and in 1919 a housing and town planning act was pioneered by an unsung hero of the early welfare state, Christopher Addison. A distinguished doctor and Liberal (later Labour) MP, Addison had been Lloyd George's minister of munitions during the war. He took on a department named the Ministry of Health, which embraced not just health care but related aspects of schools, prisons, housing, the poor law and local government generally. Addison made local councils – in London the LCC and the boroughs – responsible not just for slum clearance and out-of-town estates but for providing housing to all who needed it, with rent dependent only on ability to pay. Every dwelling also had to have a bathroom. To meet the potentially enormous cost, resources above the revenue from a local penny rate would be met by a Treasury clearly off its guard.

Whitehall's contact with local government reality was tenuous. At a time when the Geddes axe was savaging Whitehall, the Treasury was generous to council housing to the point of naivety. There was an instant explosion in public-sector supply. In 1913, 6 per cent of new houses in London were built by public authorities. By 1920, the figure was 60 per cent. Sub-contracting was chaotic and waste enormous. Materials were hijacked by a contractors' mafia. In 1921 houses in Hendon were costing the council over £1,000, three times house prices in the private sector. Builders installed 'bathrooms', but they doubled as kitchen, scullery and laundry. Two years later the Treasury cut the subsidies and costs plummeted. Addison was forced to resign.

At least houses were built. The old pre-war LCC estates at Millbank and Boundary Street had aped the work of philanthropists George Peabody and Octavia Hill. Post-1918 estates at Becontree outside Dagenham and St Helier near Sutton were like new towns, proposed for 120,000 and 40,000 residents, respectively. Fifteen smaller estates were built on greenfield sites, eventually housing 250,000 people. Unlike those in inner London, they were located far from where their prospective tenants lived, let alone where they might find work. They were pure sprawl, serviced by few trains, schools, shops or hospitals. One new arrival was reported banging on neighbours' doors pleading, 'What's happened? Why is everything so quiet?'

In 1923 Addison's old job was assumed by Neville Chamberlain, son of Joseph and MP for Edgbaston in Birmingham. A dry, hard-working intellectual with an obsession for administration – a biographer described him as 'weaned on a pickle' – he had served in 1919–21 on the government's curiously named 'unhealthy areas committee'. The experience had brought him face to face with some of the worst slums in the country. As health minister, he dedicated himself to what became the wholesale reform of public welfare, retaining this position, with one break, until 1931. On taking office, Chamberlain announced that he had twenty-five bills ready for reform, of which he was to enact a remarkable twenty-one. He even refused appointment to the Exchequer, to complete his work on what he saw as an embryo welfare state.

The 1834 Poor Law was by now almost a century out of date. The days of guardians, workhouses, infirmaries, asylums and 'outdoor relief' had long been numbered. Chamberlain's father in the 1880s had mooted incorporating them in the new county councils, and a commission proposed their abolition in 1909. But it was not until 1929 that Chamberlain was at last able to pass an act bringing the Poor Law guardians finally under local government control. This was achieved after a two-and-a-half-hour speech that was openly applauded in the commons. Had it not been for his misjudgement of Hitler in 1938, Chamberlain would be hailed as a great social reformer.

The Chamberlain act brought under the LCC the seventy-five infirmaries, fever hospitals and mental asylums of the Metropolitan Asylums Board. These ran alongside – and in rivalry with – the ancient and independent charitable hospitals. Thus the LCC's public health committee was by 1939 controlling 60 per cent of all the public sector hospitals in England. London could boast that it was 'the greatest Local Health Authority in the Empire'. In truth, the welfare state did not date from the 1945 Labour government. Its biggest boost was from a Tory health minister empowering a Tory LCC.

At the same time, the mostly Labour municipal boroughs were to prove the most assiduous innovators. Throughout the interwar period, they were torn between the socialism of Lansbury and the moderate reformism of Morrison. Lansbury's charisma was vivid, with an extraordinary talent for reducing audiences to tears. He retained his popularity throughout the twenties, even securing a seat in parliament. In 1929, when Ramsay MacDonald returned briefly to power, he made him minister for works. Lansbury blessed London with a children's boating lake in Regent's Park and a Lido in Hyde Park's Serpentine, outraging *The Times* by insisting it be mixed. To the historian A. J. P. Taylor, these were the only creditable memorials to MacDonald's benighted 1929 administration.

These boroughs, and indeed London's interwar local government of both parties, remained essentially loyal to Morrison and the Webb tradition of 'gas-and-water socialism'. There was none of the incipient rebelliousness then surging through the cities of France and Germany. The methodical Morrison was a 'new' commuting Londoner, hailing from suburban Letchworth rather than Westminster, Finsbury or Bethnal Green. Under his flag Woolwich built over a thousand council houses in the 1920s. Bermondsey won plaudits for its public health, with free tuberculosis treatment, dentistry and health visitors. It also built swimming pools and set up a 'beautification committee', which converted churchyards into pocket parks. There was even a new strain of 'Bermondsey dahlia'. Rate equalization was working as intended.

19

The Climax of the Sprawl
1930–1939

Voracious metropolis

Neville Chamberlain could reform the welfare state, but he could not handle a greater challenge, the taming of London's again rampant housing market. Local councils could build houses, but only as developers could, by simply dumping them in fields and collecting rents. They supplied no infrastructure or any pretence of planned communities. In 1927, Chamberlain had established a body grandly called the Greater London Regional Planning Committee. All it did was record three years later that green land within an eleven-mile radius of Charing Cross was disappearing at 1,000 acres a year.

In 1932, with Chamberlain now at the Exchequer but eagle-eyed over his old department, the government introduced Britain's first comprehensive Town and Country Planning Act. With London in mind, it gave councils powers to make land-use schemes, including on already built-up sites, with developers 'advised' to get council approval before demolishing or rebuilding. It was the first effort since the seventeenth century to manage metropolitan growth, other than through by-laws and building regulations. Controls were laid down on street width and structure height – the latter at a hundred feet for business property and eighty feet for residential. The act fought shy of requiring infrastructure or open space. Councils could ban the demolition of historic buildings, but only on payment of compensation, which made this a dead letter.

The act's timidity rendered it largely ineffective. The depression of 1929–31 hit London less severely than the rest of the country, but the subsequent political climate was not conducive to government restraint on enterprise. An appeal to Westminster to preserve Norfolk House went unanswered on grounds of cost. The aesthetic taste of the day did not extend to controlling the piecemeal demolition of Adam's Portland Place, or stopping Charles Holden's London University Senate House from towering over the Bedford estate. There was the occasional letter of protest to the press, as when the Arts and Crafts architect C. R. Ashbee wailed that 'any beautiful object of the past . . . that could be utilized for library, club, museum, school or parish purposes, is [instead] torn down and sold to the wreckers for its value in old materials'. It was to no avail. The thirties were to see the worst desecration of old London until the Blitz – and possibly worse even than that.

The most symbolic act of vandalism came when Morrison captured the LCC from the Tories in 1934, a victory that kept Labour in control until the LCC's abolition in 1965. Eager to show himself a serious modernizer, Morrison decided to demolish the centrepiece of every view of St Paul's from the Thames, Rennie's sublime Waterloo Bridge. He summoned the press to watch him wield his hammer to remove the first stone, declaring 'in the heart of the capital, we needed a traffic artery not an ancient monument'. There was at least an outburst of rage. The press attacked Morrison's 'aesthetic blindness bordering on philistinism' and 'vulgar utilitarianism'. The City Corporation was deterred for a further three decades from its intended destruction of Rennie's other crossing, London Bridge. Both were to be replaced with stark stone gashes, like daubing a Canaletto with whitewash. Morrison's intention, to get more traffic into the West End, was later replaced by efforts to reduce it. The loss of Waterloo Bridge began London's steady divergence from Paris and other European capitals, which continued to regard their historic centres as deserving respect and aesthetic coherence. Morrison and his successors viewed the Thames riverside as simply a series of building plots, until the advent of historic-buildings control after the Second World War.

Semi-detached city

Apart from Waterloo Bridge, movement about the capital was an LCC blind spot. No other city did so little to aid its traffic. The only new road building came from central government, and was largely confined to the Eastern and Western Avenues easing traffic through congested suburbs. North and south circular roads were projected, and a Kingston bypass built. These highways proved magnets to the new consumer businesses fleeing the East End and the docks. They included Wallis Gilbert's Art Deco Hoover and Firestone factories, and others for Gillette razors, Pyrene fire extinguishers, Curry's electrical goods, Macleans toothpaste and Smith's crisps. In 1931, at the height of the depression, fifteen factories at Park Royal were declaring a labour shortage. The same year, the American Ford motor company arrived at Dagenham, bringing employment to the LCC's isolated Becontree estate. By the end of the depression in 1933, London was supplying half of all the new jobs in Britain.

London car ownership rose six-fold from 187,000 in 1920 to just over 1 million in 1930, while the average price of a vehicle fell from £684 to £210. A 1937 report duly recommended a network of radial and orbital motorways, new tunnels and segregated fast and slow traffic lanes, but nothing was done. Matters were not helped by the extension and electrification of the railways, accelerating low-density development in the southern suburbs. In 1929 the second MacDonald government established a London Passenger Transport Board (LPTB), which by 1933 had taken over all underground and some surface railways in the capital. It became the largest public transport undertaking in the world. Its manager, Frank Pick, and designer, Charles Holden, set new standards in comfortable and stylish urban transit. Holden's Tube stations, much influenced by Sweden, were among the most exciting creations of interwar architecture, as in the field of design was Harry Beck's Tube map, based on an electrical circuit diagram. It is essentially the same map today.

The LPTB was probably the nearest London had to a planning authority in the first half of the twentieth century. The historian Lionel Esher called it 'the prime agent of London regional development', purely by virtue of where it decided to extend its railways. It presided over an exodus from the inner city to the suburbs that dwarfed all previous such expansions. The population of London between the wars increased by just 10 per cent, but its built-up area doubled. By 1939 the metropolis was thirty-four miles across, an astonishing six times its extent in 1880.

Much of this came from building over hundreds of farms in Middlesex, under the slogan of the Metropolitan Railway's 'Metroland'. Launched in 1919, this dream of suburban bliss promised to 'convert pleasant undulating fields into happy homes'. The company even commissioned a popular song, 'My Little Metroland Home'. The densities were low, land use inefficient and the call on infrastructure absurdly high. No one cared.

The neighbourhoods created by the sprawl were anonymous, their differentiation confined to price. The only areas to acquire some character were those of the Jewish north-west passage. These communities spread beyond Golders Green, where the first synagogue was opened in 1922, to Hendon, Mill Hill and Edgware. Migration into these districts, not least from Nazi Germany, was so intense by the end of the 1930s that north-west London was estimated to host a quarter of Britain's entire foreign-born population. Golders Green claimed the fifth busiest Underground station in the 1920s and one of the largest auditoriums, the mammoth 3,500-seat Hippodrome.

Southern Electric trains were at last bringing London south of the Thames fully into the commuter belt. Kent saw predominantly lower-middle-class housing, south from Woolwich into Eltham, Catford and Bexley. What was noticeable, as in north London, was that house prices rose and gardens grew in size with each extra fifty feet above sea level, as in Sydenham, Bromley and Chislehurst. To the south-west, development was closer in character to that of Metroland, as at Merton, Sutton, Epsom and round the slopes of Richmond. Building productivity became frenetic, with semi-detached houses taking less than a month to erect from start to finish. Entire farms would disappear in a matter of weeks.

A suburban culture

By now the scale of destruction of London's familiar appearance was arousing disquiet. Before the war, an attempt to build a block of flats in Kensington's Edwardes Square was fought off, but in the 1920s Endsleigh Gardens in Bloomsbury was consumed by the Friends Meeting House and the entirety of Mornington Crescent in Camden Town became a Carreras cigarette factory. The latter was the last straw for London's most characteristic townscape feature, the garden square. There seemed to be nothing to stop Grosvenor building in Belgrave or Grosvenor squares. The result was a law in 1931, specifically to preserve all London's 461 squares. The act was followed in 1934 by the LCC declaring a 'green girdle', later a belt, round its entire built-up area. It also set aside £2 million to buy land 'readily accessible from the completely urbanized areas of London' for public recreation. Only Enfield Chase and Nonsuch

Park were acquired under the plan. Grass might at last be safe, but no thought was yet given to historic buildings.

Meanwhile, London's new suburban lifestyle forced itself into the nation's consciousness. In literary circles it was treated with much patronizing cynicism. The writer Rosamond Lehmann promised to 'set fire to the latest outbreak of bungalows . . . I'd – just blow the whole thing up'. To J. B. Priestley, arriving from the north, the suburb was the new England, a place 'of giant cinemas and dance halls and cafes, bungalows with tiny garages, cocktail bars, Woolworths, motor coaches, wireless, hiking, factory girls looking like actresses, greyhound racing and dirt tracks, swimming pools, and everything given away for cigarette coupons'. To the pioneer suburban historian Alan Jackson, his subjects were seen as displaying a 'shallowness of local allegiance and lack of community spirit'. There was nothing about them to stir the interest or curiosity of outsiders. According to Jerry White, inhabitants talked 'with specious nonchalance' about 'catching the last'. Their wives said 'pleased to meet you' and set the 'preserves on a d'oyley before her whist party'.

A more dispassionate observer, the ever observant Rasmussen, was more sympathetic. He saw suburbs as the 'spreading of town centres from the city . . . so that people do not need to go into the town itself either for shopping or for pleasure'. The suburb was a new version of the city, albeit shorn of a city's services and delights. It was simply the future. The poet John Betjeman, emerging bard of suburbia, was even less critical: 'Gaily into Ruislip Gardens/ Runs the red electric train,/ With a thousand Ta's and Pardons/ Daintily alights Elaine . . .' His heroine hurries, 'Out into the outskirt's edges/ Where a few surviving hedges/ Keep alive our lost Elysium – rural Middlesex again.' Betjeman never lost his fascination with this new London. He looked out from the heights of Harrow, as if from a rocky islet at the rolling surf of suburban Wembley: 'There's a

storm cloud to the westward over Kenton/ There's a line of harbour lights at Perivale.'

A different and more potent line of attack came from a new wave
of refugee architects from Europe. Berthold Lubetkin, Walter Gro-
pius and others brought to London the spare, geometrical designs of
the German Bauhaus. Buildings such as Highpoint One in Highgate
(1933) and Maxwell Fry's Modern House in Kingston (1937) may have
been isolated eccentricities, but their austere modernism took London's Architectural Association school and the pages of the
Architecture Review by storm. A few suburban developers, such as the
New Ideal Homestead company, even tested the occasional Bauhaus
design in their pattern books. Quick-witted drivers to Heathrow on
the Great West Road can spot a few thirties 'Bauhaus' villas, with
'wrap-around' corner windows and flat roofs. They clearly did not
catch on, and some had to have hipped roofs put on top.

What the new 'modernists' did achieve was to stop in its tracks
the decorative flair of interwar Art Deco, another semi-import
from Germany. It flourished briefly in hotels such as the Savoy and
Strand Palace, in the west London factories of Wallis Gilbert and
the new suburban citadels of pleasure, the 'super-cinemas'. Many of
the cinemas were designed by the Russian émigré Theodore
Komisarjevsky. The latter's surviving Granada Tooting, with its
'Mighty Wurlitzer' organ, aimed to evoke the escapism of the new
'movies', and ease the much-publicized tedium of wives left isolated
all day on the new estates.

In terms of land consumed, the boom that ended abruptly with
the Second World War in 1939 was the most extensive in London's
history. Reaction to it had a neologism, 'metrophobia'. The Barlow
Commission, set up by Chamberlain in 1937, yet again demanded
that London's land use be properly planned, industry decentralized, slums cleared, traffic facilitated and green spaces and historic
buildings guarded. No one demurred from the ideal. Acts were

even passed, one of 1935 ambitiously called the Restriction of Ribbon Development Act. But the disconnect between government in Whitehall and reality on the ground was total. Authority could say what it liked. Nothing linked steering wheel to engine, and the engine was the market place.

Where there are people and space without regulation, the one will occupy the other. Britain's parliament was unsettled by the labour unrest of the 1920s, and by the furious revival of autocracy across Europe. It seemed to regard sprawl as a pacifying force, almost a narcotic. The truth was that Londoners craved what sprawl offered: a house, a garden and a train station. It was not their job to supply community or infrastructure. Why should government stop them when land was available? As Jackson said, the reality of the suburbs was that 'many thousands had their living standards transformed', beyond anything their parents could have dreamed. It was the same force that drove the equally careless and unplanned sprawl of 'executive estates' across the English countryside in the 2010s.

Despite the predictions of pre-war demographers, London had lost none of its allure. If its streets were not paved with gold, its suburbs were lined with grass and trees, and that was magnetism enough. London was not just the largest city on earth, but none other had so great a percentage of its people living in houses, with water and electricity, a front door, a garden and a train to convey them to work. As for the property market, the boom ran out of steam. London's growth peaked in 1939 at 8.6 million, a figure that would not be surpassed until 2019. As before the Great War, it was as if the metropolis was pausing to see what would happen next.

20

Metropolis at War
1939–1951

The Blitz

In September 1938, Chamberlain's declaration of 'peace for our time' after Munich had led to scenes of jubilation, both among the public and in parliament. Even in early 1939 there remained a lingering hope that diplomacy might curb German expansionism, or at least keep Britain out of a conflict at the time confined to eastern Europe. The invasion of Poland, its security guaranteed by Britain as had been Belgium's in 1914, dispelled that hope. But Chamberlain's declaration of war was received with none of the jingoism of 1914. Those who remember it speak of the moment only as one of numb horror.

It is known that Hitler had no desire for war with Britain. He was sceptical of his generals' invasion plan, Operation Sealion, given that the Royal Navy was still intact, while the spring 1940 Battle of Britain had denied him air supremacy. None the less, desperate contingencies were made for the defence of London, with three rings of pillboxes and machine-gun nests located in farmland in the Home Counties. To the best of my knowledge all have vanished. Reports of Hitler's plan for the occupation of London – headquartered appropriately in Bloomsbury's Senate House – were fantasies of the later Hitler industry. By the autumn of 1940 Sealion was abandoned, and the capital turned to defending itself against aerial bombardment, a different war of more dubious efficacy.

The prospect brought back memories of London's Great War, and that was indeed terrifying, given known advances in bomber technology. Bertrand Russell wrote that the capital would be immediately 'levelled to the ground on the outbreak of war'. It would become 'one vast raving bedlam, the hospitals will be stormed, traffic will cease, the homeless will shriek for help . . . the enemy will dictate its terms'. Such views were not confined to left-wing philosophers. Churchill in 1934 had warned that three to four million people would flee London into the countryside. Whitehall in 1937 predicted 600,000 dead in two weeks of bombing, and hospitals prepared 300,000 beds. As a result, London organized the evacuation of some 660,000 women and children to the provinces, including half the school population. This operation was reportedly achieved without a single serious mishap.

Half-hearted German bombing of the docks began in September 1940, but it was poorly targeted and largely random. In London a night-time blackout was imposed from the start, unpopular but regarded as effective. Metal tunnels called Anderson shelters were distributed as protection from bombs, to be erected in back gardens. They were little use in the city centre, and attempts to stop people crowding onto Tube platforms on hearing the sirens proved hopeless. Stations were swiftly overwhelmed and the authorities capitulated.

For Londoners during the winter of 1940, it was war unlike any other. They faced the nightly prospect of imminent death, much as if they had been on a Great War battlefield. On 29 December 1940, 130 bombers dropped 300 bombs a minute, enveloping the area round St Paul's in flames, though the cathedral miraculously survived. Roughly a third of the old City was hit. The bombing then ceased as Hitler turned his attention to the Russian front before returning with the 'baby blitz' of fourteen raids in 1944. These were followed by attacks from the V-1 flying bomb and the V-2 rocket from June of that year into 1945.

Experiences of the bombing varied. The writer Elizabeth Bowen remarked on how each evening Londoners would 'sense a thinning of the gap between the living and the dead . . . Strangers said Good night, Good luck, to each other at street corners, as the sky first blanched then faded with evening. Each hoped not to die that night, still more not to die unknown.' The 'Blitz spirit' has been widely debunked as a patriotic concept invented in Whitehall to boost morale. There was, rather, a grim acceptance that this was something that had to be seen through to the end. That said, thousands of evacuated children came home before the bombing had ceased, amid a feeling that government had overreacted.

Young people seemed to take it in their stride, even when the horrors were very present. In January 1941 a bomb killed 117 people sheltering in Bank Tube station. My mother, an undergraduate at the time, volunteered as an East End ambulance driver. Asked later what it was like, she would say only that it was 'like driving an ambulance', though we afterwards learned how traumatic the experience had been for a woman barely out of her teens. Away from the horrors, there was an eerie normality. Even in the bruised City, office workers adjusted to daily inconvenience. The Governor of the Bank of England, Montagu Norman, slept at work two or three nights a week, but the chief complaint was boredom through lack of business.

Citizen fortitude, rather than 'spirit', became part of the war's narrative. Little things mattered: Myra Hess's lunchtime concerts in the National Gallery; showgirls at the Windmill Theatre, which 'never closed'; a photograph of St Paul's dome amid the flames; food growing in the Tower of London moat; Noël Coward's song, 'London Pride'. The city was involved in a new sort of war – perhaps a throwback to the Thirty Years War – a conflict of whole peoples as well as armies.

This was the London vividly conveyed across the Atlantic by the American broadcaster Ed Murrow. He reported the Blitz in real time, telling of girls walking nonchalantly to work in their dresses and the rich drinking in hotel lobbies, while bombs could be heard crashing round them. One listener told Murrow that 'you laid the dead of London at our doors and we knew that those dead were our dead'. He helped destroy the idea 'that what is done beyond three thousand miles of water is not really done at all'. To Churchill, Murrow was crucial in turning isolationist America towards joining the war in 1941.

The Blitz, like all bombing campaigns against cities, was meant to break the morale of civilians and induce them to change their government and its policy. It did neither thing, in Britain or in Germany. It did not even disrupt the war effort, while the task of civil defence – air-raid protection, fire-fighting, feeding and housing the homeless – gave the public a sense of involvement they had lacked in the Great War. Subsequent surveys showed that suicides and mental distress declined and predictions of mass panic and 'bomb neurosis' were rubbish.

The Blitz, though short lived, became the defining event of London's war. Dubbed the second Great Fire of London, its civilian death toll was roughly 30,000, which contributed to the remarkable statistic that one in three Londoners who died in the Second World War were civilians rather than military personnel. In all, some 100,000 houses were flattened and ten times that number damaged. Parts of the East End saw half their properties rendered uninhabitable.

Faith in the aggressive power of the bomber fuelled the RAF's campaign to unleash similar force on Germany, which continued throughout the war. As a result, London's suffering was almost trivial compared with Germany's, where an estimated half a million civilians were killed by bombing. Its cities and even small medieval towns were attacked throughout the war, with senseless savagery. Airmen persisted in believing that their planes could win wars, possibly even without the need for ground fighting. It was to prove a destructive and costly miscalculation on both sides.

Surveying the wreckage

On VE Day, 8 May 1945, Londoners took to the streets and rejoiced. But it was more a time for licking wounds. For Britain, victory was pyrrhic. London looked more like a city in defeat – blackened, derelict, pitted with ruins. With peace, German and Japanese manufacturers raced back into production. Britain's ongoing labour inefficiencies and lack of investment were shielded behind talk of 'our finest hour'. London's chief handicap was the illusion that it had stood alone – we were constantly told it at school – and the fruits of victory were for it to enjoy. Victory had in truth largely been through the efforts of Americans and Russians. To them would go the fruits, such as they were.

As after the Great War, the expectation of the British was that a state machine that had won the war could capitalize on the peace. Labour's surprise victory over Churchill's Tories in the 1945 election, with the slogan 'Now win the peace', implied just that. Thus, while occupied Germany embarked on an astonishingly swift recovery, Britons seemed to be waiting for the government to do something. The command economy remained in place. Whitehall retained rationing of food, building materials, newsprint and clothing fabric, as if the market economy could not be trusted. There was little let-up in spartan living conditions. The winter of 1946–47 saw a bout of freezing weather and a shortage of coal. Photographs showed Londoners queuing in their hundreds to buy potatoes. Churchill was to define social-ism as 'queuetopia'.

The only brief nod in the direction of commercial reconstruc-tion was a decision in 1947 to declare the old Fairey Aviation test runway at Heathrow 'London airport', replacing the inconvenient Croydon. Its annual passenger numbers doubled in three years to 250,000, topped 2.5 million in 1955 and 5 million in 1960. Persistent pledges to the local residents that each expansion of Heathrow would be the last were flagrantly broken, as flight paths prolifer-ated over densely populated areas.

The physical destruction of London was considerable though not widespread. Thousands who had left town trickled back, but it was to ruined homes and businesses. The City had lost a third of its offices and most of its warehouses. With them went much of its remaining manufacturing and commercial activity. Finance had already seen foreign business flee, and it did not immediately return. The City's status as financial capital of the world appeared to be at an end, and American dominance was reflected in the rise of New York's Wall Street. Though the UN did hold its first meeting in Lon-don's Methodist Central Hall, its headquarters, along with those of the World Bank and the IMF, was located on American soil.

Outside the economic sphere, some signs of normality resurfaced. Dior's New Look was launched to immense publicity – and morale boost – in Paris in 1947, leaving many wondering why London design-ers were still under rationing. The Earls Court motor show resumed in 1948, though petrol was in short supply and there was a waiting list for cars. The same year saw the formation of an Arts Council, much to London's benefit, and theatres and galleries revived. The hosting by London of the 'austerity Olympics' in 1948 signalled a return to a sort of international status. I was taken by my father to the open-ing ceremony, and can recall sitting on his shoulders and seeing the lighting of the flame.

What sort of city?

In 1942, at the height of hostilities, the war cabinet had pretended to normality by publishing a report by the former director of the London School of Economics, William Beveridge, on post-war welfare reform. It was along lines he had discussed with Lloyd George during the Great War. A similar exercise in London town planning was given to Patrick Abercrombie, an academic architect who had worked on Barlow's 1937 report. He was expected to treat the Blitz as an opportunity, the start of a new era. He would report to the LCC.

The war's conclusion meant these plans could be activated. But they were to be dominated by a government set on centralizing reform, not leaving it to localities. Chamberlain's Poor Law arrangements were removed from London's control and brought under a Whitehall regime of 'national assistance'. The health minister, Aneurin Bevan, bitterly disliked the LCC's Morrison and took a particular delight in stripping London of its prized hospitals for his new National Health Service. Even in housing, 'nationalization' ruled. Before his ousting, Churchill planned to construct a million prefabricated bungalows in old Spitfire factories, to be 'erected in a matter of hours'. The outcome was a fiasco, the unit cost of the 'prefabs' proving three times that of an ordinary suburban semi. A few live on in Catford in south London, charmingly quaint and 'listed'.

Abercrombie's ideas for London's planning were on a more ambitious scale. They emerged from the revolution in planning theory that had swept Europe in the early 1930s, seizing architectural theory in dictatorships and democracies alike. Hitler's Albert Speer envisaged Berlin as a new Germania, laid out on an imperial scale. Soviet Russia was implementing Stalin's apocalyptic urbanism. Whole cities in eastern Europe were to be cleared and avenues of state-owned structures erected in their place. Though such ideas owed something to classical geometry and imperial grandeur – Hitler saw Berlin as a new Rome – their autocratic implications were devastating. They had no respect for Europe's urban culture as it had evolved over time, nor for its historic buildings.

These ideas were heavily influenced by the Swiss-French architect Le Corbusier. Born Charles-Édouard Jeanneret, he had inspired the pre-war modernist movement known as CIAM, which saw 'architecture as a social art . . . an economic and political tool that could improve the world'. A London offshoot known as MARS was formed in 1933, with Le Corbusier calling on its members 'for the rational re-equipment of whole countries regarded as indivisible units . . . to enable us to carry out our vast undertakings'. They had to 'brighten the homes and thus the lives of millions of workers', a goal to be pursued 'in a spirit of grandeur, nobility and dignity'.

Young architects were mesmerized by Le Corbusier. As an omnipotent state had put technology to the aid of war, now it should 'wage' peace, dictating the future of human habitation, with architects as its field marshals. Le Corbusier told them to think of the great French rulers Louis XIV, Napoleon Bonaparte and Napoleon III, 'golden moments when the power of the mind dominated the rabble . . . men can be paltry. But the thing we call man is great'. As the leading British modernist Maxwell Fry put it, architects should address 'ourselves only to those capable of understanding us, and let the rest go hang'.

In most professions, Le Corbusier and his followers would have been thought mad. He proposed demolishing the entire right bank of the Seine in Paris for rows of sixty-storey concrete blocks. London's Architectural Association answered with a plan for London. It showed little left standing other than the Tower of London, St Paul's and the British Museum. Round them were strewn giant slabs and motorways. It was as if the Blitz was a facilitator, a mere overture to architecture's operatic enterprise, to refashion all of urban life after its own vision. I recall apprentice architects still talking like this at the Architectural Association in the late 1960s. No one was joking.

Ideology in practice

Abercrombie had been secretary of the new Council for the Preservation of Rural England. But he was also professor of town planning in his native city of Liverpool, and he spoke the language of the moment. He raged against London's past as a time of 'obsolescence, bad and unsuitable housing, inchoate [sic] communities, uncorrelated road systems, industrial congestion, a low level of urban design, inequality in the distribution of open spaces, increasing congestion of dismal journeys to work'. He emerged from Nick Barratt's history of London planning as possessed of 'that love of neatness and beautiful shapes on maps that is endemic in planners, but that sadly and rarely takes account of what is already there'. Abercrombie's fingers, said Barratt, 'itched to demolish and rebuild'.

The plan's central principle was borrowed from John Gwynn in the 1760s, that London had grown too big at the expense of the rest of the country and should be curbed. A green belt, first mooted before the war, should become sacrosanct, reserved for farming and leisure. Within that belt, the city should be adapted to the age of the motor car, with five 'ringways' and radials galore. An inner ringway was to encircle the City, Southwark and the West End, passing where possible through blitzed districts. A second ringway was to run through Notting Hill, Primrose Hill, Islington and down to Rotherhithe, Peckham and Clapham, later dubbed the Motorway Box. A third was the North and South Circular. Two more were proposed further out. The City for its part would have none of this and proposed a ring road of its own, outside the line of the old walls. Fragments of the City scheme were actually built, including a dual-carriageway along 'London Wall' by the Barbican, and Upper and Lower Thames Street along the river.

Abercrombie's roads alone would have cost billions of pounds and involved evicting more Londoners than the Blitz. But they were nothing on his plan for the London in between. This London, he said, was 'worn out', with 'drab and dreary' old buildings unfit for modern living. Over half a million people should be moved to eight new 'satellite towns' in the Home Counties, including 40 per cent of the population of the East End. Industry would be banned from areas designated residential. Roads everywhere would be bordered by parkland. No one would be asked permission.

Densities, land usage and building heights would be rigidly controlled. 'Bad and ugly things', undefined, would be eliminated. Abercrombie was sensitive to what he called 'organic communities', historic 'villages' such as Kensington, Islington, Hackney and Stepney. These would be fenced off and left isolated in traffic-free peace, like urban museum objects. The rest of London would have to start again. The new metropolis would see an end to 'violent and competitive passion' and be a place of 'order and efficiency and beauty and spaciousness'. The plan survives in a short black-and-white film, available online, called *The Proud City*.

Not since Wren had one man sought to treat the metropolis as a canvas for his personal vision. Wren had the excuse that he had a cleared site. Abercrombie was disposing of a city of 7 million living souls. In 1947 his plan was weaponized with a new Town and Country Planning Act, the first to insist that local government actively control future development. It gave councils power to permit or refuse buildings, without compensation for loss of profit. This included the protection of historic buildings, lists of which would be prepared. Public development would be financed by a proposal from the wartime Uthwatt Committee, to impose a 'betterment levy' of the surplus profit on private building. Only 'cases of extreme hardship' would be relieved, drawing on a central fund of £300 million.

Meanwhile however, a parallel renewal was taking place, on a par with the City's response to Wren's plan after the Great Fire. An act passed in 1944 had already allowed the immediate rebuilding of blitzed buildings, even those only mildly damaged. Any domestic properties that had been used as wartime offices could also stay as offices. In addition, a 'third schedule' loophole in the 1947 act allowed 10 per cent to be added to the cubic volume of any bombed structure to aid restoration, an easement that could override normal zoning.

This battery of supposed emergency measures, however well intentioned in their devising, proved to be Abercrombie's undoing. The 1947 act was a powerful disincentive to renewal, yet also an invitation to exemption and evasion, indeed rampant corruption. The third schedule loophole was blatant. The responsible minister, Lewis Silkin, later admitted, 'We did not realize it could be abused,' but he did nothing to correct it. It was in the long tradition of Whitehall's ineptitude in planning the capital. As with any plan, the only question for Abercrombie's was how long it would survive first contact with the enemy.

The city hits back

Abercrombie's enemy was the bruised soul of post-war London. In fairness to all sides, the city looked terrible. Buildings were dark and dirty. Pollution and soot obscured the visual detail that had delighted Victorians and Edwardians and was all but invisible to 1940s Londoners. It was near inconceivable at the time to see these blackened hulks of stone as remotely attractive. Bombed streets had a gap-toothed appearance, filled with rubble. In his history of the rebuilding, Lionel Esher described 'where the dingy terraces stood still, rotting sandbags oozed onto the pavements, rats infested cellars, summers of uncut grass choked the back gardens'. The overwhelming colour was black, relieved only by the occasional green of a tree and the bright red scattering of buses, telephone kiosks and pillar boxes. I shall never forget those reds, which always seemed just to have been repainted. They were London's smile amid adversity.

Yet something was moving through the dust. Observers of London's streets on the mornings after the Blitz would have noticed men, notebooks in hand, wandering the ruins. Their interest was not in Corbusian utopias, it was in profit. Many had graduated from the pre-war London College of Estate Management, and won their spurs demolishing and redeveloping old West End mansions. They were the outriders of a new boom. Their method was to ring round estate agents the morning after an air raid, seeking dazed owners desperate to sell. They knew that no living city can stand still while others dream. London was now, as in 1666, in a fight for survival. People needed somewhere to work, and work meant offices. Revenue had to flow. As the bombs stopped falling, intellectuals such as Abercrombie were the last thing landowners, tenants or developers needed. As it raised its head from the dust, London looked at the denizens of Whitehall and County Hall and said no.

Some of these entrepreneurs wanted shops. Henry Price built his Fifty Shilling Tailors empire on the ruins of the Blitz, as did Montague Burton, 'the tailor of taste'. Others just wanted land on which to build. These included such names of the future as Harold Samuel, Joe Levy, Charles Clore, Felix Fenston, Jack Cotton and Max Rayne. In the 1960s Oliver Marriott, a young business journalist, was intrigued at how a handful of unknown Londoners suddenly became millionaires. In *The Property Boom* (1967) Marriott recorded these men as they played on the gullibility of London's planning community and the defects and loopholes in their 1947 act. As the forties came to a close, a new war front seemed to open. On one side were the forces of a drastic ideology, on the other a guerrilla army of irregulars, bursting with ambition and not a little greed. Between them lay the battlefield of the London property market.

Festival interlude

The year 1951 saw a sort of truce. It was an epitaph on post-war Labour, celebrated in a Festival of Britain on the South Bank. The festival site was laid out round a new concert hall, with an ideal of Britain produced not by the modernists but by a pre-war liberal establishment. The satirist Michael Frayn dubbed it 'herbivore', as against the modernists' carnivore. It paid no respect to the new Corbusians and Abercrombie, other than in fulfilling the latter's desire for a culture quarter on the river. It was light hearted and picturesque. Festival pavilions displayed the wonders of British science and industry, glowing warm and colourful in the heart of the metropolis. Esher wrote of approaching the site from Trafalgar Square 'down the gloomy chasm of Northumberland Avenue', over a temporary Thames bridge to a playground of whimsy and eccentricity. It was all 'Victorian balloons, penny-farthings . . . Emmett trains . . . sweet ration, Ealing comedies'.

I remember it as a creation from an *Eagle* comic, drenched by the wettest London summer on record. Twenty-five years later, I interviewed many of its surviving authors for a BBC anniversary documentary. Time and again they recalled how eager they were to seem optimistic and enthusiastic, the dreams of their youth so battered by war. It was hard for me, a younger generation, to comprehend the depth of the trauma to which they were responding, coupled in some cases with a fear that the modernists might yet triumph.

Churchill regarded the festival as socialist propaganda. When he returned to office in 1951 after its closure, he ordered the total clearance of the pavilions, the Dome of Discovery and the Skylon, with only the Festival Hall left standing. The site promptly suffered 'festival blight', the curse of all locations designed for one-off events. Though on valuable land, it degenerated into dereliction until seized by the LCC's architectural department. In 1968 it erected the concrete Hayward Gallery on a site next to the Festival Hall, its anonymous 'creative team' said to revel in its ugliness. The two outdoor sculpture galleries have never been used, and the site has defied affection and demolition ever since. Together with the more stylish National Theatre next door, by Denys Lasdun and opened in 1976, the Hayward group stands as monument to a revolutionary episode in London's cultural history. The rest of the upstream site was left a car park, as much of it remains. At least the equally controversial 2000 Millennium Dome contrived to survive, and be reborn as a successful entertainment vennue.

21

The Great Property Boom
1951–1960

The guerrillas take over

By the 1950s a more confident London was emerging. Young people were restive, finding a new generational identity from across the Atlantic in all things American. They took to rock-and-roll music, coffee bars, jeans and leather jackets. The American Bill Haley and his Comets had the distinction of being the first band to induce a riot, on arriving at Waterloo Station in 1957. His explosive dance music pre-dated Elvis Presley and the homespun Cliff Richard, whose first hits came in 1956 and 1958, respectively. Gradually a divide opened between young and old London, between those for whom the war had been a life-changing experience and their children, who soon tired of hearing about it.

One wartime hangover was the mild glamour attaching to the black market, immortalized by Pinkie in the film *Brighton Rock*. A craving for light-heartedness amid the gloom was captured in a series of comedy films from Ealing Studios. The hardships of post-war London were satirized in *Passport to Pimlico* (1949), *The Lavender Hill Mob* (1951) and *The Ladykillers* (1955). A 1959 musical, *Fings Ain't Wot They Used T'Be*, bewailed 'Once our beer was froffy/ Now it's froffy coffee.'

Confident was not a word applied to an increasingly weakened County Hall. Both Labour and Conservative governments since the war had nipped in the bud the interwar surge in metropolitan sovereignty. The LCC had lost health and hospitals, and the

boroughs and guardians had lost their poor. Only education, housing and planning survived of the former pillars of London
democracy. Morrison was now in Whitehall, and there was no
more talk of home rule for London. Moreover, three-quarters of
the land area of 'London' now lay outside the LCC's boundaries. It
was as if the seventeenth-century dysfunction of the City versus
Westminster was being replicated in the Home Countries.

More drastic was the decision of the Conservatives, on coming
to power in 1951, to dismantle wartime controls, good and bad. The
housing minister, Harold Macmillan, drew many of the teeth from
the 1947 act, and thus from Abercrombie's plan. He declared his
ambition to 'set the people free . . . to help those who do things; the
developers, the people who create wealth, whether they are humble or exalted'. Few were by now humble. In 1953 and 1954 all
building licences were ended, as was the defunct Uthwatt levy and
controls on building supplies.

The message was to let rip. The third schedule loophole was not
withdrawn until 1963. Dubbed a 'spiv's charter', it helped devastate
the visual coherence of post-war London streets. Walk across St
James's Square, Portland Place, Bayswater Road and you can almost
tell where bombs had fallen. Infills rose at least two floors above
neighbours, scarring composition and group aesthetic. It is the most
obvious difference between London and post-war continental cities.
London saw the worst sort of planning – planning by exemption.

While the Treasury taxed income, it astonishingly did not think
to tax capital gains. Loans flowed to property companies as pension
funds saw swift pickings in soaring property values. London's new
ground landlords were the Pearl, the Prudential and the Norwich
Union. Harold Samuel's Land Securities, the biggest developer of
them all, went up in value from zero in 1944 to £11 million in 1952 and
£204 million in 1968. In the years following the war, Marriott listed
110 millionaires, their wealth created often from just a few hundred

pounds. Value that should properly have accrued to London as a whole was syphoned off to a very few individuals.

Waiting like lambs for these killings were London's old estates, crippled by bombing, depopulation and estate duty. Zoned for residential use, their owners had little idea of the value of their property, if granted a little ingenuity. The Bedford estate sold its marginally less elegant streets and squares in north Bloomsbury to the burgeoning University of London, which proceeded to demolish or deface them. An extensive site to its south, partly of tenements opposite the British Museum, was earlier sold to the museum for a new British Library. It fell foul to a successful early conservation battle, and the planned library was deposited on the Euston Road next to St Pancras, where a piazza that should have complemented Smirke's great portico was – and is – just a waste of space.

The Portman estate sold 150 acres of Marylebone to Max Rayne, who demolished and developed much of Baker Street and the area round Portman Square. He and another developer, Maxwell Joseph, took over much of the Church Commissioners' Bayswater estate, where they flattened acres of stucco townhouses. Marriott described Eastbourne Terrace, next to Paddington, as costing Rayne just £1,000 to negotiate, demolish and rebuild, before walking away with £2.9 million in profit. In 1950 the Grosvenor estate decided to let go all of Pimlico, whose leases had deteriorated and gone over to multi-occupancy. It was only Cubitt's quality as a builder that saved them from demolition. Within two decades an 'independent' Pimlico had recovered its old class.

A hesitant public realm

Though Abercrombie's plan, finally approved by the LCC in 1953, lost its coherence as the fifties progressed, it was still the only plan in town. As the LCC dithered, it tried at least to retain control of a few heavily blitzed development areas. These included the surroundings of St Paul's, Elephant and Castle and the East End 'village' centres of Stepney, Poplar and Bow. The results were disappointing. The south side of St Paul's, once enclosed by buildings, was left pointlessly empty. A raised piazza on the north side, designed by William Holford, was so avoided by City workers it was subsequently demolished. The hub of south London at Elephant and Castle, intended by LCC planners to become 'the Piccadilly Circus of the South Bank', was eliminated entirely in favour of two large roundabouts, with pedestrians forced into tunnels.

Abercrombie's ambition was met in one respect. At least 260,000 Londoners were moved out to new towns in the home counties, to Stevenage, Hemel Hempstead, Welwyn, Hatfield, Harlow and Crawley. The villagers of Stevenage were outraged at having the East End, as they saw it, dumped on their doorsteps, naming it Silkingrad after the minister. Post-war London was to Hertfordshire and Essex what pre-war London had been to Middlesex. The outward migration also embraced more distant towns such as Chelmsford, Luton, Southend, Maidstone, Dorking, Bracknell and Reading. East End boroughs such as Stepney lost roughly half their families and much of their communal soul.

The practical impact of Abercrombie was thus simply to expedite what the market had been doing for half a century, to give new impetus to London's outward spread. It leap-frogged the now statutory green belt and expanded across the south-east region. London decentralized as intended, but it did so by filling the centre with offices and removing their workers further afield, thus adding to the strain on public and private transport. The existing built-up area did not densify, while building consumed ever more countryside. London needed no Abercrombie plan to do this. The market had been doing it for centuries.

One thing the LCC did know about was council houses, and here it forged ahead. Initial efforts, by both the LCC and the boroughs, took a lead from the pre-war estates, as epitomized by Becontree and St Helier. In central London the result was mansion flats, mostly with front doors, stair wells, Georgian windows and sloping roofs. These were rarely more than six storeys high and mimicked the private-sector flats of the Edwardian era. They were popular, creating new neighbourhoods along streets or round courtyards.

The mid-fifties saw a complete shift from this style. As the modernists moved into the ascendant at County Hall, under chief architects Robert Matthew and Leslie Martin, design policy was contemptuous of individual houses, traditional streets and terraces, as much as they were of interwar suburbia. The new metropolis should be of towers and slabs, deliberately anonymous entrances, corridors and shared open spaces. These ideas were carried to Whitehall, where civil servants after 1956 offered council subsidies for high-rise flats, the amount increasing with each additional storey.

The earliest manifestation of the new style was Westminster council's Churchill Gardens estate in Pimlico, the design of two young graduates of the Architectural Association, Philip Powell and Hidalgo Moya, victorious in a competition as early as 1946. They proposed a thirty-two-block estate of nine to eleven storeys, demolishing more Pimlico houses than had the Blitz. The estate is now a period piece, its windy acres softened by later landscaping. The terrain has even seen the insertion of a few rebellious cottages and private gardens.

In 1952 the City of London broke the habit of a lifetime and built a block of its own council flats, albeit outside its boundary in Golden Lane, north of the Barbican. This design competition had been won by three teachers from the Kingston school of art – Peter

Chamberlin, Geoffry Powell and Christoph Bon – with a slab block of sixteen storeys, at the time the tallest housing in Britain. It breached the London height limit of a hundred feet, but no one seemed to worry.

The LCC was not to be outdone. In 1958 it moved 'out of town' to the Alton estate on the edge of Richmond Park in Roehampton. This estate, designed by Rosemary Stjernstedt, was of eleven-storey slabs set on a slope overlooking the park, self-consciously modelled on Le Corbusier's Unité d'Habitation in Marseilles. This was softened by a 'mix' of four-storey maisonettes, as if to excuse the offence which the slabs blatantly caused the rurality of the park. Roehampton's influence on public housing nationwide was immense.

London's high-rise living was never about density. Tower-block estates rarely housed more people per acre than former terraces; indeed, today the densest London housing is in Victorian South Kensington. Alton's a hundred persons to the acre was the standard suburban ratio. Even the cliff-like estates of Brixton's Loughborough, Southwark's Brandon and Lewisham's Pepys estates were little over 200. In Hong Kong at the time, British colonial officials were cramming Chinese workers at 2,000 to the acre.

These buildings were always a political statement, the imposition of a new style of urban living in defiance of that preferred by London's traditional housing market. Some high-rise blocks harnessed ground-level imagery, calling themselves 'streets in the sky' or 'vertical streets'. Rear gardens, now impossible, were supplanted by 'community open space'. Tenants in no sense owned their flats, even as co-operatives. They had to rely on 'the council' to maintain them. The community was not one that emerged from the nature of the street, but one ordered from above.

As if galvanized by the new ideology, the City of London decided in 1957 to extend its Golden Lane enterprise by developing the entire Blitz-damaged Cripplegate ward of some forty acres as one grand design. Begun in 1965, the Barbican was to spread north of London Wall, coded as Route 11, along which were to be placed six bland office towers. Marriott gave a hair-raising account of the corruption, incompetence and fleetness of foot involved, not least, by a former lord mayor. The estate, again designed by Chamberlin, Powell and Bon, was planned on Corbusian principles as an overpowering visual unity. The surrounding streets were given over to traffic and lined by three storeys of car parking, supporting a podium. This podium was to be a 'street in the air', forming the base for thirteen slab blocks and three residential towers of forty-four storeys, the tallest in Europe.

The Barbican's brutalist language was the first extensive example of what Abercrombie and his adherents envisaged for the whole of London. It was intended as the start of a City deck, from St Paul's north-east to Liverpool Street and round to the Tower of London. As urban design it was a fiasco. There was no evidence that the public wanted to walk concrete decks three floors up in the air, nor did anyone think to ask it. The City was reduced to paving the edges of the surrounding streets with cobbles to make it impossible for pedestrians to walk at ground level. The result was that few Londoners, except residents with keys, went near the place. Even to Esher at the time of its construction, it was all 'Piranesian grandeur' and 'Stygian gloom', 'where spaciousness is mere space if crowds don't take to it, and it seems doubtful they ever will'.

Half a century on, there was no take-up of the pubs, shops and community centres intended for the podium, while the public is excluded from the gardens, mostly empty as residents are increasingly absent. Admired by brutalists the world over, the heavily gated Barbican must be the most deserted thirty acres in the heart of any European city. The long-term future of the estate must be dubious. Never in the history of modern urbanism can so much space have been allocated at such opportunity cost to the exclusive convenience of so few. The Museum of London, located on its fringe, had an exterior so hostile and inaccessible its trustees pleaded with the City to be allowed to escape to a new site, a wish that was subsequently granted. The museum was allowed to move to the comparatively un-brutal surroundings of the former Smithfield meat market.

Friends in high places

For all the faults of public housing in the 1950s, by the end of the decade councils had built as many houses as had been destroyed in the Blitz. This in itself was a real achievement. Roads fared less well. One reason was that the LCC did not have remotely enough money to acquire land for road building, widening or realigning. This led in turn to the final denouement in the Abercrombie saga, not a confrontation between the public interest and developer capitalism but a collusion between the two.

The LCC wanted to ease the path of London's traffic. Developers offered a way for them to do so, at a price. They would secretly amass sites, notably at road junctions, and make them available to the LCC in return for waivers from height and density controls on adjacent land. While continental cities formulated and obeyed rules for the density of streets and the appearance of skylines, London was putting them up for sale. As under the Elizabethans and Stuarts, authority developed a vested interest in undermining its own rules. The discovery that planning permissions were 'negotiable' bred a whole new chapter in the property boom – one that has corrupted London's planning ever since.

A first such deal was reached in 1963, to allow Harry Hyams's Centre Point at St Giles Circus to rise to three times the permitted plot ratio. Its office space increased so fast in value that Hyams left it empty as it appreciated on his balance sheet – a device others later repeated with luxury flats. In exchange, the LCC secured land for a roundabout at the junction of New Oxford Street and Charing Cross Road, though it was one it subsequently found it did not need. There was no inquiry, public debate or even announced decision. For an outlay of £3.5 million Hyams walked away with £11 million of profit, profit that under Uthwatt would have come to London. An emerging 'Tin-pan Alley' district of Soho had been wiped out, and for nothing but an empty office block.

Towers and slabs suddenly erupted across the landscape, with central government, the LCC and the boroughs conspiring to defy their own rules. Protocols governing high buildings round the parks, along the Thames or in the central West End disintegrated. A slab on the old Stag brewery site in Victoria overlooked a gyratory roundabout of a scale more suited to a suburban bypass. It was supposed to avoid the need for traffic lights: they now festoon it.

On Euston Road, Joe Levy was allowed a tower looming over Regent's Park in return for an underpass that doubles as a traffic jam. For £2 million of tunnel Levy netted a profit of £22 million. In Knightsbridge, a busy intersection had life sucked from it by an office block built for Bowaters by Harold Samuel, an LCC plan for a 400-foot tower with deck access having been abandoned. It neutralized the neighbourhood and was later replaced by an even bleaker block of mostly empty flats by the architect Lord Rogers. Knightsbridge was never to recover its character, its vitality moving down the Brompton Road. London's planners could create developer profits, but not people magnets.

It was not only the West End that played host to this unholy alliance of private capital and public authority. Jack Cotton was allowed to erect a dreary tower and slab either side of Notting Hill, in return for a marginally wider street. Other former hubs of London life were destroyed for new crossroads, at Whitechapel, Vauxhall, Hammersmith and the Angel Islington. It is worth comparing them with neighbourhoods that avoided this fate, such as Borough Market, Fulham Broadway and Camden Town.

The most celebrated close shave was at Piccadilly Circus. In 1959 the LCC agreed to support Jack Cotton's Monico office development, intending to do to Piccadilly what Centre Point would do to St Giles. It was halted by central government only when Cotton publicized details of his deal, to be stunned by the resulting outcry in the press. The other end of Haymarket was less fortunate. When even the LCC balked at an eighteen-storey tower for the New Zealand government, in flagrant breach of a St James's height restriction, it was overruled by the cabinet on the grounds that a Commonwealth tower must be all right. The result at the junction with Pall Mall must be the West End's bleakest street corner.

Macmillan as prime minister allowed Conrad Hilton to build a hotel overlooking Hyde Park, in defiance of a ban on high buildings round the parks or overlooking royal palaces. Hilton had apparently appalled Macmillan by saying London would 'never get a Hilton' if his tower was refused. The decision freed the defence ministry to follow suit, with a lofty residence for its cavalry officers at Knightsbridge, rising over an obsolete stables for army horses. A threat by Shell to move its headquarters to the Netherlands again led the government to overrule County Hall and allow a block of Muscovite proportions on the South Bank.

The LCC's planning committee was presided over during this period by two councillors, Bill Fiske and Richard Edmonds. They were not so much corrupt as out of their depth, while their staffs enjoyed a revolving-door relationship with developers. The official LCC history by Eric Jackson relates that any plot-ratio variance 'was mostly carefully investigated . . . in relation to any other nearby development'. This was patent nonsense. One report estimated that the planning committee spent an average of just four minutes on each application.

These early developers overwhelmingly turned to a single architect, the amiable Richard Seifert, in their dealings with the planners. A Royal Engineer during the war, the Swiss-born 'Colonel' Seifert developed a reputation for twisting officers round his little finger. More important, he worked in secret and delivered on time and on budget, a talent rare in his profession. Seifert was the deviser of Centre Point and a dozen prominent slabs and towers, becoming the most prolific London architect since Wren, with a turnover of £20 million a year by the mid-Sixties. His signature was lozenge-shaped transoms and mullions. *Building* magazine attributed 600 buildings to his firm in London alone. Always personable, even to those who crossed him in conservation battles, he blighted London's streetscape with no feel for context or horizon. I last encountered him in 1989, during the struggle to salvage the Rose Theatre site from beneath one of his towers in Southwark. His sole concern was his reputation for completing on time.

There can be no argument that this group of men supplied in a very short time what London urgently needed, offices in which to work. They vastly enriched themselves. Other than those who inherited wealth, the likes of Samuel, Hyams, Levy, Cotton and Clore became the richest men in Britain. They were on a par with the privateers of Elizabeth I's day, wildcat operators set loose on the high seas to grab what they could from the anarchy round them. Francis Drake at least had to share his winnings with the crown. The developers mostly vested theirs in capital, and needed to share little of it with the taxman.

The failure of planning to order the post-war recovery from the Blitz set the tone for later, meagre attempts to control London's growth. Developers grew arrogant, careless about what they did to the urban environment, while planners shrugged and, for a while, still pretended to be enacting Abercrombie. As each new Barbican, Hilton and Centre Point rose, the case against the next one weakened. Each clearance of a perfectly sound set of buildings validated the next. The early squares, Hanover, Grosvenor, Berkeley and Portman, vanished as compositions of individual townhouses. They became just building sites, like any others.

On one matter concerted action was taken, though again it was no thanks to London – or central – government. The capital since the days of Dickens had been 'foggy London town'. The city and fog had become synonymous, to the extent that 'smog' was almost part of London's character. Tourists practically expected it. In 1952 there occurred an eerie repeat of the Great Stink of 1858, the worst 'pea-souper smog' in living memory, created by freak weather conditions. It was so thick it penetrated buildings and called a halt to West End shows, as audiences could not see the stage. It was proclaimed as the cause of 8,000 premature deaths.

A backbench MP, Gerald Nabarro, introduced a private Clean Air bill to control coal emissions in the capital. Unbelievably, the bill was opposed by the government under pressure from the coal lobby, an echo of its reluctance to clean up the Thames. A persistent campaign followed, and an amended bill was finally passed in 1956. The slow conversion of London to smokeless fuel became a full ban in 1968, and pea-soupers became a thing of the past. Other less visible pollutants of London's air soon took their place.

22

Swinging City
1960–1970

Permissive capital

The 1960s form a curious golden age in London's history, a decade when the metropolis supposedly emerged from an era of post-war inhibition into 'swinging' modernity. In 1960, in a hugely publicised case, a London court rejected a government ban on D. H. Lawrence's novel *Lady Chatterley's Lover* as obscene, despite it having long been available 'under the counter'. Trivial in itself, it released a surge of liberalization, covering both social and cultural behaviour, initiating what came to be called, by champions and opponents alike, the permissive society. London's global image was transformed.

A year later, the contraceptive pill was introduced, at first 'under prescription to wives only'. In 1964 the election of a Labour government, after thirteen years of Tory rule, brought to office the most radical home secretary of the post-war years, Roy Jenkins. Within a year, both judicial execution and corporal punishment by 'birching' had been ended. In 1967 Great Britain joined a small group of mostly Scandinavian countries in legalizing homosexual acts. Abortion was also sanctioned up to twenty-eight weeks' gestation. In 1969 divorce after two years' separation was permitted. Theatre censorship by the Lord Chamberlain came to an end.

Though in most cases reform was as yet partial, the impact on the open and fluid society of a capital city was immediate. Gay pubs and fringe theatre proliferated. Barely a weekend passed without some sort of demonstration or march. Nudity in the musical *Hair* caused a sensation in 1967. The Beatles arrived in London from Liverpool, their first hit, 'Love Me Do', appearing in 1962. Beatlemania went global. 'Mods' in cashmere fought style wars, and sometimes real ones, with 'rockers' in leather. Americans whom I showed round London at the time were amazed by the shortness of girls' skirts and the sight of same-sex hand-holding in the street.

In 1966 Frank Crichlow's Mangrove restaurant off Portobello Road organized the first Notting Hill carnival, a boisterous evocation of London's West Indian culture that became an annual event. London's demography began to change, and with it the city's established enclaves. The clothes trade side-stepped Bond Street and Regent Street, and colonized Mary Quant's King's Road and John Stephen's Carnaby Street. Theatres branched out of the West End into pubs such as Islington's King's Head. A club scene largely confined to traditional jazz erupted into discotheques, from the Saddle Room in Park Lane to 2,000 'twisters' crammed nightly into Hammersmith Palais. West Londoners discovered Bengali cafes in Brick Lane and Chinese restaurants in Limehouse. The bistro and the coffee bar took business from the traditional pub, with its not-so-subtle hierarchies of public, saloon and private bars.

The Jenkins reforms constituted a sort of pact between the postwar state and a new generation of Londoners. A city which since the war had seemed to languish in cultural deference to New York and Paris came alive. Its markets responded to the taking down of cultural and social barriers and the release of creative energy. Fashion magazines and colour supplements boomed. London was now celebrated in cult films such as *Blow Up*, *Alfie* and *Darling*, with no more demure Ealing-comedic references to sex, class or the war. A strident group of novelists and playwrights emerged, 'angry young men' such as Arnold Wesker, Kingsley Amis, David Storey, Harold Pinter and John Osborne. Women were represented by Shelagh

Delaney and the director Joan Littlewood. Visits to Littlewood's Stratford East theatre were exhilarating treks to a foreign land, notably in 1970 to see *The Projector*, a revival of an eighteenth-century attack on London property development. The concept of a London season took on a new edge, with the annual march of the Campaign for Nuclear Disarmament from Aldermaston to Trafalgar Square, beginning in 1959.

In 1966 America's *Time* magazine came to London and portentously declared it a 'swinging city'. Its youth was now a 'class' of its own and was shedding the capital's 'smugness and much of the arrogance that often went with the stamp of privilege'. Instead it was displaying 'a coziness and a mixture [of] social circles that totally eludes New York'. London was exhilarated by the accolade, as if it had won an urban Oscar.

London landlords began an operation which at the time seemed Herculean. They honoured the clean-air statutes of the 1950s by starting to wash and restore colour to what were still overwhelmingly black buildings. A wholly new city emerged in shades of dark red, sandy pink, grey, cream and white. This led to a new awareness of the quality and detail of Victorian and Edwardian architecture, long seen as incorrigibly gloomy. The portico of St Paul's went from black and white to pure white in 1965, with the critic Ian Nairn deploring the 'loss of chiaroscuro'.

Meanwhile the post-war burst of property speculation peaked in 1962, having added 50 million square feet of offices in central London, five times the amount destroyed in the Blitz. This was the opposite of what both government and LCC planners had intended, which was to disperse offices out of the capital. The 1964 defeat of the Tories was fuelled in part by public aversion to the anarchy and ugliness of much of this renewal. The new Labour government immediately enforced a total ban on private office building in the capital, and pursued a policy of office decentralization.

At the same time, the new government committed what was generally agreed to be a serious blunder. The economic affairs minister, George Brown, decided London needed more hotel beds, and duly offered a Treasury subsidy of £1,000 per room for new ones. The result was pandemonium, as recession-hit office developers rushed to the trough, their favoured architect Seifert in the lead, fearing the bonanza might end.

Since the subsidy was per room, irrespective of size, some dozen so-called 'rabbit-hutch' hotels erupted, most designed by Seifert, in Knightsbridge, Lancaster Gate, Cromwell Road, Edgware Road and even one overlooking Kensington Palace. The last time a government had directly sponsored public buildings on this scale was for the Queen Anne and Waterloo churches, designed by the notable architects of the day. The 'Seifert hotels' were dire structures and still are. Situated near parks or Georgian squares, they inevitably were a precedent for future intrusions.

The government of London, again

The Tory government had acknowledged the failings of the LCC by in 1960 commissioning a report by Sir Edwin Herbert. He proposed simply to abolish the LCC and the metropolitan boroughs, replacing them with a vastly expanded Greater London Council (GLC), embracing all Middlesex and parts of Surrey, Kent and Essex. Beneath that tier would be thirty-two new London boroughs, each double or treble the size of the former ones.

The new GLC's powers, like those of its predecessors the LCC and the MBW, would be limited and 'strategic'. It would prepare a new Greater London Development Plan (GLDP), charged with updating Abercrombie and concentrating on major roads and comprehensive developments. It would have residual housing powers, largely over the old LCC estate, and responsibility for both tall and historic buildings. It had no control over the police, which remained with the Home Office, or public transport, which remained with a nationalized London Transport.

More significant were the powers granted to the new boroughs, described by Herbert as London's 'primary unit of local government'. These included housing, social services, local roads, refuse collection, planning and development control. The GLC administered virtually nothing. The boroughs were reinforced at the coalface of local government. Herbert thus emphasized the balance of power in the metropolis, as engineered by Lord Salisbury at the end of the nineteenth century.

The Herbert proposals were battered by local politics. Labour had controlled the LCC for decades and the Conservative government saw widening its boundary into Tory shires as the only way of ever winning back the capital. But while Middlesex gave up the ghost, Tory Surrey and Kent had no desire to lose territory and fought back, though with little success. Kensington and Chelsea contrived to keep their names in a merged borough. Camden embraced old Holborn, St Pancras and Hampstead. Kilburn and Marylebone joined a new City of Westminster. Herbert tried ingeniously to combine rich and poor areas of the inner city. Yet for all these efforts, the Tories were unable to win the first GLC elections in what was a golden year for Labour, 1964. They lost by thirty-six seats to sixty-four.

Nothing so typified the ongoing confusion over government in the capital as the fate of education. The new outer boroughs fought to keep their schools against Herbert's recommendation of a new London education authority under the GLC, while the old inner ones fought to remain united. A compromise was an Inner London Education Authority, a ghost of the old LCC, comprising relevant members of the GLC. This curious hybrid survived thirty-six years, almost always under Labour control.

High rise, low rise

The new GLC had a difficult legacy. Not only did it run almost nothing, its 'strategic' decisions either required co-operation with the boroughs or conflicted with them. It did have early successes. One of its functions was to list and protect the capital's historic buildings and allot 'blue plaques' to homes of distinguished former residents. In this it was remarkably active. Guided by a team of historians and architects, it set a new standard of building preservation, saving hundreds of otherwise doomed London streets and monuments.

Less successful was the council's supposed policy on high buildings. With the pass already sold at Centre Point, the Hilton and the Seifert hotels, County Hall effectively gave up. There was talk of the need to cluster tall buildings and keep them away from the Thames, but vague proposals that they be allowed 'where appropriate' opened the door to years of corruption and exception. The only specific control was on views of St Paul's, at least when seen from the smarter west side of London and from Greenwich. London remained unique among ancient world cities at the time in having no policy at all on its skyline. In 1969 Paris allowed the erection of the Tour Montparnasse, to such a universal cry of anger its city centre was never so defiled again.

In one respect, opinion was changing. By the time the new GLC arrived, the housing department in County Hall was experiencing doubts about high-rise council flats. These were proving hard to let and unpopular with all but the most desperate of tenants. A survey of Bethnal Green by Peter Willmott and Michael Young as early as

1957 reported that residents wanted to retain the intimacy and vitality of their old street communities. 'We don't look on [Bethnal Green] as a pile of stones,' said one. 'It isn't the buildings that matter. We like the people here.' They felt they associated more freely in streets than in tower blocks. No one actively preferred the latter.

Critics of the new age of mega-estates were emerging on all sides. A local historian, Nicholas Taylor, wrote of those in his native Greenwich, 'Into these castles-in-the-air were stacked the thousands of council tenants who had no choice in the market, but had to acquiesce in the judgment of elected committees and their professional advisers . . . [their] spectacles misted over by the sheer political beauty of utopia rising heroically out of ruin.' Hackney's Patrick Wright later wrote of streets of perfectly sound houses pulled down simply to benefit from government rebuilding subsidy. A result was that the borough was failing to house as many people as it was evicting. Its gigantic GLC Trowbridge estate, built in 1966, leaked and became a slum almost from the start. Its towers were dynamited twenty years later.

To the planning historian Lionel Esher, by the mid-sixties London's official architects were no longer attracted to 'new urban patterns to dramatize a revulsion, a revolution, against the old or to symbolize a victory of the powers of light over the powers of darkness'. The LCC's chief architect from 1953 to 1956, Leslie Martin, escaped to Cambridge, where his students concluded that the best housing would be to lay 'four tower blocks on their sides round a rectangle of open space'. To Esher, this was merely the London format invented by the Georgians, which Martin and his colleagues had spent a decade demolishing.

Government policy took time to catch up with this change of heart. It was taking up to a decade to build a modern estate – they were still being erected into the 1970s – against just weeks to restore Victorian terraces to the same densities. By 1970 the GLC had erected 384 blocks over ten storeys high. Quite how they were to be 'laid on their sides' was not clear, and became the subject of numerous cartoons in the architectural press.

One devastating answer came in 1968 on an estate in Canning Town in Newham. The twenty-two-storey Ronan Point was typical of the cheaply constructed blocks created in a decade of council subsidy-chasing. A gas cooker exploded on the eighteenth floor and blew out the tower's load-bearing side panels, collapsing an entire corner to the ground. Four tenants died and seventeen were injured. The building was repaired, but few chose to live in it. After sixteen years, the estate was demolished, to be replaced with two-storey terraces.

By now the high-rise council estate had become as much a feature of poorer London as the Georgian square was of the richer. Flats tended to go to problem families and recent immigrants, adding to their unpopularity. I researched estates in Wapping and the Isle of Dogs at the time, and saw many that had clearly passed out of council control. Corridors on the Samuda estate on the Isle of Dogs were infested with feral dogs. Rent books for Wapping flats were said to be on sale in Nigeria.

Enthusiasts for high-rise living later switched their attention to the private sector, where they found more receptive takers among young people without families and with money to pay for concierges. These tenants had less need of a sense of neighbourhood. They were well off and often sought a pied-à-terre rather than a permanent 'home'. When the architects Alison and Peter Smithson were asked about the swift degeneration of their brutalist Robin Hood Gardens in Poplar, they complained it had 'the wrong sort of tenants'. The implication was that modern architects had not been serving the right class of Londoner.

By the time of Ronan Point, the fashion for high-rise public housing had lasted barely two decades. Yet it housed an estimated quarter of council tenants relocated since the war. The busy diversity and chance encounters of a city street were replaced by anonymous corridors and lifts. Back gardens were replaced by unpoliced open space. Rather than house more people, the new blocks housed fewer. From 1950 to 1970, London's population fell by 9 per cent and that of Inner London by 17 per cent.

The concept of a city neighbourhood was analysed at the time by the American sociologist, Jane Jacobs, in her *The Death and Life of Great American Cities* (1961). Jacobs's account of why people liked streets was rooted in her understanding of their social geography. It was that of the front door, its steps, the line of vision down a road from overlooking windows, and less tangible factors such as the nature and continuity of tenancy, family structure and employment. Jacobs saw the street as both communalizing and 'self-policing', as in effect a miniature polity. She took urban conservation, in the widest sense, out of the realm of nostalgia into practical sociology. The book was read and acclaimed by architects and planners, but its message was ignored. Even with the demise of high-rise, London architects no longer built traditional streets. It was if they had lost the art.

What should replace towers was another matter. Some councils sought to recreate the London terrace but in novel garb. Westminster produced Lillington Gardens on Pimlico's Vauxhall Bridge Road (1961). Redbrick and ground-hugging, it was covered in greenery, each flat struggling for individualism. There was a brief craze for elevated or 'grandstand' streets on decks, such as the Brunswick Centre in Bloomsbury, termed an 'ideograph of city-centredness'. Others were built in Reporton Road in Fulham and in Camden's 'ziggurat' of 520 flats in Alexandra Road, St John's Wood. They cost ratepayers £100,000 for each flat completed, a sum that was considered a wild extravagance.

As long as central subsidy continued, council architects continued to demolish streets and seek new geometries for new Jerusalems.

Most popular was the high-density, low-cost, 'system-built' slab, as demonstrated in two giant estates, Aylesbury and Heygate, erected at the end of the sixties in Walworth in Southwark. I later toured Aylesbury, reputedly the largest housing 'complex' in Europe, with a proud government minister, Sir Keith Joseph, whose own company, Bovis, had built it. The central concept was that of the street in the sky, wide enough for a milk-float to get down it. But it did not behave like a street as it required a temperamental lift to reach it, while residents were separated from their cars. Heygate was blighted by crime and later demolished, and Aylesbury was expected to follow.

The most dramatic exemplar of the new low-rise ideology was London's own 'new town', located on the Thames marshes west of Greenwich at Thamesmead. This was the GLC's first attempt at a modernist 'Barbican-on-the-water'. Launched in 1965, it was composed of concrete-built flats set round a yachting marina, designed to house 60,000 people and with a third of the houses private. The project replicated the Barbican's brutalist aesthetic, which seemed out of place in a Thames-side meadow. It also repeated the failings of the LCC's Becontree, in that little thought was given to transport, shopping or other infrastructure. Ground floors were declared uninhabitable because of the risk of the river flooding.

The isolation of the site, nowhere near a Thames crossing, made it hard to let, and a third of its properties went to recent immigrants. Thamesmead was used as the set for Stanley Kubrick's dystopian film *A Clockwork Orange*. In 1972 the plans were scaled back to 45,000 people, and the whole project was later handed over to the Peabody housing trust. Fifty years on, Thamesmead's central shopping area is bleak. There are no yachts in the basin, just rubbish, but a Victorian clock tower was imported somehow to cheer things up. Thamesmead was never rooted in humane town planning but in architectural fantasy.

In 2019 Peabody anticipated having to spend £1 billion on a new town centre, in the hope of revitalizing an area of London to be expanded one day to equal the size of Westminster.

A different form of 'place-making' was inspired by the new borough of Croydon. In 1965 the ambitious leader of Croydon council, James Marshall, produced plans to create what he dreamed would be a 'mini-Manhattan of the suburbs', or at least a mini-Abercrombie. He constructed as many offices as Birmingham did at the time, threading his new town centre with dual carriageways and underpasses. Despite this determination, the blocks lacked architectural inspiration, and the result never took hold. Croydon did not have the magnet of a preserved historic core, unlike suburbs such as Ealing and Richmond. But at least one corner of London had tried to honour the planners' vision.

A future in the past

If London's new architecture in the 1960s failed to respond to the revolution in the city's culture, the seeds of a different form of revival were sown. In 1967 a Tory politician, Duncan Sandys, introduced a measure in parliament empowering local councils to map what were called conservation areas. A Civic Amenities Act authorized them to declare neighbourhoods of architectural or historical importance, within which they could forbid or control development, with a presumption in favour of forbidding.

Sandys's conservation areas took hold across a metropolis clearly hungry for some such discipline. Within a decade they had spread to every London borough other than Barking. Two hundred and fifty were in place by 1975, mostly in former Georgian and early Victorian neighbourhoods. They eventually expanded to cover most of residential Westminster, Kensington and Chelsea, much of Camden and

Islington, and with pockets across the rest of the metropolis. Conservation areas were to become a planning tool with greater impact on London's appearance than anything in its history. It was a poor comment on London government that the two most beneficial innovations in late-twentieth-century London – this and Nabarro's Clean Air Act of 1956 – required the initiative of private MPs in parliament, not in town or county halls or even in Whitehall.

The initial effect of the areas was to freeze property values, since by definition they made demolition and redevelopment impossible. In time, however, ground landlords found that, far from losing property value, conservation enhanced it. Demand sent prices ahead of the cost of rehabilitation, drawing private money into the renewal of previously depressed areas. The reality was that when urban demolition and rebuilding fell out of favour as government policy – not least for their cost – so did the public money to finance them. Conservation replaced public with private money. Large areas of central London began to change character as home owners and landlords sold to those able to spend on restoration. This was inevitably controversial, as existing residents were gradually replaced by newcomers, a process described by the sociologist Ruth Glass as gentrification.

A Rent Act in 1957 had partly decontrolled rents, still leaving so-called sitting tenants with a degree of security. But there was now an incentive for landlords not just to increase rents but to induce tenants to leave, to make way for renovation and sale. The most notorious early practitioner of what came to be called 'winkling' was Kensington's Peter Rachman. He concentrated on ousting elderly tenants and selling to West Indian and other immigrants, often profiting from overcrowding. This led to belated measures to curb such action. Rachman's core properties, off Westbourne Park Road, were later cleared by Westminster for its Westbourne Gardens estate.

As it was, gentrification soon developed a degree of self-mockery.

The estate agent Roy Brooks published advertisements in the *Observer* promoting semi-derelict properties as 'challenging . . . promising . . . in need of love . . . would suit desperate writer in search of something sordid'. Middle-class parents would profess shock at the parts of London into which their children were moving. Where once 'pioneers' reached into Primrose Hill, Notting Hill, Islington and Camberwell, they now began to 'colonize' Fulham, Battersea, North Kensington, Kilburn and Kentish Town. This was understandably opposed by longstanding residents who felt duly invaded.

The customary form of clearance was simply waiting for older tenants to die, and for renewal to take place around them. Surveys suggested that, under the 1957 act, less than 10 per cent of tenants were actively in conflict with their landlords. The issue was not so much the eviction of former residents as the type of community created by the new ones. It was the question of to whom does a London neighbourhood 'belong'. I return to this below. Many of the newly conserved areas had been built for middle-class Londoners, only drifting downmarket in the twentieth century as their occupants fled for the city's cleaner and less crowded outskirts. In this sense, they were being 'regentrified'. In some areas, including where I was living in Camden, councils responded by buying streets in conserved areas and using them as social housing for existing residents. The result was to create successfully 'mixed' neighbourhoods, and more cheaply than by demolishing and rebuilding.

London's traditional communities could have been preserved – and gentrification diluted – had this policy been pursued more vigorously after the war. As the critic Tom Dyckhoff has noted, old streets did not appeal only to the rich. Both rich and poor 'had come to share a love for values inherent in the dense, historic city, its aesthetic form, its layers of history, its ability somehow to encourage neighbourliness or its sheer excitement'. Somewhere in this catalogue of virtues lay what I can only term the soul of the city. Its attempted destruction in the decades after the war I still regard as a gross professional crime.

The shift to conservation at the end of the 1960s was helped by a volte-face in government policy. The 1969 Housing Act, passed in the aftermath of Ronan Point, replaced subsidies to high-rise with what amounted to the opposite, improvement grants for rehabilitation. 'Improvement areas' replaced redevelopment areas as focus of planning attention. By the 1970s London's streets and squares were being seen as assets rather than obstacles to the city's renewal. A decade that had begun with one cultural revolution ended with another. An inner-city of the sort that across much of America was being deserted by its middle class and left to the destitute poor was being reused rather than obliterated.

23

Recession Years
1970–1980

The seventies strike back

Decades rarely perform the task expected of them, by tidily encapsulating the character of their phase in history. Yet the 1970s in London seemed to reverse the 1960s. The capital had been galvanized, its cultural, social and territorial arteries opened to new blood. Tourism to the swinging city boomed, possibly doubling over the decade (tourism statistics are unreliable). The metropolis had developed a magnetic attraction, draining youth and talent from the provinces and even from abroad. By the 1980s London was said to have more immigrant communities of over 30,000 people even than New York.

As throughout history, newcomers were a cause of friction. Acts restricting Commonwealth immigration in 1962 and 1968 were introduced by governments of both parties, and the issue came to prominence in politics. There had been much-publicized race riots in 1958, but inflammatory speeches in the late sixties by the Tory politician Enoch Powell sent London's Conservative vote soaring (despite Powell's dismissal by the Tory leader Edward Heath). At the 1967 GLC election, the Tories won an extraordinary eighty-two seats to Labour's eighteen, and the party took control of twenty-eight out of the thirty-two new London boroughs. Though the Tories were assisted by Labour's devaluation of the pound, their poll was noticeably high in immigrant areas, such as traditionally

Labour Lambeth, where a twenty-four-year-old John Major (later prime minister) found himself catapulted into the chair of the housing committee. Three years later, in 1970, Heath's party was strong enough to defeat Labour nationally and form a new government.

Immigrants were consolidating their historic enclaves. The Irish remained concentrated in Kilburn. West Indians had been arriving in Brixton and North Kensington ever since the initial *'Windrush'* recruitment by London Transport in 1948. They were followed by large influxes of Asians, first from Pakistan, India and Bangladesh, and then as a result of their expulsion from East Africa. Immigrants tended to settle in previously depressed areas, the Sikhs in Southall, Indians in West Ham, Vietnamese in Kingsland Road and Bangladeshis in the Whitechapel now being vacated by the Jews.

A Georgian chapel on the corner of Fournier Street in Spitalfields embodied these exotic shifts in London's population. It had been built as a Protestant church by Huguenots in 1743, then was converted into a synagogue and is now a mosque. North Kensington's Notting Hill carnival was undaunted by the neighbourhood's rapid gentrification, or by periodic confrontations with the police. It went from strength to strength, to become the world's largest ethnic street festival, transforming a now sedate North Kensington into a vivid demonstration of London's diverse personality.

In 1973 the Heath government secured admission to the European Common Market. This offered new trading opportunities but also new competition. London's financial status was now also fighting for pre-eminence with the commercial centres of Paris, Frankfurt, Brussels and Amsterdam. Its staple industries of financial and professional services were suffering, as before in the City's history, from 'closed shops' and restrictive practices it found hard to reform. The same applied to the docks and motor industry. London would have to update itself to face European competition. London in the seventies suddenly found itself on the defensive.

At the moment of Britain's Common Market entry, the western economies were traumatized by a quadrupling in the price of oil by the producers' cartel OPEC. This coincided with a wave of strikes against state-imposed statutory wage restraint, making it illegal to pay more than a stipulated pay rise. By 1974, Tory government inspectors were actually vetting wage slips of journalists on my newspaper. Power supplies and public services were crippled. Not even during the war had businesses been limited to a three-day week. Nocturnal London was an eerie sight, with streets in some neighbourhoods lit while adjacent ones were in darkness. I remember driving across a blacked-out Barnes towards a dazzling Roehampton on its distant hill.

Trade union power was now demonstrated more aggressively than ever since the General Strike. A desperate Heath government sought re-election in 1974 by asking 'Who rules Britain?' The answer from the voters was 'Not you'. But the return of a Labour government under first Harold Wilson and then Jim Callaghan saw no let-up in the troubles, rising to a pitch in the 'winter of discontent' in 1978–79. Cemetery burials were suspended and rubbish piled high in Leicester Square. The London of the sixties had become divided and confused. The once-swinging metropolis seemed gripped by *die Englische Krankheit* (the English sickness), the continental idiom for rickets now widened to caricature Britain's tottering economy.

Policing a capital

Though little noticed at the time, there now appeared the first signs of what would become a London plague, in some places as serious as the gin menace of the eighteenth century. This was the consumption of narcotic drugs. In the late sixties, cannabis and LSD were available in pubs and nightclubs, but 'harder drugs' were mostly confined to a few thousand registered addicts, who could obtain them on prescription. Reporters would interview the nightly queue outside the Piccadilly Circus chemist, Boots as the next day's supplies of heroin were handed out.

In 1971 the Misuse of Drugs Act withdrew those supplies, with devastating effect. It drove hard drugs underground into what became a booming illicit industry. Within a decade the estimated number of heroin users shot from 6,000 nationwide to 60,000. Dealers were better salesmen than Boots. For poorer parts of London, harsh penalties for drug possession and dealing gave London's criminal gangs a new source of blackmail and income that became embedded in London's so-called informal economy. The act also stimulated police corruption. The Metropolitan Police, under Home Office control, had long been a freemasonry apart. Since the nineteenth century, the force's relationship with London's criminal community had bordered on reciprocal tolerance. In the sixties and seventies, the Kray and Richardson families ran empires of sex, night clubs and extortion under the eyes of the authorities, touched with a seedy glamour.

The 'Met' was headed from 1972 by a reforming chief commissioner, Sir Robert Mark, in alliance with Roy Jenkins, who came back to the Home Office on Labour's return to power in 1974. Mark publicly declared that 'a good police force is one that catches more crooks than it employs'. With Jenkins's support, he wound up the Met's criminal investigation department (CID), ending its cosy collaboration with East End gangsterism. When journalists challenged him on the need for such radicalism, Mark replied, 'Just watch bank robberies drop.' The robberies had been a monthly diet of the London press, and Mark was right. After the demise of the CID they virtually ceased. Mark retired in 1977, before his officers found a more lucrative source of income in the narcotics economy.

Motorway Boxing

London's government could by the early seventies claim to have met one cardinal duty laid on it after the war: it had ended mass slum housing. Slumdom might live on in the stairwells of tower blocks and the overcrowded basements of Rachmanism. But for all the grotesques of modern architecture, money had been spent and hundreds of thousands of Londoners, old and new, rehoused. By the mid-1970s, there were said to be more houses than households in a capital now steadily losing population.

There was less to show for the GLC's other specific duty, to keep the capital moving. Across Britain, cities were having their Abercrombie moments. Birmingham, Bristol, Liverpool, Nottingham, Newcastle and Glasgow tore into their still-grand Victorian centres for inner relief roads, gyratory traffic schemes and ringways. The cost to taxpayers and ratepayers was astronomical. The loss of civic institutions and civic dignity was tragic, while the gain in faster journey times was trivial.

London was, ironically, lucky in that its Abercrombie plan, reborn under the LCC and taken over by the GLC, was simply too ambitious. For a while, the GLC was undaunted. Guidance on implementing the post-war road schemes had been supplied by Sir Colin Buchanan, in a 1963 report titled *Traffic in Towns*. It was sensational. In the 1940s, the *Architecture Review* had preached 'traffic modernism'. Honouring it, said Buchanan, meant a 'traffic architecture . . . so people could live at peace with the motor car'. This would best be done by devoting the city's ground floor, Barbican-style, to traffic and allocating pedestrians upstairs to a city-wide 'deck'.

The deck became the holy grail of London planners. Buchanan declared it would supply 'the things that have delighted man for generations in towns, the snug, close, varied atmosphere, the narrow alleys, the contrasting open squares, the effects of light and shade, and the fountains and the sculpture'. This paradise would connect with the traffic teeming below by means of escalators and lifts. An illustration showed Fitzroy Square sitting lost amid a maze of slabs, decks, feeder roads, dual carriageways and spaghetti junctions, all to replace a traffic light at the top of Tottenham Court Road. The Smithsons declared a future London as a 'grid of expressways' weaving through a city of decks and towers as 'acupunctures into our moron-made cities'.

The prospect dazzled GLC councillors, who would reply to all critics by saying, 'but we are told this is the future'. Buchanan, like Abercrombie, came of a planning caste whose utopianism was ingrained. He protested that his ideas were not 'recommendations', merely a 'least absurd alternative'. He did not describe what might be the most absurd. His concept of traffic separation required at least in theory the rebuilding of the entire city. The GLC's development plan (GLDP) reduced Abercrombie's five ringways to three, but the bill for the inner Motorway Box alone was £500 million (or £7.5 billion in 2019 prices). Some 100,000 houses would need to be destroyed, their replacement consuming London's stock of new public housing for a generation. The evictions would be horrendous and the external costs enormous.

At the same time as these proposals were mooted, a curiosity unrelated to the GLDP was about to emerge, a relic of an old Whitehall plan for an urban motorway to link the Euston Road to the A40 to Oxford. Called Westway and running over North Kensington, it was opened in 1970 by the then transport minister, Michael Heseltine, amid local fury. The television satire *Yes Minister* suggested the road's sole purpose was to help MPs back to their old university. A similar link planned from Pentonville to the M11 (and Cambridge) was never built. The public reaction to

Westway offered politicians and the public a taste of what the Motorway Box would encounter as it drove its way across central London. The GLDP went out to consultation, with the Box as its star exhibit. Councillors and officials attending meetings in affected areas such as Islington, Camden, Chelsea and Wandsworth were lucky to escape unharmed.

In the event the London Tories were defeated in an election in 1973, and the incoming Labour Party abandoned the Box and all mention of it. Short stretches had been started and still remain. They include parts of the East Cross Route at either end of the Blackwall Tunnel, and 400 yards of the West Cross Route north of Shepherd's Bush roundabout to Westway. Connoisseurs of planning archaeology can see the butt-end of a slip road to the non-existent Box, jutting menacingly from the Westway junction towards Ladbroke Grove.

Other legacies of the Buchanan era were more bizarre. For a period, all new buildings in the City and West End were required to incorporate an elevated podium, pending the age of the deck. Of these the Barbican remains the most complete, but 'decked London' includes Lower Thames Street, New Zealand House in Pall Mall and old Castrol House on Marylebone Road. The mind boggles at how they were expected to link together.

A curio of the deck ethos was *The Economist*'s fifteen-storey tower-and-plaza off St James's Street, designed by the Smithsons in 1964. I worked in the tower for five years and recall frantic attempts to entice pedestrians to use the deck for its intended purpose as a 'town square' for St James's. As at Paternoster Square and the Barbican, Londoners simply refused to desert what they regarded as 'the ground'. They would rather picnic on the pavement than upstairs and out of sight. The tower's 'listing' prevented the piazza's replacement by buildings in a 2018 renewal.

At the same time, a more down-to-earth County Hall was

engineering two major benefits to movement in London, bus lanes and the new Victoria and Jubilee Tube lines. The Victoria Line, completed in 1971, was the first in half a century, finally linking a neglected swathe of north-east London with the centre. The Jubilee Line followed in 1979 and linked the north-west. They were inexpensive and unobtrusive, compared with the later Crossrail. At the same time, a Thames barrier was being constructed at Woolwich, to open in 1984. It was to protect London not so much from high tides as from storm-water surges upstream meeting an incoming tidal flow. For the time being, London seemed safe.

Gunfight at Covent Garden corral

While argument over the Motorway Box raged, another battle was being fought over what was to prove a last attempt by the GLC's planners to restructure inner London. The benighted Piccadilly Circus, rescued from Jack Cotton in 1962, was handed to Westminster council, who proposed three Centre Point-style towers and a giant deck, designed by the architect Lord Holford. This was rejected in 1972 by the government, on the grounds that it left 'insufficient room for traffic throughput', increasing it by 20 per cent rather than the required 50 per cent. Within a year, traffic was no longer a god, the plan was dead and Piccadilly was left in peace.

Not far to the east lay the equally vulnerable Covent Garden, a neighbourhood of warehouses north of the old fruit and vegetable market. The market was due to move in 1974 to Nine Elms on the South Bank, and a plan had been drawn up by County Hall's architects to redevelop the area. It would again be decked and surrounded by dual carriageways along Holborn and the Strand, demolishing 60 per cent of the area's buildings and 80 per cent of its housing.

With the council already under attack over the Motorway Box, local reaction to the Covent Garden plan from residents, businesses and politicians alike was explosive. It was opposed by London's *Evening Standard*, whose editor, Charles Wintour, accurately judged the mood if not of all London then certainly of his readers. That London's historic fabric could be dismissed as 'obsolete' was at last becoming unthinkable.

Officials with whom I dealt as a journalist at the time were confused and angry at such fierce opposition to what they regarded as 'the city of the future'. At one hearing, a GLC engineer told the inspector that the demolition of the whole of Maiden Lane and building a dual carriageway along the Strand was essential, 'otherwise we can assure you the West End will grind to a halt'. These people, many of whom I came to know, seemed unaware of how they were now trying the emotions of a large section of the London population, and so doing with mendacious futurology.

The Covent Garden plan was killed in the climactic year of 1973 by a bizarre act of political sabotage. A government minister, Geoffrey Rippon, sympathetic to the protestors, had his officials list for preservation 250 buildings chosen strategically across the Garden area. This instantly stymied the plan. When Labour took control of the GLC later that year, that plan passed with the Motorway Box and Piccadilly Circus into oblivion. Covent Garden in its entirety was declared a conservation area under the new Civic Amenities Act.

The campaign saved the area, but controversy shifted to whether London had saved its body, but not its soul. As new users poured into Covent Garden it was argued that its old community had been destroyed for what amounted to 'commercial gentrification'. In reality, city-centre communities are constantly shifting sands. The Earl of Bedford's estate was for aristocrats. The subsequent market was for porters and salesmen, replaced in turn by a fragmented neighbourhood of older council tenants and low-rent newcomers in buildings requiring renewal. The only question was who would pay for that renewal and whether it would be drastic or gradual.

The GLC subsequently protected its tenancies in the area, but nothing was likely to stop Covent Garden, rescued from Barbican-style neutering, from blossoming into one of central London's most appealing, colourful and popular neighbourhoods. Theatres and the Covent Garden opera house were balanced by the retail dynamic of Long Acre, and by the charming back streets of Seven Dials and the triangular enclave owned by the ironmongery firm Comyn Ching. The triangle was admirably restored by the architect Terry Farrell after its rescue from demolition. It is the fabric of a city that dictates its use, not the other way round. In Covent Garden a neighbourhood of adaptable buildings was saved to receive the next tide of Londoners to sweep over its borders. No such tide was admitted to the Barbican.

Epitaph on an era

The sagas of the Motorway Box, Piccadilly Circus and Covent Garden signalled 1973 as a revolutionary moment in London planning. The Bastille was stormed but the full revolution still lay ahead. At the start of the 1970s, the Heath government had decided on a wholly new Whitehall enclave, demolishing the area between Downing Street and parliament in favour of high-rise slabs. Gilbert Scott's Foreign Office, John Brydon's Treasury building and Norman Shaw's New Scotland Yard would all have gone. Another proposal was to demolish Nash's entire Carlton House Terrace. British Rail wanted to demolish St Pancras station, having obliterated Euston in 1961. Only the decking of Knightsbridge and Piccadilly Circus had been abandoned.

In the City, the corporation wanted to be rid of Leadenhall and

Billingsgate markets. The British Museum pressed for the flattening of south Bloomsbury. The Royal College of Art sought to demolish the north end of Queen's Gate in Kensington. Bankside and Battersea power stations were at risk after decommissioning. The City Club in Old Broad Street was to go, as was the Langham Hotel opposite the BBC. It remains difficult to conceive the city envisaged and planned by London's government at the start of that decade.

By its end, these losses were averted not by official action or change of heart, but by popular protest, orchestrated by groups such as the Georgian Group, the Victorian Society and SAVE Britain's Heritage, with assistance from the media and local activists. A campaign fronted by the poet Robert Graves rescued Albert Bridge in Chelsea from the wreckers. A central pier was found to be perfectly adequate as a support. The Langham, the City Club and St Pancras were saved. Another campaign mounted by the *Evening Standard* in 1974 evicted civil servants from Somerset House and their cars from Horse Guards Parade.

Battles were not always won. A terrace of magnificent Rothschild family mansions disappeared from the Hyde Park Corner end of Piccadilly, to be replaced by a bland modern hotel. The Norfolk estate's enclave of eighteenth- and nineteenth-century streets south of the Aldwych was wiped out, for replacement buildings so ugly they have since been demolished. Georgian north Bloomsbury suffered terribly from London University's architectural vandalism. Woburn and Torrington squares were almost eradicated. Imperial College smashed the Victorian Imperial Institute to the ground, leaving only its tower. Arts and educational bodies proved to be the most ardent destroyers of London's heritage.

There were grievous losses in the City, including the Coal Exchange by the Monument and Barings Bank on Gracechurch Street. Dozens of old warehouses lining Upper and Lower Thames

Street went for the City's miniature bypass, later to be reduced to a single lane each way. By the 1980s probably none of the historic buildings and streets demolished in the previous thirty years would have gone. Time was not on their side.

The 1970s ended on a depressing note. The decade had marked a post-war low in the city's morale. Prospering cities do not lose people, and London's population had fallen from a pre-war peak of 8.6 million to 6.7 million. Demographic predictions since the turn of the twentieth century, that London's glory days were past, seemed at last to be plausible. Growth in the capital was subsiding. In 1977 the 'old Labour' GLC of Sir Reg Goodwin was voted out after just four years. It was replaced by the Tories under a buccaneering right-winger, Sir Horace Cutler.

By then the modernist consensus on housing, motorways and comprehensive renewal had collapsed, leaving the GLC with no intellectual direction. In 1979 the council built fewer than 900 houses, half of them in Thamesmead. The attempt to upgrade London's main roads had ended in total failure. The South Circular in particular was ridiculed as 'back streets linked by road signs'. Road capacity was now treated as finite and movement in the capital was handed over to London Transport. As for strategic planning, there was none worth the name.

When I look back on this period, I recall only a constant battle against what seemed a great mistake, made by a generation who found themselves in charge of a great metropolis with no concept of what kept a city living, breathing and changing. Though constitutional responsibility lay with those voted for by the public, in truth the elected were taking advice from the unelected, a coalition of architects, planners and contractors. To criticize the politicians was akin to blaming a patient for obeying doctor's orders.

For these doctors, I have little sympathy. Many were friends of mine, but where London was concerned they showed no humility, only arrogance. Trained in the early post-war years, they treated the metropolis as their professional foible and source of gain, leading gullible politicians of the left and right up an ideological garden path to a false utopia. From 1950 into the mid-1970s they inflicted greater destruction on London, and the rest of urban Britain, than all Hitler's bombs. The cost of rectifying that destruction as the century drew to a close was to be immense. To the best of my knowledge, the architectural profession has never held an inquest on this period, let alone shown the slightest remorse.

24

Metropolis Renascent
1980–1997

Showdown at County Hall

London at the end of the 1970s faced a peculiar challenge. Margaret Thatcher's election as prime minister in 1979 changed the political weather. She despised consensus, and did not mind who knew it. She also had distaste for local government, possibly through her father's experience of it. This was despite the GLC being led by a Tory, Sir Horace Cutler, who supported Thatcher and was eager for reform. In 1978 he had asked the experienced Leeds city councillor Sir Frank Marshall to come up with new ideas for governing the capital. The result was a plan to give the GLC responsibility for strategic planning, roads and railways, while housing and social services should go entirely to the boroughs. He also suggested giving London's health services (back) to County Hall. This was truly Morrisonian and did something to restore a little dignity to London's civic authority.

All was to no avail. In 1981, with Thatcher embarked on a programme of national austerity and with the economy in recession, Labour recaptured the GLC. The day after the election, the party's moderate leader, Andrew McIntosh, was toppled in a coup by Ken Livingstone, a radical activist with no executive experience. Livingstone was to prove a refreshing as well as an alarming presence on the London stage. He hailed from Norwood in south London, moving to Hackney and then to Camden. His sole occupation appeared to be migratory councillor/agitator, with a caustic wit, off-the-shelf left-wing views and a reputed love of newts. Above all, he displayed a blind hatred for everything Thatcher was trying to do to rescue Britain from the trough of the 1970s.

For the next five years Livingstone did not govern London, but rather used the GLC as a political weapon, leading many Labour notables to desert to the new Social Democratic Party. He was never dull. He decked County Hall in banners blazoned with the capital's unemployment rate. Bus and Tube fares were cut (until stopped in the courts), the GLC precept on local taxpayers was doubled and large grants were distributed to far-left groups. Livingstone even gave local activists a plot of GLC land for 300 tenants in Coin Street on the South Bank, downstream of Waterloo Bridge. It remains today, like a modest suburban housing estate deposited on one of the capital's most valuable sites.

Livingstone was inviting Thatcher to react, and react she did. A 1983 white paper, cynically entitled 'Streamlining the Cities', dismissed London's government as 'an overhead'. The GLC was to be abolished, lock, stock and barrel, and the capital would be run by its boroughs. If further oversight was needed, it would be supplied by a minister in Whitehall. The Stuarts' Court of the Star Chamber was reborn. No other city in the world experienced such humiliation. The abolition of London government was opposed by all sides of the political divide. For the first time since the Metropolitan Board of Works, the capital's affairs were overseen by no locally elected body. Livingstone gleefully accepted municipal martyrdom. The GLC died in March 1986 with the most spectacular firework display London had seen, as if Livingstone was trying to re-enact Guy Fawkes. The surviving Inner London Education Authority limped on until 1990, when it too was disbanded and its schools devolved to the boroughs, many of them passing to central government as 'academies'. London was ruthlessly centralized.

County Hall was deliberately left empty. The year after abolition I held a farewell party in its empty, dust-coated chamber, with Livingstone even taking the 'chair'. The rest of the building became part hotel, part hostel, part aquarium. In a gesture of superior contempt, the government then dwarfed it with a giant Ferris wheel. The once beating heart of London's government was reduced to Disneyland.

The London boroughs had little more luck. Thatcher in 1985 capped the rates of those she thought spendthrift, mostly Labour ones. This led to battles reminiscent of pre-war Poplar, between compliant and militant councillors. Some, such as Hackney and Lambeth, descended into factional chaos, with considerable help from a freelancing Livingstone and friends. Thatcher's granting of the 'right-to-buy' to council tenants was furiously contested. The arguments for the policy – that the tenants were anyway de facto holders of an asset for life – was plausible, but undermined by the houses being sold at discounts of 30–70 per cent, with half the revenue going not to the councils that built them but to the Treasury.

London was soon creaking for lack of self-government. Services such as transport, fire brigade, parks and waste disposal required oversight, and were being run out of Whitehall by a plethora of 'quangos' – on one count as many as a hundred. A bizarre London Residuary Body continued some GLC functions. The government even set up a half-hearted London Planning Advisory Committee, while Thatcher created a Government Office for London, notionally under a minister 'for London'. Whatever abolition had done, it had not abolished a bureaucratic overhead. People did not appreciate democracy until deprived of it.

Thatcher's view of local government showed itself most emphatically in a reckless decision to do away with local property taxes, known as rates, in favour of a poll tax. Rates, like most taxes, were unpopular, but they were easy to understand and collect, based on a house's assumed market value. They were also progressive, increasing with a house's value. The new poll tax was a universal flat rate on rich and poor alike. Although it was hardly penal – eventually about £400 a head – it was a gift to left-wing agitation, culminating in a violent riot in Trafalgar Square in 1990. The tax's unpopularity played a part in Thatcher's fall the same year, leading to its replacement by her successor, John Major, with a marginally more progressive council tax.

Target London

As Britain's capital city, London could not escape involvement in the tribulations of national politics. Ever since the resumption of militant Irish nationalism in the 1970s, it was hit by IRA bombings. These were mostly the work of so-called 'sleeper cells' and hard to prevent. Initial targets were West End stores and hotels, such as Harrod's and the Hilton, intended to disrupt tourism. Thatcher's hard line with republicanism meant that barely a month passed in the early 1980s without an incident somewhere in the capital.

In 1984 an attempt was made on Thatcher's life and that of her entire cabinet, in the blowing up of the Grand Hotel in Brighton. A lull followed, but attacks resumed after her departure in the nineties, with mortar attacks on Heathrow and on No. 10 Downing Street, followed by a devastating bomb in 1992 outside the Baltic Exchange in the City. This killed three people and caused £800 million of damage. The City's planners allowed the demolition of the ravaged but still magnificent Exchange, once fulcrum of global shipping, to make way for Lord Foster's strange Gherkin. It was vandalism on a par with the 1930s destruction of Soane's Bank of England.

The bombings ceased with the Good Friday agreement of 1999,

by when London had seen some 500 IRA attacks and fifty deaths. At times they almost seemed part of London life. The newspaper newsroom would echo to the periodic shout of, 'Bomb! Stop the presses.' Publicity-seeking terrorism was the price London paid for being a capital city and, on the whole, it took it in its stride. The contrast was glaring with the paranoia that overtook the security agencies and others in response to later Islamist attacks. Either way, London was the place to 'send a message', from CND and the anti-Vietnam protestors of the 1960s to the climate change activists of 2019. It was still truly a global capital.

Docklands renaissance

One achievement lay to the credit of the 'direct rule' years. The GLC's planning lethargy had frozen in dereliction much of London's former industrial landscape. Through the seventies, the docks were gasping their last. In 1975 the value of goods passing through them was overtaken by Heathrow, Gatwick and soon Stansted, and in December 1981 the last ship loaded a London cargo. The baton of a mighty industry passed downstream to Tilbury, while in east London miles of riverside land lay deserted.

The parallel decline in manufacturing was almost as dramatic. Jobs in the sector fell by 80 per cent between 1960 and 1990, and for the first time since the war, London's unemployment in the eighties went above the national average. Britain's seven worst unemployment black spots were in inner London boroughs, particularly hitting recent immigrants. De-industrialization was clearly outpacing the growth in the service economy.

A final burst of despairing militancy came from a well-organized group of workers, the printers. These so-called 'aristocrats of labour' enjoyed closed-shop working practices dating back to the invention of typesetting in the Middle Ages. Each print-room function was guarded by meticulous rules, hopelessly outdated by computers. The migration of newspapers from their historic home in Fleet Street was facilitated by a Labour environment minister, Peter Shore. In 1979 he gave permission for the newspaper magnate Rupert Murdoch to demolish Europe's finest array of Georgian warehouses at London Docks for a new print works. What might have become the Covent Garden of the East End was levelled to the ground.

Shore was unaware that Murdoch's intention was to use the walled docks to break the print unions' power. The result was London's last sustained campaign of labour violence, the Wapping riots of 1986–87, aimed at preventing Murdoch operating his new plant with non-print-union workers. The activists did not enjoy wide support, and the protest drained away. Wapping led to the demise of the printing 'chapels' – as the London unions were called – and the slashing of production costs across the newspaper industry. It left London with a remarkable ten daily and evening titles, a range of reading unique among western cities.

At least the London Docks now had a new use. Other dockland sites lay dormant and government action was clearly needed. The GLC had appointed a joint committee of the relevant boroughs to investigate their future, but it seemed as inert as the land it was discussing. An early decision by Whitehall in 1981, even before the GLC's demise, was to vest the entire area in a London Docklands Development Corporation. Local boroughs were furious, but could hardly complain. As the environment secretary, Michael Heseltine, pointedly said, 'We took their powers away from them because they were making such a mess of it.' A year later, on the initiative of the chancellor, Sir Geoffrey Howe, the Isle of Dogs docks enclave was even declared an 'enterprise zone', free of planning controls and taxes for a decade.

The Isle of Dogs was an island only by virtue of its docks. It was a London apart. In 1970 a self-appointed 'president', Ted Johns, had declared 'unilateral independence' of the local Tower Hamlets council, a short-lived but much-publicized enterprise. The island's old West India Dock round Canary Wharf had become an artistic hangout of warehouses and attics, billed as Poplar's creative quarter. The LDDC in 1982 brought this to an abrupt halt, inviting mostly overseas speculators to take land in London's first free port. The venue appealed to few London investors, who fought shy of a location so far from the city centre.

After a number of false starts, Canary Wharf was acquired by a Canadian firm, Olympia and York, owned by the Reichmann brothers, to whom Thatcher took a personal shine. Their faith in the site was extraordinary. They tried to pre-let three towers, including the tallest in Europe by the celebrated American architect, César Pelli. London office tenants still stayed away, and with barely 60 per cent of the development let, in 1992 Olympia and York filed for receivership. It was said to be losing £38 million a day. I predicted at the time that Canary Wharf would be like Ozymandias's 'vast and trunkless legs of stone', an ill-conceived venture in a ruined wilderness, the wrong place at the wrong time.

The City returns to global

In this prediction, I was mistaken for two reasons. In October 1986 London experienced possibly the most radical ever upheaval to its commercial structure. The then chancellor, Nigel Lawson, deregulated the City's financial institutions, disbanding their monopolies and overriding their restrictive practices, dubbed the Big Bang. It was an overnight revolution. Lawson's financial wild west was aided by the recent eruption in the global Eurodollar and petrodollar markets, on which a free-wheeling London was well placed to capitalize.

Foreign banks poured into what seemed freedom city. Though there was an immediate loss of jobs in traditional banking, incoming firms led to rents in the City shooting up by 52 per cent between 1985 and 1989. Canary Wharf itself was rescued by a Qatari sovereign wealth fund, while foreign banks lapped up the Wharf's cheap accommodation. They did not care where Poplar was, so long as it had a computerized trading floor, no taxes and no meddlesome government. By the end of the 1990s, the Isle of Dogs was employing 50,000 people, with its own new residential quarter spreading along the banks of the Thames. Seen from the island's urban farm, the Mudchute, a mile to the south, the Wharf's towers rose eerily over grazing sheep and llamas, like a film set in Dubai.

There was a second reason I was wrong. Canary Wharf, the symbol of private capitalism, was massively bailed out by big government. Shocked by the venture's initial failure, Thatcher threw money at it. Her friendship with the Reichmanns had already led her to dig a new road tunnel under Limehouse to the Wharf entrance. This cost £300 million and was claimed as the most expensive mile of tarmac in the world. Even more extravagant, Thatcher ordered work to proceed on an extension to the Jubilee Line from Westminster to the Wharf. Its stations, each by a celebrity architect, are among the finest modern buildings in London, notably Sir Richard MacCormac's Southwark and Sir Michael Hopkins's Westminster. At £3.3 billion this was also the world's most costly railway. The government even conceded a union demand that it run with drivers, though it was designed for none. This was hardly Thatcher the free-market fundamentalist.

Including the cost in rates and taxes forgone, Canary Wharf was the most extravagant public sector renewal project in Britain, estimated at some £8 billion, in a capital that arguably least needed such largesse. It galvanized this part of Docklands. The Wharf's new Jubilee Line station, by Lord Foster, was worthy of a grand London terminus. Residential towers rose on every side. The development was virtually a gated city, isolated from Poplar and the London round it. As with medieval Westminster, a new civic entity was created by public patronage, as a rival to the old one.

Beyond Canary Wharf lay a greater challenge. The distant Royal Group of docks saw service as the City airport, begun in 1986, adjacent to a virtually inaccessible exhibition centre. It was linked by a driverless overhead railway that, absurdly, did not feed into the Tube network (until a later terminus at the Bank). In reality, the LDDC was replicating the unplanned sprawl of the metropolis over the previous century. It was following wherever the market led.

Little thought went into social infrastructure or the cohesion of the new east London. There were no attempts at community building, no high streets or even crossings of the Thames, to bring south London within the embrace of the new wealth. The most noticeable revival was in high-rise living for young private buyers. But the resulting townscape was bleak. The guarded edifices of the docklands estates were a far cry from the intimate terraces and street-based neighbourhoods of the old docks. Time alone will tell if this London can find a distinctive personality.

A new commercial economy

The impact of the Big Bang on the City was dramatic, if two-edged. Beforehand, wrote David Kynaston, the City was seen as 'an unpatriotic casino which pays itself obscenely high salaries for dancing on the grave of British industry', dominated by old-school networks and monopolies and soon to be overtaken by faster-moving cities in Europe and elsewhere. With the 1980s this changed almost overnight. In 1986 I interviewed an executive with the American bank

Morgan Stanley, tasked with assessing various cities as its European headquarters. He reported back that London beat Paris, Brussels and Frankfurt, not just on deregulation but on office availability, professional services and the quality of 'prime West End' accommodation. The city, said the banker, 'had the best expatriate package, no language barriers, houses with gardens, human-scale buildings, a living Disneyland, a bond between past and present'. Frankfurt's Deutsche Bank was finding younger staff pleading to be posted to London, until more worked there than in Frankfurt.

The Big Bang was undeniably disruptive. A year later in October 1987 came Black Monday, with an abrupt collapse of stock markets round the world. London share prices saw their biggest fall since 1929. This coincided with a great storm, when London was hit by record-breaking winds of up to 100 mph, causing the loss of a third of the trees in Kew Gardens. I noticed that fallen plane trees in Bloomsbury could not be sawn up as the chainsaws kept snapping on fragments of wartime shrapnel embedded in the branches. London never lets us forget its history.

The recovery that followed did not last. A threat of inflation and a rise in bank rate to 15 per cent in October 1989 sent office and house prices into a sudden fall. In 1991, 230 property companies went bust, and office rents fell 30 per cent between 1989 and 1992. The Broadgate development in the City was no sooner declared open by the Queen than its developer, Rosehaugh, went into receivership with debts of £350 million. An extraordinary one-third of office accommodation in the City and Docklands was reported vacant. The residential market peaked and home ownership experienced 'negative equity'. Housing 'crisis' had once meant soaring prices, but now meant plummeting ones. They did not recover until 1994.

None the less, London's economy was firmly set on a new course, with financial services in the driving seat. The City Corporation was able to claim that the number of foreign banks in London, seventy-six in 1959, had reached 580. Sixty per cent of global Eurobond business was processed through London's exchanges, with their currency transactions outstripping New York and Tokyo together. There were said to be more American banks in London than in New York, and more Japanese ones than in Tokyo. The city had restored its financial status lost after the Second World War.

Over the 1990s, jobs in financial services rose from 600,000 to nearly a million, fully a quarter of the metropolitan workforce. Given the multiplier effect of those jobs, London was virtually a one-industry town – or two industries, with tourism. Average earnings of Londoners by the end of the decade were running at 30 per cent above earnings nationally, and the capital's wealth was shielding the British economy from a collapse in its balance of payments.

A shift now emerged in the nature of London's workforce. Roughly a third of a million newcomers were arriving in London each year from every corner of the globe, mostly young, mobile and eager to work in jobs that locals were reluctant to do. This led to the rise of low-wage, freelance employment in services such as tourism, fast food, messengers, home deliveries and minicabs. An upmarket version of this was the growth in labour-only agencies for teachers, nurses, social workers and home carers. Such a fragmented, non-unionized labour force was a throwback to the casualization of the nineteenth century.

Divisions and contradictions

London at the start of the twentieth century was still remarkably free of the ethnic and group tensions often experienced in less prosperous parts of England, and in cities in France and Germany. The metropolis had grown used to immigrants, not least because its economy depended on them. But there was a price to pay, in the character of the housing market. The newcomers were not settled Londoners waiting patiently for their number to come up on the housing list, nor could they mostly afford the rising price of owner-occupation. They were seeking simply a place to lay their heads in a London whose housing market seemed not to reflect what was still a declining population.

Local boroughs were required by law to accommodate families, if not individuals, British and foreign who presented themselves as homeless at their door. But traditional council estates had never recovered from the reputational crisis of the high-rise 1960s and 70s. Public subsidy to council-house building under Thatcher virtually dried up. Such money as was available was redirected to not-for-profit housing associations, mostly working on smaller and rehabilitated sites. For the poorest Londoners, help with housing switched to means-tested housing benefit, often paid direct to private landlords. One result was that overall state support for public housing actually rose in real terms under Thatcher, switched from house building to rent subsidizing. Money went more directly to those in urgent need.

Thatcher's granting council tenants the right to buy their homes had a number of consequences. It clearly reduced the size of the council estate, and with it the long-term stock of public housing. However, in parts of London as many as a third of houses sold under the scheme moved into the lettings market, often leased back on short lets to the councils that previously owned them. They were then occupied by recipients of state housing benefit. In some areas this proportion was as high as 80 per cent.

The buy-to-let market benefited from tax advantages that were hard to justify, but it did inject supply into the cheaper end of the housing market. I studied housing in Newham, a borough under acute pressure, and was told that the council could not possibly have handled at times as many as 5,000 immigrants a year without the surge in buy-to-let tenancies. I was shown a street of some fifty former council houses, each previously occupied for life by one or two elderly tenants. They had moved to the seaside while each of their houses was occupied by up to twenty people. Regulation of such properties was inadequate and their condition often deplorable, but bed-spaces there were. The supply of available social housing increased.

London under Thatcher and her successor, John Major, saw a period of undoubted resurgence. But like many revolutions, it had been binary. It was private sector against public, open markets against closed, new outsiders against old insiders. The gap between rich and poor neighbourhoods widened, with deprivation still extreme in the latter. In the 1990s, seven of England's ten poorest local government areas were in the capital, including Tower Hamlets, Newham and Southwark. London in the 1990s differed from the sixties in being harder-edged, more pecuniary, more classless, diverse and rootless. Old barriers were tumbling. The marriage of the Prince of Wales to Diana Spencer in July 1981 won a global audience, interpreted as heralding somewhat improbably a more classless form of royalty. Black politicians were gaining prominence, with the first black MPs for London, Bernie Grant, Paul Boateng and Diane Abbott, all elected in 1987. Gay festivals celebrated homosexual freedom.

Even London's voice, long a delineator of class boundaries, saw a subtle change. It began to standardize into a demotic deadening of 'received pronunciation', as it acquired elements of so-called 'estuary English'. BBC newsreaders spoke in cadences quite different from a quarter-century before. Yes became yeh. Consonants were dropped and slang, even swear words, entered daily speech. The subjects of Caryl Churchill's satire on the period, *Serious Money*, were not 'toffs' but upwardly mobile 'yuppies'. The new vulgar was pink champagne and a Porsche, the new leisure venues east not west of the City, notably in the burgeoning neighbourhoods of Hoxton and Shoreditch.

One consequence was a shift in political allegiances. London's working class was moving rightwards and a middle class of civil servants, academics, the media and 'creatives' moved to the left. Labour votes were safer in gentrified Islington than in fluid Tower Hamlets and Southwark, where 'poor whites' were turning to the right. I noticed this vividly when I saw a group of leather-clad despatch riders cheering Thatcher when she appeared on a fish-and-chip shop television screen. London's first right-wing British National Party councillor was elected for the Isle of Dogs in 1993, where the East End once elected communists.

To sociologists, this process was one of social atomization. As high streets deteriorated, libraries closed and churches emptied, there was a loss of communal coherence. London's independent borough newspapers disappeared almost completely. People noticed their neighbours changed with ever greater frequency, and came from ever more distant lands. In his social history of the capital, written in the recessed early 1990s, Roy Porter was gloomy. London, he said, had been lucky in avoiding 'the horrors of religious persecution, ethnic pogroms, political violence and all-out war'. But he saw a city in decline. Its population was still falling, and there was no reason to believe this would halt. The computerized, digital workplaces of the future, predicted Porter, would be in the expanding 'ex-urbs' of the south-east, in towns such as Maidenhead, Reading, Reigate, Sevenoaks, Basildon, Chelmsford, Watford and St Albans. To him, 'only a blind believer in the benevolence of the free market' could think London's economy safe in the long term. There was 'a new pessimism, a new anxiety about the future'.

This mood was reflected in the writings of those recalling old allegiances and certainties. London's writers at the time tended to share Porter's pessimism. Peter Ackroyd's impressionistic biography of the metropolis was suffused with melancholia, though it ended on a mild upbeat of 'resurgam'. To Ackroyd, London had always been in a 'state of becoming'. Patrick Wright's evocation of old Dalston, *A Journey through Ruins* (1991), was a sigh of woe at the changing face of Hackney, dedicated ironically to Thatcher. Iain Sinclair's observant studies of suburbia were shot through with nostalgia for a departing good neighbourliness. A harsher dystopia ran through a generation of London novelists, from J. G. Ballard's *High Rise* (1975) to Martin Amis's *London Fields* (1989) and Zadie Smith's *White Teeth* (2000). To them all, London seemed a city upheaved by Thatcher's disruption, ill at ease as it faced a new century.

25

Going for Broke
1997–2008

Camelot-on-Thames

If any city bore comparison with London at the start of the twenty-first century it was New York. Appearance aside, they were two sides of one coin, culturally as well as economically. They shared not just banks, shops, brands, fashions and food, but plays, musicals, television shows, best-sellers, journalism and, above all, the English language. American accents proliferated on London radio and in London's streets. The world's two largest English-speaking cities were twins, albeit non-identical.

In 1996, in the dying years of the Major government, the American magazine *Newsweek* sent a team to report on the metropolis surveyed by its rival, *Time*, thirty years before. What was swinging London now like? *Newsweek* solemnly reported that London had moved on from 'swinging' to become a more mature, grander, deeper though no less fashionable place. It was now 'the coolest city on the planet . . . a hip compromise between the nonstop newness of Los Angeles and the aspic-preserved beauty of Paris'. It seemed a reasonable verdict.

The accolade was seized on by Tony Blair, Britain's new political broom, eager to sweep away the pains and divisions of the Thatcherite past. Elected in 1997, he announced the birth of 'Cool Britannia', while his publicists suggested that Downing Street was nothing less than a new Camelot, a reference not to Arthurian legend but to the Kennedy White House. A sceptical MP, Tam Dalyell, compared it instead with the court of Louis XVI. Peerages were distributed to London's arts 'luvvies', who crowded the steps of Downing Street to be photographed with the JFK of the new age.

Vanity projects tumbled from Whitehall into the lap of an eager capital: a bid for the 2012 Olympics, a lavishly over-engineered Tube line, Crossrail, a new Tate gallery on Bankside, even a dubiously needed super-sewer down the Thames. London had itself a sugar daddy. Investment in its infrastructure was soon running at two-and-a-half times that in the north of England, or so the northern outpost of the Institute for Public Policy Research bitterly calculated.

The metropolis became the stage for the enactment of the Blair 'project', one of style rather than content, described by Blair's aide Jonathan Powell as 'Napoleonic'. So-called New Labour did not reverse the structural reforms of the Thatcher era, but almost parodied them. It increased the use of private finance for hospitals, schools and public services and, in 1997, proceeded with the sale of London's Tube network, forming two companies to run the track. One was bankrupt within five years, and both were eventually taken back into public ownership under Transport for London.

A mood of reconciliation after the contentious Thatcher years was undoubtedly welcome. It saw its inadvertent consummation in the death of Princess Diana in 1997, shortly after Labour took office. It proved an event comparable with her marriage sixteen years earlier as Blair hogged the limelight, espousing Diana's memory as 'the people's princess', while London hosted an outpouring of what seemed a global grief. A mountain of plastic-wrapped flowers piled up outside Kensington Palace and there were moves, swiftly resisted, to rename Heathrow airport and the M25 after the dead princess.

A safe city or not so safe

Blair's earliest achievement was to settle the conflict in Northern Ireland, relieving Britain of thirty years of intermittent terrorism. For London the respite was short lived. Blair's desire for a role on the world stage led to him seizing on al-Qaeda's 9/11 attack on New York in 2001 to join America's George Bush in retaliatory wars in the Middle East. That on Iraq in 2003 led to global protests, including almost a million people on London's streets. The government initially denied the marchers access to Hyde Park, 'out of concern for the grass', but soon relented. It was probably the largest assembly ever seen on the streets of the capital.

Far from Blair's claim that the invasion of Iraq would make London safer, the metropolis became the target for a new bout of terrorism. In July 2005 a four-bomb attack on its transport system caused fifty-two deaths, the capital's largest ever loss to such an incident. As with later attacks, it was hard to link the perpetrators with any organized conspiracy. Most if not all were 'lone wolves', their actions hard to prevent or to treat as part of a co-ordinated 'war on London'.

In the case of the IRA, successive governments had refused to grant terrorists the 'oxygen of publicity'. Islamists, on the other hand, were given publicity in abundance. Despite pleas not to 'give in to terror', central London from the early 2000s came to resemble a city under siege. The area round Parliament Square and Buckingham Palace was filled with barriers, bollards and armed police. Automatic weapons were visible outside parliament and even at railway stations. Bags were searched in shops, theatres and museums.

Foreigners were surprised at London's loss of sang-froid. I once counted forty police officers 'guarding' the Changing of the Guard. Britain's Middle East venture, far from protecting its capital, had turned it into the most embattled city in Europe. London's well-established Muslim population was now 12 per cent of the total and approaching the city's largest practising faith group, but it found itself singled out as a collective risk to public safety. Once in place, the security industry became a vested interest against ever reducing the 'threat level'. The barriers that went up across the West End remained un-removed.

While policing the capital was distracted by terrorism, a darker menace was the market in illegal drugs, and the street gangs that thrived on them. A third of young Londoners professed to regular or occasional drug use, mostly of ecstasy and cannabis. This market inevitably attracted supply. Unregulated circulation drove up crime and blighted immigrant neighbourhoods, in some of which drug dealing was the major source of income. The result was that a quarter of London's prisoners were incarcerated for drug use or related criminal activity, and the prisons themselves became major consumers of drugs. At a drugs seminar I attended in Bethnal Green, where possible legalization was discussed with local social workers and others, two well-dressed young men tackled me afterwards and accused me of 'wanting to do us out of business'. Britain's government was adamantly wedded to suppression, despite all the evidence that it was doing more harm than good.

The Blair boom

By the start of the new millennium, London had sloughed off much of the rancour of the Tory eighties and nineties. The economy had recovered from the 1992–94 blip, and was on a long-term upswing. It now experienced a new source of inward 'investment', as its banks and property market became a bolt-hole for the world's migratory wealth. Blair's aide Peter Mandelson surprised some in his party by remarking that he was 'intensely relaxed about people getting filthy rich . . . as long as they pay their taxes'. Few of the immigrant rich paid any taxes, being allowed to classify themselves as 'non-domiciled'.

At the same time and as if overnight, London's population decline halted. It had fallen to a low of 6.6 million in 1985, but against expectations surged on the turn of the century, to reach the 9 million mark in 2019, topping its previous peak in 1939. The booming sectors were financial services at roughly 25 per cent of employment, but also domestic and overseas tourism at 15 per cent, and personal services such as private health and education. Most marked was the rise in the creative industries, identified by the American economist Richard Florida as the key drivers in twenty-first-century urban regeneration. A London that a century before had depended on money, manufacturing and distribution was now turning more towards design, marketing, the arts and the media. 'Creatives', however defined, were estimated to embrace as many workers as finance.

These new activities, often in small-scale, freelance and 'start-up' ventures, were peculiarly attracted to older parts of town, to off-West End basements and former warehouses, to Clerkenwell, Shoreditch and Southwark. In Marylebone, some of the world's most advanced diagnostic medicine was buried beneath Harley Street. Soho's back streets saw the highest-tech studios for film post-production. Buildings designed for horses and carts played host to the most cutting-edge technologies.

This was the new economy that the digital revolution had promised would disperse wealth from the metropolis. It did the opposite. Workers needed places to congregate and network. Coffee houses proliferated as if imitating the seventeenth-century City. Once-doomed cultural activities strengthened. Publishers found themselves producing more books, while specialist and weekly magazine sales increased even as conventional newspapers moved online. The West End theatre stopped predicting its imminent demise and pushed up prices. In the 1970s I had wondered at there being thirty live stage performances in London each night. By the 1990s the list had more than doubled. Expanding too were auction houses, comedy clubs and even public lectures and debates.

All attempts to decentralize economic activity out of London were in abeyance. Every new government proposal – high-speed trains from the north, new runways at Heathrow, subsidies to first-home ownership – aided the capital. London's gross value added per person rose to 70 per cent above the national average. At a business meeting in Manchester at the time, I heard nothing but pleas for London 'to stop stealing our best people'. The capital was referred to by Scotland's leader, Alex Salmond, as 'the dark star economy, inexorably sucking in resources, people and energy from the rest of the UK'.

The 2001 census confirmed the upturn in London's population, also indicating that 37 per cent of Londoners were now born overseas, with 55 per cent declaring themselves as other than 'white British'. The property market surged. What had happened to Covent Garden in the 1980s was replicated in the once-derelict rim of the old central area, in King's Cross, Old Street, Bermondsey and Vauxhall. Shoreditch town hall, where I once watched scruffy East End boxing matches, became a Michelin-starred restaurant. When my parents' old flat in the Barbican was sold in 2001, the estate agent described it as 'convenient for fashionable Hoxton'.

Further out, residential gentrification expanded into longstanding working-class suburbs. Newspaper property supplements once focusing on north-west London began to feature north-eastern and southern areas such as Hackney, Clapton, Stoke Newington, Walthamstow, Bow, New Cross, Peckham, Balham and Wandsworth. The writer Iain Sinclair ingeniously traced London's 'ginger

line' along the route of the orbital overground train. It was supposedly the point beyond which Starbucks no longer ventured, and
where 'you can still get a bedsit for two hundred'. It was also the
limit of that continental shelf of London gentrification, the Victorian terrace.

Turn again, Livingstone

On one matter Blair was as good as his word. In 1994 the Commission for Local Democracy pressed to restore self-government
to London in the form of an elected mayor. As its chairman in
1995, I lobbied Blair, then in opposition, to pledge such a reform.
He was initially reluctant, having no more sympathy for local
government than had Thatcher or Major. But he warmed to the
idea when he realized the mayoralty might circumvent local
Labour parties, with whom he was increasingly at odds. He over-
came strong opposition from his local government spokesman,
Frank Dobson, and the measure appeared in the party's 1997
manifesto.

London held a referendum on whether to become a mayoralty
in 1998, with 72 per cent voting in favour, and in 1999 an act of
parliament restored democracy to the capital in the form of a
Greater London Authority (GLA). It was its fourth such version
in just over a century. As with the MBW, LCC and GLC, the
institution's powers were vague and 'strategic'. The mayor would
be responsible for roads and transport, though not for the surface
railway. For the first time, London was given oversight of its
own police forces, though the power had to be shared with the
home secretary, chaotically, as it proved. One London police
chief, John Stevens, told me he was accountable to twenty outside bodies.

The new mayor answered to an elected London Assembly, which could veto but not amend the GLA budget. Since central government retained control of virtually all local spending, this meant little. The most immediate argument was over where the mayor's office should go. The obvious choice was County Hall, and every effort should have been made to repossess it. Instead a decision was made to build an egg-shaped City Hall, on the South Bank opposite the Tower of London. It was designed by Lord Foster, increasingly the Seifert of modern London architecture.

Again the issue of the City Corporation was dodged. It remained like a lavish Vatican in its Mansion House, even holding fast to the title of Lord Mayor. This caused much confusion among visitors as to who was the 'real' mayor of London. The City's chief contribution was to manage some of London's parks, including Hampstead Heath and Epping Forest. It also jealously clong to its own planning and development control.

An election for the first mayor took place in 2000 when, in a fitting historical nemesis, it went to Ken Livingstone. The former GLC leader professed himself a changed man, representing not just a militant leftist clique but 'all Londoners'. He turned up at any occasion likely to capture the public eye. His election was at least useful in placing the office on the political map. It was inconceivable anyone would abolish the office in future.

The one area in which the new mayor could exercise some authority was transport. Livingstone unsuccessfully contested the government's Tube privatization. He introduced a travel pass, the digital Oyster card, and began to replace the double-decker Routemaster buses with an articulated and single-decker 'bendy' version. He also initiated an electronic congestion charge for private vehicles entering a central zone. Since barely 12 per cent of vehicles in the central area were private cars, it had little impact on congestion. Livingstone was unable to end a much-deplored legacy of Thatcher's direct rule, the deregulation of London roadworks. Their ubiquity undid any benefit from the congestion charge and cursed London's traffic, in noticeable contrast to the more disciplined streets of Paris and New York.

The property boom returns to vertical

Livingstone had one other policy priority, and its impact was noticeable and permanent. He was fascinated by skyscrapers. He once told me he wanted London 'looking more like Manhattan'. According to journalist Peter Bill, he would shout at planning meetings, 'Make it higher.' Virtually the only specific policy in his 2002 London plan was for fifty-storey skyscrapers next to commuter stations. The City, under its activist chief planner, Peter Rees, shared this enthusiasm. Initially it held to a policy of clustering tall buildings east of St Paul's, beyond the line of Gracechurch Street and Bishopsgate. But having already allowed the Barbican and the old NatWest tower west of this line, the discipline was hard to enforce.

Towers now arrived on the skyline thick and fast. They acquired gimmicky marketing tags such as Gherkin, Shard, Cheese-Grater, Can of Ham, Scalpel, Helter-Skelter, Walkie-Talkie and Pinnacle (later abandoned). The Walkie-Talkie was curved outwards to maximize lettable space, with the result that its reflective windows could warp cars and fry eggs on the pavement below. The structures were virtually immune from restriction since there was simply no policy against them. Even the supposed ban on sightlines to St Paul's was flexible. The architect Rem Koolhaas was allowed a bland box immediately east of the cathedral on the grounds that he was designing for the banking aristocrats the Rothschilds. The policy of not building high along the Thames corridor was abandoned, as was the ban on a visual 'wall' behind St Paul's. Each breach of policy became a precedent for the next.

Since a tower by the river at Millbank had been allowed in the 1960s, it was harder to object to a forty-nine-storey proposal at St George's Wharf in Vauxhall almost opposite. This structure was regarded as a developer's 'try-on'. It would dominate the Thames from Westminster to Chelsea, and even the normally quiescent borough of Lambeth turned it down, as did a government inquiry. It was described as setting 'a precedent for the indiscriminate scattering of very tall buildings across London'. Yet in 2005 Livingstone backed it, as did the environment secretary, John Prescott, and it went ahead. The Vauxhall tower was the most serious intrusion yet on the London horizon. It performed no civic function and its luxury flats were virtually all empty. The *Guardian* later reported that 131 of its 214 units were held overseas. The £10 million penthouse belonged to an absent Russian, and there were just fourteen names on the electoral roll.

The same controversy overtook the ninety-five-storey Bermondsey Shard, which was to become, temporarily, the tallest building in Europe outside Moscow. The Shard was the foible of an East End shopping magnate, Irvine Sellar, whose architect, Renzo Piano, explained its motivation as being merely that Sellar 'has a desire to build it'. No other borough but poverty-stricken Southwark would have tolerated such a structure, with not the slightest nod of respect to its location in low-rise Bermondsey. It was approved by Prescott in 2003, but building was delayed by financial trouble and a deluge of objections from landscape and heritage organizations.

Though undeniably a serene obelisk when seen from a distance, the architectural critic Owen Hatherley justly described its landing in Borough High Street as bullying it 'into silence . . . an act of urban thuggery . . . sheer aggression and arrogance'. Pedestrians were forced through a maze of walkways just to cross the site. Like the Gherkin in the City and the London Eye, the Shard forced itself into iconic status in the modern city by its sheer size.

Office towers were seldom popular among commercial tenants and few made money. They were expensive and required a high ratio of servicing to lettable space. As the developer Stuart Lipton told *Estates Gazette*, 'They take twice as long to build, cost fifty per cent more than a ground-scraper, and are at least five per cent less efficient than a conventional building.' He illustrated his point when in 2016 he came to the City's rescue by taking on the financially cursed site of the formerly proposed Pinnacle at 22 Bishopsgate. He erected a sixty-two-storey slab of glass with a floor space so wide and a facade so bland it even defied a nickname.

A succession of high-rise deals ended in woe. The Shard proved near unlettable, and had to be rescued by that last resort of London's extravaganzas, a Qatari wealth fund. The Gherkin cost more to build than its valuation on completion. The bulging Walkie-Talkie was saved by Chinese money. But yield mattered little to overseas investors. What they wanted was secrecy and security, which London's light-touch regulators offered in abundance.

The inevitable result was for investment to proceed from commercial to high-end residential properties. In 2007 Livingstone obtained new powers to override local boroughs and encourage more skyscrapers, where they 'contribute to regeneration and improve London's skyline'. He claimed all his residential towers would be 50 per cent 'affordable' – an echo of the high-rise council estate of the 1950s. It was a claim he had no intention of enforcing. All the towers approved by Livingstone – some 200 of over twenty storeys built or under way when he left office – were for private investment, and many if not most were largely empty of occupants.

The image of high-rise living clearly underwent a transformation. Towers might be unpopular when occupied by poorer tenants with families, and when owned by councils with little interest in their maintenance and supervision. But as pieds-à-terre or stand-by investments for the international market they proved ideal. In cities such as New York, Berlin and Singapore, local laws and leaseholds often stipulated that properties had to be owned by nationals or be occupied for given amounts of time. In 2017 New Zealand simply banned foreigners from buying property without proof of permanent residence. In other words, city planning should consider the impact of a particular built form on its neighbourhood and community.

London planners and their political masters showed no such concern. The new towers that rose over the metropolis in the first two decades of the new century appealed to their purchasers precisely for the reasons they should not have been allowed. They offered privacy, secrecy, gated security and a lack of nosey neighbours. With their ownership often hidden behind offshore companies, the towers were bank vaults in the sky. Square footage was bought and sold, often before being built, like company stock. A block in Canning Town was acquired by a Chinese investor and left almost entirely as a shell.

Each year, London's planners, architects, councillors and developers would gather at the annual construction industry fair known as MIPIM in Cannes. The event saw lavish entertainment and relentless wheeler-dealing. On my last visit, one developer told me he reckoned more decisions about London's appearance were made on the beach at Cannes than in any London council chamber. Local opposition to a project would be met by councils demanding so-called 'section 106' concessions. This involved the developer making a handful of flats available at 'affordable' prices – usually a 20 per cent reduction – or paying for a primary school or swimming pool elsewhere in the borough. The payment in 2018 to Tower Hamlets for 'Spire London' in Docklands was reportedly an enormous £50 million. As the payment did not go to an individual, it was termed a 'legalized bribe'. London had come full circle from the days of Hyams and Levy. Planning was a matter for 'negotiation'.

As if to symbolize this new balance of power, Blair in 1999 abolished the Royal Fine Art Commission, an independent champion of architectural standards and longstanding thorn in the side of many commercial architects. He replaced it with a Commission on Architecture and the Built Environment (CABE), astonishing even the developer community by appointing as its chairman their elder statesman, Stuart Lipton. CABE welcomed the Vauxhall tower as 'clear and attractive' – though it did object to the Shard.

The Blair boom was a long one. It had inherited the upturn in the economy in the later years of the Major administration, and was aided by a declining pound following Britain's departure from the European Monetary System. The metropolis had emphatically recovered from the depths of the 1970s. By the time Blair gave way to his colleague Gordon Brown in 2007, morale in the three main pillars of London's prosperity – finance, tourism and property – was extraordinarily high. Few thought that pride might be coming before a fall.

26

Constructs of Vanity
2008 to the present

Johnson's star ascendant

In 2008 London was hit by a banking failure originating in America and soon consuming all Europe. It saw the worst collapse of financial confidence since the 1930s, and pushed Britain into a brief but severe recession. As on similar occasions before, London survived relatively unscathed. Though a provincial bank, Northern Rock, failed, none was allowed to go bust in London thanks to government support for two of the most prominent, RBS and Lloyds. The outgoing Labour government of Gordon Brown (2007–10) and the incoming coalition of David Cameron and Nick Clegg (2010–15) pumped liquidity into the credit system and forestalled serious harm.

For London the story was rather one of belt-tightening. The property market hesitated, fell for a year and then levelled out. The biggest hit was taken by local government, and a severe austerity policy was pursued by the chancellor, George Osborne. Over the next decade, London's local councils lost between 40 and 50 per cent of their central government grants. This was to cost them 37 per cent of revenue per head, against 29 per cent in the rest of the country.

In the recession year of 2008, the London mayoralty passed from Livingstone to the Conservative Boris Johnson. Educated at Eton and Oxford, Johnson was a marked contrast to Livingstone's 'cheeky chappie' image, but he shared his predecessor's unconventional humour and lack of cant, virtues in civic leadership. Nothing about his past, his classical metaphors, incessant gaffes or colourful private life seemed to dent his popularity. His liberality with public money became near obsessive.

On taking office Johnson, an avid cyclist, took over Livingstone's bicycle network as his own, its bikes being dubbed 'Boris bikes'. They were to lose £160 million a year. At the same time, the mayor reconfigured a route through the West End for cycle lanes, to the delight of cyclists and the rage of taxi drivers. The main Embankment road was reduced to a single lane each way, forming a perpetual jam. By 2018, the only free-flowing thoroughfare across inner London was the Marylebone/Euston road. Post-war Buchanan was truly dead.

The LSE's London expert, Tony Travers, estimated that in New York, where the city government was in charge of all roads, some 90 per cent of them were available for through traffic. In London, where side roads were a borough responsibility, one-way streets, 'mazes' and on-street parking confined such traffic to barely 20 per cent of space. The result was that acres of tarmac in the capital lay unused except for access and on-street parking, land denied to housing, shopping, playing or even gardening. London's use of space was extravagant.

Johnson performed a personal U-turn on tall buildings. Having accused Livingstone when in opposition of creating 'Dubai-on-Thames', he became high-rise's most ardent advocate. The independent forum New London Architecture (NLA) reported the number of tall buildings passing through the planning system as doubling under his regime. He also commissioned vanity projects worthy of Blair at his most extravagant. He backed a loss-making cable car over the river in the East End. He spent half a million pounds on a giant helter-skelter on the Olympic site in Stratford – 'an icon to match the Eiffel Tower' – and ordered unusable water cannon for the police.

With George Osborne's help, Johnson approved a £60 million 'garden bridge' over the Thames at the Temple, supposedly at no cost to the public purse. It turned out that each had promised £30 million of public money, with Johnson underwriting any losses. The potential cost rose to £175 million and the project was cancelled after £43 million had vanished into the pockets of 'consultants'. Soon afterwards, the neglected Hammersmith Bridge had to be closed for want of £30 million as no one would take responsibility for its maintenance. London government was not in good shape.

Johnson scrapped Livingstone's 350 single-decker buses and ordered new double-deckers, promising a return to Londoners' much-valued freedom to hop on and off a rear platform at red lights and at will. Each old bus was put on the market for £80,000, while the new ones cost £350,000. In the event, the rear platform proved almost unusable and the order was cancelled by Johnson's successor. Bus use in London started to decline in 2014, by some 3 per cent a year. By his departure in 2016, Johnson's mayoralty was clearly seen as just a calling-card for a return to higher things at Westminster.

Riotous city, Olympic city

In August 2011 an incident occurred of the sort that periodically caused London to pause and think. Riots broke out following the police killing of a black suspect in Tottenham. For most of a hot summer week youths went on the rampage, from Wood Green, Streatham, Enfield, Woolwich and Croydon even to Oxford Circus. The targets were mostly shops, many gutted by fire. The police stayed in the background, with magistrates hard-pressed to fix penalties for the theft of goods found lying in a street. The riots showed how fragile was the border between tranquillity and violence even in a usually stable city.

In 2016 a new mayor was elected, Labour's Sadiq Khan, ushering in a calmer, duller mood at City Hall. As with Johnson, the mayoralty, always limited in its powers, was coming to seem less a matter of civic leadership than a promotional platform for an aspiring politician. Far from increasing 'home rule for London', the new office strangely drained the capital of political traction. London failed to imitate Manchester, which in 2015 negotiated control of both its health service and its railways away from Whitehall. In railways, London still controlled only its underground lines. With elected mayors active in Birmingham, Liverpool, Bristol and South Yorkshire, London reverted to its lethargic past. When in 2018 the new Crossrail failed to open on its due date and soared over budget, there was little outcry.

The biggest challenge to Khan was a sharp rise in gang and knife crime, the Met police now being notionally his responsibility. After two decades in which the capital's overall crime rate had been drifting downwards – and continued to do so – knife attacks mostly on young males surged. The cause appeared to be territorial battles between drug gangs, to which the police had no answer beyond controversially stopping and searching large numbers of black teenagers. What was not explained was why the incidence of these crimes had taken a sudden upturn, other than the familiar culprits of a booming drugs economy and a rise in youth club closures through austerity. Whether London might one day take up the challenge of legalizing its drugs market, as in the Netherlands and an increasing number of American states, seemed doubtful. The open trading of cannabis – with police increasingly turning a blind eye – led to anarchy without resolution. Few noted the eighteenth-century parallel with London's gin menace, when taxation, regulation and enforcement, rather than prohibition, eventually proved an antidote.

The 2011 riots led to concern at what pictures of flaming buildings might do for the image of the London Olympics the following year. The worries were needless. London 2012 was an impressive display of gaiety, security and expense. The city became a global television set. With Johnson pleading for non-ticketholders to stay away for fear of congestion or trouble, London that August seemed a ghost town. Special trains conveyed visitors to the games site in the Lea Valley near Stratford. Official Olympic vehicles were given special traffic lanes and clickers to turn the traffic lights to green. Sponsors demanded rival advertisements be cleared from Olympic routes, and there were logos even on lavatory seats. Tourism declined 8 per cent that year.

With no cost control, the Olympic bill soared from an initial budget of £2.4 billion to £9.5 billion. Subsequent estimates later put the total cost at nearer £15 billion. All was forgiven when the games were declared a success, with the prime minister, David Cameron, promising they had been worth £13 billion in exports, an absurd figure. But there was no question a pride surged over London that summer, as Nero's bargain held, of 'bread and circuses' for public contentment. London 2012 saw a curious inversion of London's traditional modesty.

Housing crisis – or not

A sense of suspended hysteria followed the 2012 Olympics, including much controversy over their 'legacy'. Tourism did not rise, sports activity fell and a huge site at Stratford stood aching for reuse. On one thing all agreed, the legacy must have to do with housing, for housing was 'in crisis'. Nothing could banish the phrase from the political lexicon.

Despite appearances, house prices in London throughout the 1990s and 2000s were not out of line with those in other successful cities.

In the decade following the 2008 crash, London's property index actually lagged behind global trends. It rose annually by 3 per cent in real terms, against New York's 5.5 per cent, San Francisco's 13 per cent and Stockholm's 14 per cent. Cities such as Melbourne, Singapore, Paris and Brussels all experienced intense upward pressure on housing costs. The reason was the same. Big cities at the turn of the twenty-first century were attracting more residents than their housing markets could supply. New building was not the answer, despite the pleadings of the construction lobby for permissions. Cities such as Melbourne and others in California were building in plenty. New building could never add more than a percentage point or two to supply each year, while in London they represented barely 14 per cent of annual purchases. With ten people arriving to live in London every hour, more bodies had to be accommodated in the available space. The issue was how could this best be achieved.

London was exceptional in one respect, the inefficiency of its use of land and buildings, resulting in centuries of low-density sprawl. The geographer Danny Dorling gave London one of the lowest population densities of any big city anywhere. The LSE 2005 cities survey showed New York, Moscow and Tokyo all far more concentrated than London. In Paris density was quadruple, at 20,000 people per square kilometre. Nor was that all. The 2011 census showed London properties with more bedrooms than occupants. The estate agency Savills reported in 2015 an estimated million London homes were 'hidden' by under-occupation.

The predicament was aggravated by Londoners' preference for houses over flats of any sort. They had long devoted a large portion of their income to investing in privacy, living room and, if possible, a garden. According to the London Wildlife Trust, 2 million out of 3.8 million households in the capital had garden plots of some sort, a proportion far beyond any comparable city. And governments since the war had pandered to this preference, with mortgage subsidies, first-time buyer subsidies and help-to-buy subsidies. The cumulative effect of these benefits was that policy persistently subsidized housing inefficiency.

As if this were not enough, London's property tax – council tax after 1993 – was minimally related to value, the top valuation band being just three times the bottom. In 2019 it was revealed that a £100 million penthouse overlooking Hyde Park Corner would pay roughly £2,000 in local tax, while a similarly priced property in New York paid $250,000. In addition, heavy stamp duty on house purchases exceeding £1.5 million – up to 12 per cent on expensive properties – deterred older owners from downsizing. This disincentive to move was the last thing needed by housing supply in a booming city. It led to overinvestment, 'space hoarding' and price inflation, and discouraged market fluidity and densification. British central government remained, as always, a poor governor of the metropolis. Public housing limped along in the backwash of these political and market pressures. Councils were still wrestling with the legacy of their 1960s and 1970s estates, many requiring demolition or rehabilitation. Most were now passed over to housing associations, new custodians of social housing in the capital. As noted, the whole of Thamesmead went to the Peabody trust, while the burden of housing poverty continued to shift onto housing benefit. A 2013 study showed a third of recipients – probably the poorest – were in private sector tenancies.

After almost a century, the concept of a public sector housing 'estate' seemed as outdated as that of a private 'great estate'. In 2016 Lambeth announced that it wanted to build 1,000 new council houses, but these were for 21,000 people on its waiting list, with over 1,850 homeless families and 1,300 more in severe overcrowding. Awarding just 1,000 of them a lifetime asset seemed a bizarre use of public money. Yet public housing lobbies, egged on by housebuilders, pressed not for densification of the existing housing stock, but for ever more new building. Such investment could only divert resources from those in real housing distress. They were not those eager for a cheaper 'more affordable' home, as the jargon put it, but those in genuine need of adequate housing. As in the nineteenth century, policy seemed to concentrate on the 'deserving' poor. London's housing 'crisis' lay in distorted housing policy not a lack of house-building.

The inevitable consequence for councils wishing to continue building for social rent was to cross-finance 'affordable units' by selling parts of their old council estates to the private sector. This was the case with the large Pepys estate in Lewisham, and Heygate in Southwark. The new Heygate, dubbed Elephant Park for its proximity to Elephant and Castle, was of high architectural quality, its borders carefully integrated into surviving fragments of Victorian Walworth. But political protest erupted when only 25 per cent of the 2,700 new flats were available at reduced prices and just seventy-nine were let to 'social' tenants, defined as those in extreme need.

Given that 55 per cent of housing in Southwark was council-owned, some shift towards gentrification might seem reasonable. This did not appease those who saw an erosion of the public estate in parts of the city that had long been seen as reserved for London's poor. As London experienced acute inwards migration, it was an argument almost impossible to resolve. What was undeniable was that Walworth had been torn apart by its elected council not once but twice in living memory.

Where the 1960s tower blocks were due for renovation rather than demolition, the risk was of cutting corners, and worse. In 2017, North Kensington's Grenfell Tower burst into flames after a small kitchen fire took hold of its external cladding and turned it into an inferno. Seventy-two people died. It turned out that many more blocks were similarly at risk from faulty cladding and inadequate fire protection. These buildings had clearly gone beyond a council's capacity to maintain or even monitor them. Fifty years after the disaster at Ronan Point, London still had not come to terms with the dangers inherent in high-rise living.

A London cosmopolis, of sorts

By the second decade of the twenty-first century, the inflow of foreign money on a scale impossible to quantify was having a noticeable impact on wealthier neighbourhoods. They were emptying. Livingstone's theory that the inflow would help boost social housing was absurd. Estate agents were reporting 80 per cent of 'prime West End' sales going overseas. A survey in 2019 indicated that 30,000 high-end London properties were foreign owned and probably unoccupied, 10,000 of them in Westminster. This was certainly an underestimate, with even the East End affected. Of 800 new flats sold in Robin Hood Gardens in Poplar in 2017, just seventeen went to London buyers before the rest were marketed overseas.

An evening walk through the once populous streets off Chelsea's King's Road or Kensington's Phillimore estate would reveal almost no rooms lit at night. Whole floors at new luxury developments such as One Hyde Park in Knightsbridge or One Kensington Gardens beyond the Royal Albert Hall were entirely dark, many of them clearly unfurnished. The 2011 census showed Kensington and Chelsea as the only English borough south of the Wash to see a fall in population. In some neighbourhoods the fall was precipitous, leading to shop closures, under-used GP surgeries and vacant residents' parking bays.

One consequence of this occupancy freeze was an abrupt end to the westward drift of London's population, familiar since the seventeenth century. New Londoners were moving east, colonizing once-vacant acres of Docklands with gated high-rise estates. There was no shortage of land in London, merely of land initially of appeal to private developers. In 2014 the agency Stirling Ackroyd identified enough developable sites in Greater London to house half a million people, mostly to the east. Nor was there any problem with demand, at least from global investors. The tallest residential building in Europe was planned for the Isle of Dogs, the sixty-seven-storey Spire London, comprising 861 flats, to go on the market at an average of £1 million each.

East of Docklands lay yet another London, as yet little developed. Dagenham, Rainham and Dartford rarely appeared in any strategic plan, let alone in any London guidebook. The eastern reaches of the Thames were still as described by Conrad in *The Heart of Darkness*, 'resembling an immense snake uncoiled, with its head in the sea, its body at rest curving afar over a vast country'. Occasional attempts were made to give the area new names, such as East Thames Corridor and Thames Gateway. To wander these parts was to imagine oneself at the mouth of the Humber or the Severn, or the empty acres of New York's Long Island. It was also to realize that, for all the claims of London running out of land, there were still new areas to settle. In the 2000s, Johnson's idea of a new city airport in the Thames estuary was dismissed as unrealistic, at a time when Hong Kong was building that very thing. As congestion and pollution enveloped ever more of west London and battle was joined over yet another expansion of Heathrow, it was clear that points east could still hold the future of the metropolis.

The end of a boom

By 2016 the impact of a decade of property resurgence was apparent. London house prices had plateaued and then begun actually to fall, though the amounts varied by area and survey. Anecdotal reports suggested sales plummeting in richer neighbourhoods by

10 to 20 per cent. London's first skyscraper, Centre Point, which had been converted into luxury flats, found them unsellable and half were left empty. In 2018 estate agents reported that London had 54,000 flats coming to market at or around the £1 million mark, for which there were an estimated 4,000 buyers a year. NLA's model of London present and future at their Store Street offices showed the metropolis like a pin-cushion, with no fewer than 540 buildings of twenty storeys or more in the planning system, in addition to some 250 already erected or under construction.

These were overwhelmingly intended as upmarket flats. After half a century of decline since its starring role in post-war council-house building, the London high-rise had returned to centre stage, to become what the square was to the Georgian city, the defining feature of its built environment. The only question was who, and at what income level, would ever buy them. Given the high service charges in these blocks and the market's dependence on foreign buyers, London was paying the price, yet again, of its historic inability to regulate its growth or curb rampant property speculation. It was building homes but making no effort to ensure they were occupied – or to decide by whom.

Gradually the outcome of the capital's recent planning history became evident. Between a quarter and a third of central London was now conserved, a remarkable achievement which effectively stabilized its nineteenth- and twentieth-century appearance for all time. But these areas were beginning to look like clearings in an urban jungle, surrounded by decontrolled strips and patches of dense high-rise. Thus three-quarters of Westminster was conservation area, punctuated by tower clusters round Victoria and Paddington Basin, and wherever else a developer could slip through the net, as at Marble Arch and Hyde Park Corner. With no plan or co-ordination, developments would erupt unannounced along Islington's City Road, round Elephant and Castle and at seemingly random points along the river.

The Thames was losing its battle to avoid becoming a canyon. London's horizon was now effectively deregulated.

Attempts to ascertain the reaction of Londoners to the new appearance of their city were remarkably scarce. An NLA poll in 2014 confirmed a longstanding preference against living in towers, with 70 per cent of those aged over thirty-four against it. Opinion was more evenly divided on whether skyscrapers 'improved the skyline', with 45 per cent in favour and 40 per cent against. They were equally divided on whether tall buildings made London look better or worse.

My own view was that dwellers in modern cities saw their evolution as somehow inevitable – unlike rural villages, which were defended by their inhabitants with meticulous attention. It was as if their sheer size rendered them ordained by fate. Certainly they appeared at the mercy of the market economy, and where large sums of money were at stake the market often spoke loudest. The power of numbers to crush all attempts at planning or regulation remains evident in the great cities of the developing world, as anyone who has flown over Mexico City or Lagos will attest.

Cities in autocratic states behaved quite differently. Such places have often decided to destroy and rebuild themselves after the fashion of the age. Haussmann did it in nineteenth-century Paris. In the 1960s I saw bulldozers obliterate the old boulevards of Bucharest and in 1983, I saw them obliterate the ancient quarter of Chengdu in China, the more heart-breaking for my knowing they would one day regret it. In London, the free market and the crush of numbers was always in contention with decisions. The ancient settlement took its shape from the decisions of its Roman governors, and later from the residency of the crown at Westminster, as well as from the denial of new bridges over the Thames and from the failure to plan the railway. The statutory intervention of conservation areas in the 1970s had a dramatic impact on the capital, possibly more than anything since the Great Fire. Another decisive moment was the debate over the comprehensive renewal of inner London after the Blitz and through into the 1970s.

By the end of the twentieth century, the virtual collapse of strategic planning and the power of the property interests left little scope for public decision or public patronage. However, some areas still had to be planned. These were chiefly a number of large industrial sites, formerly of docks, railways and utilities. Decisions were awaited on three such sites in the inner area, at Battersea power station, the Lea Valley north of Stratford and old railway land at King's Cross. In each case, the outcome illustrated the strengths and weaknesses of London's government at the turn of the new century.

Battersea, Stratford, King's Cross

At Battersea the central issue was the preservation of a mid-twentieth-century power station, with four celebrated chimneys. The government required that the power station be left in place and, without much explanation, that the site should have its own spur from the Northern Line Tube. In return developers would be allowed what became the drastic overdevelopment of the site itself.

A Malaysian consortium was granted permission for 4,239 flats on the site, twice the size of the Barbican. Architects such as Norman Foster and Frank Gehry were asked to design cliff-like slab blocks divided by narrow canyons. To add to the project's appeal to its intended investors, the main square was named Malaysia Square, and fashioned round that country's national flower, the hibiscus. The whole was called, with heavy irony, a 'village'. There was no pretence of the development being for Londoners, and it was launched in January 2013 by Malaysia's 'minister for local government' in Kuala Lumpur, where the mayor Boris Johnson went in 2014 to help with sales. As the market weakened in the mid-2010s, the minimal 'social' housing component was slashed to just 386 flats. The project met financial headwinds in 2018 and had to be rescued by the Malaysian government in a deal later investigated for corruption.

The pattern set at Battersea was continued downstream on formerly commercial land at Nine Elms and Vauxhall, centred on a new American embassy, built like a secured cage in a moat. Here a sequence of high-rise blocks accommodated some 20,000 luxury flats. There were no planning requirements for mixed tenure, job opportunities or community facilities. Nine Elms echoed the nineteenth-century suburb, with developers just building and pocketing the cash. As a result, a sizeable acreage of central London was in effect acquired and shipped abroad. It is hard to imagine what this area will be like in fifty years' time, should foreign investors cash in and the market collapse. There must be a risk of Nine Elms mirroring the Victorian Ladbroke estate – and passing through a phase of collapsing values and ruination.

A more interventionist approach to urban renewal was attempted north of Stratford in east London in the wake of the Olympics extravaganza. The site was handicapped by the government's refusal to demolish the stadium, too big for most team games and even then in only intermittent use. It was more than the government could bear to admit that £700 million had been wasted on two weeks of entertainment. The stadium was eventually gifted to West Ham United FC for £15 million, to be much disliked by the club's fans for its size and lack of intimacy. Like the adjacent aquatic and volleyball centres, these large structures serve only to 'hollow out' neighbourhoods.

The so-called London Legacy Development Corporation rejected any traditional street layout for the site in favour of a spread of exceptionally large buildings, let to developers in the hope of recouping some of the cost of the games. The former athletes' village became an estate of flats, mixing market rents with 'affordable' ones to achieve a degree of social diversity. It is currently the most successful area of the site, giving onto a small park along the River Lea.

The most adventurous decision was to imitate Victorian South Kensington along a bank of the canal, with a blood transfusion of cultural assets such as the V&A, Sadler's Wells ballet, the College of Fashion, the BBC and even Washington's Smithsonian Institute. The £1.1 billion cost was to be offset by 600 luxury flats, including at one point a forty-storey block. When it was discovered that this would be visible behind St Paul's even from Richmond Park twenty miles away it was abandoned, a visual sensitivity rare in London's recent history.

A classic London contrast lay in the district immediately to the west across the Lea, the enclave of Hackney Wick. It was a neighbourhood of hipster studios, bars and workshops that had colonized the old riverside warehouses, merging with new and old houses and flats, some public, some private. An intriguing option would have been to have serviced the Olympic site with simple infrastructure and leased it as a low-rise enterprise zone, perhaps a 'greater Hackney Wick'. A version of this was initiated to the south, at the mouth of the Lea on the Thames. Trinity Buoy Wharf, built in part from disused containers, became a remarkable colony of informal 'creative' uses under the gaze of Canary Wharf. Instead, Stratford seems likely to witness a familiar London tale of property boom and bust.

In the 1980s, the question facing the British Rail board at King's Cross was whether its redundant goods site would play host to a Barbican, a Canary Wharf or a Thamesmead. After a series of false starts the developers, Argent, were required to retain the existing warehouses, gasholders, nature park and canal, as well as create a new mixed community for Camden Council within the perimeter of the scheme. This was a tall order. In return they could have a medium-rise office zone near the station.

Argent immediately let the warehouses to the University of the Arts, attracting a cluster of galleries and restaurants that gradually came on stream and conditioned the development as it progressed. The contrast with Stratford could not have been more stark. The Coal Drops Yard opened as an upmarket shopping enclave in old Victorian buildings. The community sector was a mix of public and private housing, with its own shops, clinic and school. The office zone was densely developed, but not overpoweringly so, and was chosen by Google for its London headquarters.

The canal-side steps soon became a popular picnic venue, and the warehouses a visitor destination in their own right. There can be little doubt that the key factor was the meticulous integration of the new fabric and new uses into old ones. The same had been achieved with the rehabilitation of former industrial land to the west of the site at Camden Lock, after yet another battle against an office development in the 1970s. King's Cross was much the most successful of these London renewals.

Brexit-on-Thames

In 2015 the Cameron government won a general election with a pledge to allow a referendum on Britain's membership of the European Union. Throughout history, London had benefited from the exchange of trade, investment and people with continental Europe. It was a European city and always would be. At the same time, its primary concern with business held it aloof from many of Europe's conflicts and crises, usually to its advantage. It had always been semi-detached, for the past century conspicuously with one foot in Europe and another in New York.

While the United Kingdom as a whole voted to leave the EU, London voted 60:40 to remain. Many observers saw the vote as less a rebuff to Europe and more a protest by provincial England at London's perceived self-centredness and success. But even London's vote was far from unanimous. Many boroughs were as disaffected as the provinces. Havering in the East End registered one of the highest leave votes in the country, at 70 per cent. This was a reminder that, for all its wealth, the capital possessed pockets of intense poverty. Its citizens had a lower than average UK disposable income after housing costs. Its child poverty was above average, and its rate of inward migration gave it the most overcrowded housing and the highest numbers sleeping rough. In other words, it had failed to overcome the familiar downside of success.

As I write, the final outcome remains unclear, but past experience suggests that Brexit would not severely affect London's long-term prosperity. While some activities might disperse to the continent, the city's global status looks secure, as does its cultural appeal as an educational and tourist destination. More likely, Brexit would signal what had been coming for some time: a mild recession and the toning down of an overheated economy. Whatever was to happen at Westminster, London would always be what it always was, Britain's bridge to the continent.

Epilogue

The corner of Borough Market on a Saturday morning is an astonishing sight. A jumble of Victorian alleys, railway arches and warehouses are crammed with food stalls and open kitchens. The crowds can be impenetrable, as thousands of shoppers mingle with passers-by and tourists. They spill into the surrounding streets, the riverside wharves and the cathedral churchyard. It is Southwark as it was in Chaucer's day – scruffy, vital, irresistible, a London seething with life.

Looming over the scene just a stone's throw to the east, is an apparition. The gleaming flank of Bermondsey's Shard rises into the sky, vast, silent, largely empty, its windows blind and its entrances guarded as if against imminent assault. The edifice seems without purpose, the pavements round it dead. Perhaps one day the Shard will swarm with people, while Borough Market will lie a vacant heap of dust. I doubt it.

London is a composite of such contrasts, and I acknowledge that this is part of its appeal. It is a place of diversity and eccentricity, where citizens have grown accustomed to clashing streetscapes, to a present in perpetual contention with the past. All cities are a resolution of such forces, between the demands of the property market and the efforts of authority to direct that market to some wider purpose. London was initially unusual. It did not begin life as a fortress or a focus of religious faith. Its purpose was trade, and the requirements of trade dominated its early growth. Authority sought to regulate that growth, though with little success. As a witness in the twelfth century, William Fitzstephen, said in summing up the London of his day, it was 'Truly a good city – if it has a good lord.' Rarely has this been the case.

From the Tudors onwards the argument over how the city should grow has always preoccupied it. Planning the first Covent Garden, the Star Chamber dictated the design of the piazza and even named the architect, Inigo Jones. One of the earliest permissions, for Lincoln's Inn Fields in 1643, sought to 'frustrate the covetous and greedy endeavours of such persons as daily seek to fill up that small remainder of air in those parts with unnecessary and unprofitable buildings'. The word 'unprofitable' meant 'to the public'.

From the Great Fire onwards, governments assumed powers to license building beyond the City's authority, and to ordain the safety and form of the streets. It might not concern itself with the health or well-being of the citizens, or with the 'noisome trades' settled anarchically east along the river. But to the west the crown collaborated with the owners of the land over which London was to expand, to ensure its 'profit' to the metropolis. From the layouts of St James's Square, through the building acts of the eighteenth century to the enterprises of John Nash and Thomas Cubitt, there was a consensus on how London should look.

Better-off citizens thus enjoyed streets and buildings that were probably cleaner and more spacious than those of any other city anywhere. The house style was classical but never ostentatious – at least not until Nash – with classes of property fixed by statute to serve all tiers in society, other than the very poorest. The resulting buildings proved extraordinarily adaptable as the property market ebbed and flowed. Even today, the attic of a back-street mews may hide a digital start-up, while the shell of a Spitalfields mansion may hide a rag-trade sweat shop. The most expensive commercial floor space in the world is not in some City skyscraper but round eighteenth-century Berkeley Square. Nor was it true that the terrace and square reflected a purely bourgeois taste. When in 1984 the BBC sought a proletarian setting for its London soap, *EastEnders*, it chose not a council tower block but Victorian 'Albert Square', based on Fassett Square in Dalston.

London was dilatory in moving on from the regulation of its buildings to showing a concern for its infrastructure and for the living conditions of its poor. The market-led arrival of the railways was crucial. These disrupted the property market more than anything since the Great Fire, and focused public opinion on the acute poverty in which, according to Mayhew and Booth, a quarter of Londoners were now living. From the 1840s to the 1880s argument raged, first over the state of the city's water and sewerage, and then over the housing of the poor. In the latter case, response came first from philanthropy and then from the slow and painful birth of municipal democracy. Only with the twentieth century did London acquire governing institutions which other English cities had enjoyed since the 1830s.

Even then, galvanizing the LCC and the metropolitan boroughs into urban renewal took a long time. It allowed the continual ripples of suburban expansion to meet the burgeoning demands of all Londoners to escape the slums, with little more assistance than statutory 'workmen's trains'. The expansion grew and grew. In the half-century from 1880, London's land area increased a phenomenal six-fold, with new suburbs absorbing almost all of Middlesex together with portions of Essex and Surrey. Meanwhile the inner city saw 'reverse gentrification', as early Victorian leases came to an end and dilapidated streets were occupied by those who could not afford suburban flight.

The result was an open door to Abercrombie's 1940s revolution, to his dismissal of London as an 'outdated city' and his proposal to renew its core fabric from the ground up. London, he said, had to be 'made fit for the motor age', its historic neighbourhoods reduced to quaint enclaves. From this emerged unquestionably the most destructive period in London's history, as hundreds of thousands of working-class Londoners were decanted into council estates, many so poorly designed as to require early demolition. Communities were upheaved, and immense sums wasted, while residents were driven from Victorian homes that could more cheaply have been restored. Demoralized planners and confused politicians eventually admitted defeat, leaving a property market free, for the most part, recklessly to write its own rules. Having survived one potential affliction the metropolis faced another.

The strategic planning of London at the turn of the twenty-first century would appear to have all but given up the ghost. There was no debate on whether London's continued growth was to be encouraged or discouraged. Older areas that survived the Blitz and Abercrombie were largely safeguarded by local designation. But wider planning was limited to documents and good intentions. The new London showed no obvious concern for how modern buildings should sit alongside old ones, common practice in cities abroad. Tall buildings rose with no relation to their streets. There was little effort to guide density, use and social mix. Shopping in local high streets was left to wither. The London horizon was abandoned to fate.

The most vigorous debate was over to whom London 'belonged'. Large swathes had, since the nineteenth century, been increasingly one-class towns. This changed rapidly. As middle-class boroughs accepted pockets of public housing in the 1960s and 70s, so gentrification took hold of many working-class ones. It was never clear to what degree these changes should be quantified and organized, nor on what theory of urban demography such organization should be based.

In my view, no one is 'entitled' to the ownership of a great city. London has always been a vehicle for immigration and emigration, for Olsen's incessant 'comers and goers'. Its economic vitality has depended on it. In the twenty-first century, with a third of London citizens born abroad, the idea of a no-go area for immigrants was unsustainable. Equally, the idea of 'freezing' any district to a single group or class, as had seemed the intention in the mid-twentieth century, was unrealistic. I recall Sir Robin Wales, for twenty-six years leader then mayor of Newham, telling me the problems of his borough could be summed up as, 'We just don't have enough ABC1s'. Newham lacked a critical range of spending power and local enterprise, largely through an excess of council ownership.

At the same time, London has never been a city without local personality. It is a collective of communities, of citizens who in an age of democracy naturally seek a degree of control over their neighbourhoods. They want protection from the harshness of the property market, from the disappearance of places of work, leisure and shopping. They want some social mix in their communities. Anna Minton's account of the suburban dispersal of Heygate's residents in 2008 replicated, albeit less harshly, the Southwark dispersals that followed the coming of the Victorian railway.

Modern cities should be able to show more social concern than has resulted from the distorted housing strategies described in the last chapter. A well-ordered city balances the flow of the property market against the needs of poorer and migrant workers and the virtue of neighbourhood continuity and cohesion. It cares for its homeless and incapacitated

The metropolis, in other words, 'belongs' to all its citizens, to its nation and to the world. It is a matter of political decision how, at any stage in history, they divide it up between them. This is why I have devoted so much of this book to London as a built phenomenon, to the city whose fabric will survive long after each generation of its citizens has come and gone from its streets. When I look at those streets, I try to imagine the range of occupations, classes and nationalities that must have walked their pavements and lived under their roofs. I agree with the critic Rowan Moore in summing up London as 'a city of the present, too pragmatic to be a utopian ideal of the future, too messed-up to be a model from history, but able to give shape to whatever forces are running through the world'. It is what drives me to conserve as much as we can of the buildings that have proved themselves over the centuries to be popular, lasting and adaptable.

Perhaps since my first memories as a child are of a townscape bombed, polluted and overwhelmingly black, I see today's London as incomparably a better place to live, cleaner, richer, more diverse and more diverting than it has ever been before. Its public transport is improved, its food immeasurably so. The faces seen and languages heard in the streets are those not of one nation but of a world city. Its greatest and most recent loss has been of tens of thousands of houses and commercial buildings that would today be popular and throbbing with life, when so many of their replacements are costly, energy consuming and often empty. But we can still try to design a new city in the spirit of the old.

I am glad to have been present during the 1970s when London's history was at a sort of turning point. Walking through Covent Garden long after its rescue, I encountered a former local councillor who had sought its demolition to make way for another Barbican. I asked if he did not prefer it the way it had turned out. He grudgingly admitted that he did, but he could not quite explain where he and his colleagues had gone wrong, other than to blame 'the planners'. Across London, I wondered how many politicians, architects and builders might have agreed with him.

My response to today's London is best illustrated in two of my favourite walks. To me they offer the same variety and delight as a naturalist derives from a walk through field and forest. They are rich in animal, vegetable and mineral, and constantly changing with the seasons. My first is in the City. It passes from the buzz of Ludgate Circus through the back alleys of Carter Lane and Apothecaries Hall on the slopes south of Ludgate Hill. It threads through alleys between the occasional surviving townhouse and the old St Paul's Deanery. The route crosses Queen Victoria Street to regain intimacy in Huggin Hill with its Roman baths, Trinity Lane and College Street, then down to the ghost of the Walbrook stream at Dowgate, where Romans once worshipped Mithras.

With the great towers of the Gracechurch Street cluster to our left, we dive down Laurence Pountney Hill and Lovat Lane to Wren's exquisite St Mary-at-Hill, before passing the bombed ruin of St Dunstan's to emerge at the Norman Tower of London. We have traversed a millennium of history – two millennia if we count the Roman baths. Our scenery is owed not to any Wren or Abercrombie, but to the medieval aldermen and vestries who embedded these old lanes so deep in the soil of London that no road-builder has dared eliminate them and no architect dared crush them.

A second quite different walk runs across the West End north from the Embankment through the Adelphi into the back streets of Covent Garden. It passes tiny Brydges Place, at its narrowest barely forty centimetres, to run up to London's most humble roundabout, Seven Dials, before turning west into exotic Chinatown. Unlike in the City, the streets here are mostly straight, Georgian in scale, their upper storeys still boasting the dimensions of the eighteenth-century building acts. What is intriguing here is not the buildings but their uses. Today's Soho is impossible to categorize. It is part red-light district, part upmarket dining area and then, north of Brewer Street, doors, windows and name-plates indicate the hallowed shrines of the movie business and the editing suites of the world hub of post-production. The citadels of Hollywood must dance attendance on the basements of Soho. The true measure of the productivity of these conserved neighbourhoods is that Georgian Soho's employment density at 1,300 per hectare, is more than half that of massively renewed Canary Wharf, at 2,300.

To the west, we find colourful Carnaby Street, surviving still as a promiscuous retail promenade, a relic of the 1960s in the shadow of pompous Regent Street. Beyond lies one of London's unnoticed delights, the Edwardian rebuilding of the facades of New Bond Street, like a cartoon strip of baroque Rome. Bond Street's 'suburb' Avery Row, is the Crown Estate's model restoration of what was a scruffy 'borderland' of studios and warehouses, running through to the deserted streets of west Mayfair.

These are streets that have prospered where the city has kept its nerve and not run screaming into the market place. They are where fabric was the essence, offering a welcome to whatever the transient market ordains. London has its clusters and some of them are splendid. But it is clear that the creative juices that keep the city constantly on the alert crave the patina of time passing. The neighbourhoods through which I walk can be replicated in Paddington, King's Cross, Clerkenwell, Shoreditch, Bermondsey and Lambeth. Their secret lies in their buildings because it lies in the people their buildings attract.

I used to fantasize that one day I would see London finished. I would see every construction site completed and every roadwork tidied away. I would look out from Primrose Hill and consider the metropolis a job well done. Successful cities are never like that. My London has no hours, no seasons, no years or centuries. It is always going about its business. We can take it or leave it, but it does not care. It may be a flawed masterpiece, but it is a masterpiece without question, the most exhilarating human construct in the world.

A Timeline of London's History

43	London founded in reign of Emperor Claudius
60	Boudicca's revolt; London sacked
80–90	Building of London Bridge
c.120	London extensively damaged by fire
410	Roman withdrawal; the city abandoned
604	Mellitus first Bishop of London; St Paul's founded
c.830	First Viking raids on the Thames
886	Alfred the Great retakes London, declares it a burgh
1018	Cnut crowned king
1042	Edward the Confessor bases court at Westminster
1066	Norman Conquest spares London expropriation
1087	First great fire of London; St Paul's destroyed
1189	First mayor elected in the City
1209	London Bridge rebuilt
1290	Expulsion of the City's Jews
1348	Black Death arrives
1381	Peasants' revolt; Wat Tyler killed
1397	Dick Whittington mayor for first time
1476	Caxton sets up press at Westminster
1536–41	Dissolution of the monasteries; mass transfer of wealth from church to crown
1571	Opening of Gresham's Royal Exchange, modelled on Antwerp's
1576	Burbage's Theatre opens in Finsbury Fields
1580	Elizabeth I's first edicts against London growth

1598	Stow's survey of the metropolis published
1616–19	Inigo Jones's Queen's House in Greenwich and Banqueting House in Whitehall
1630	Earl of Bedford licensed to build Covent Garden piazza
1649	Execution of Charles I in Whitehall (the Tower rejected for risk of riot)
1653	First coffee house opened
1660–69	Pepys's diary records events in the capital
1665	Earl of St Albans wins licence for St James's Square
1665	The Great Plague
1666	Great Fire of London destroys 80 per cent of the City
1673	Wren begins rebuilding of St Paul's
1683–84	Frost fair on the frozen Thames
1688	William of Orange arrives; he and Mary establish palace at Kensington
1694	Founding of the Bank of England
1702	First London newspaper, the *Daily Courant*, appears
1712	Act to build fifty 'Queen Anne' churches, twelve finished in the capital
1717	Handel's *Water Music* played on the Thames; 'Whig' Hanover Square and 'Tory' Cavendish Square laid out
1721	Grosvenor Square laid out
1729	Opening of Vauxhall pleasure gardens, followed by Ranelagh in 1741
1739	Thomas Coram founds Foundling Hospital
1748	Henry Fielding appointed first stipendiary magistrate at Bow Street
1750	Opening of first river crossing since London Bridge at Westminster
1751	Act to tax and curb gin consumption begins to control the gin menace

1768	Royal Academy founded, moved to Somerset house ten years later; John Wilkes elected to parliament for Middlesex
1769	New toll bridge at Blackfriars
1774	Building Act lays down classes for Georgian houses
1780	Gordon riots, London's worst civil disturbance
1812	Nash publishes his plan for a 'royal way' from Carlton House to Regent's Park
1818	Church Building Act heralds 'Waterloo churches'
1820	Work on 'royal way' begins
1825	Cubitt acquires Belgravia leases from Grosvenor estate
1829	Metropolitan Police Act
1832	Great Reform Act updates parliament, initiates Poor Law reform
1834	Destruction of Palace of Westminster by fire; competition demands gothic replacement
1836	Opening of first London railway from Greenwich to London Bridge
1837	Railway links Birmingham and Euston
1841	Repeal of Corn Laws reduces London prices and aids boom
1851	Great Exhibition initiates Kensington building boom
1858	The Great Stink spurs reform of London sewerage; building of Embankment begins
1863	First underground train runs from Paddington to the City under Marylebone Road
1866	City bank failure and collapse of London shipbuilding
1867	Hyde Park riots lead to Second Reform Act; most male Londoners enfranchised
1870	Forster Education Act sets up elementary board schools; women vote and stand for school boards
1871	Hampstead Heath saved from development and left 'wild'

1880	First luxury flats built by Norman Shaw next to the Albert Hall
1888	London County Council replaces Metropolitan Board of Works; women can vote in local elections
1890	First 'tube' train runs, from King William Street to Stockwell
1891	Arrival of first trams
1899	Vestry government outside City boundary replaced by metropolitan boroughs
1903	Works starts on Yerkes's Piccadilly and Bakerloo lines
1904	LCC takes over board schools
1907	First petrol buses take to the streets
1915	Zeppelin bombing raids over London docks
1919	Addison's 'homes for heroes' leads to rampant house-building boom
1929	Formation of London Passenger Transport Board, later London Transport
1929–31	Wall Street crash and recession have little impact on London
1932	First Town and Country Planning Act
1934	LCC declares a 'green belt' around London
1940–41	The Blitz
1944–45	V-1 flying bomb and V-2 rocket attacks
1947	Town and Country Planning Act gives teeth to local planning
1948	London stages 'austerity' Olympics; NHS removes hospitals from LCC control; *'Windrush'* recruits arrive for London Transport
1951	Festival of Britain
1953	Abercrombie report approved as London Plan
1956	First Clean Air Act in response to worsening London smog

1963	Secret deal to allow Centre Point, London's first skyscraper
1965	LCC replaced by larger Greater London Council; Barbican building begins north of London Wall
1966	First Notting Hill Carnival
1967	Civic Amenities Act establishes conservation areas for London; Tory landslide in local elections, winning 28 of 32 new London boroughs
1968	Collapse of Ronan Point tower block
1973	Planning revolution as proposals for Piccadilly Circus, Motorway Box and Covent Garden all fail
1981	Livingstone takes control of GLC; last London dock closes
1984	Thames Barrier opens
1986	GLC abolished; Big Bang transforms City
1990	Poll tax riot in Trafalgar Square
1997	Labour attempts to sell off London Underground
1999	GLA established
2000	London mayoralty election won by Livingstone
2001	Census reveals London's population rising again
2003	Huge London demonstration against Iraq war; Prescott approves Shard for Bermondsey; London's high-rise boom takes off
2005	Islamist bombs explode on public transport, causing 52 deaths
2008	Boris Johnson elected as mayor, launches civic bike scheme
2012	London Olympics at Stratford
2016	Sadiq Khan elected as mayor
2016	Londoners reject Brexit in national referendum
2017	Grenfell Tower fire causes 72 deaths

Author's Note

This book completes a trilogy of short histories, previously of England and Europe. They are intended to offer a more concentrated view of the past than large general histories but, I hope, without over-simplifying. In the case of London, it was a delight to burrow slightly deeper into one place, but as before the art lay not in what to include but what to leave out. I apologize, if I have omitted a favourite neighbourhood or landmark. The narrative is chronological, since I believe there to be no other way to relate events to causes. This especially applies to my emphasis on London's physical appearance, a less familiar topic for most London biographies. No city in the world, in my opinion, wears its changing years so visibly on its sleeve.

My sources are derived from a lifetime living in London, from hundreds of books (some listed in the Further Reading section below) and countless conversations with people in its political, business and cultural life. London has had its epic biographers, most recently, the grand surveys by Stephen Inwood, Jerry White and Peter Ackroyd. Ben Weinreb and Christopher Hibbert's *London Encyclopaedia* remains indispensable, as are the Secker and Warburg histories, the researches of New London Architecture, the Pevsner guides, the shelves of the London Library, the blogs of the Londonist and Wikipedia's London contributors.

I have traipsed the streets of London with too many friends to mention. Tony Travers of the LSE has been a constant help in this volume, notably in matters of London's government, and in exploring London's less familiar suburbs. So too has been my brother Tom.

Marcus Binney, with whom I and others founded SAVE Britain's Heritage (SAVE) in 1975, and after that the Twentieth Century Society, has been a friend and unceasing campaigner for the protection of London's old buildings. I also pay tribute to countless volunteers of the city's civic, conservation and amenity societies, without whose unpaid and unsung efforts London would look utterly different today. As was said of Wren, *Si monumentum requiris, circumspice.*

I would like to thank the experts who read and commented on an early version of the text, Caroline Barron, Richard Hingley and Tony Travers. Any errors that survived their strictures are my responsibility, and I welcome correction for later editions.

Further Reading

The following books are cited in the text or have been used as sources.
I have not included strictly local histories.

Ackroyd, Peter, *London: The Biography*, 2000
Barratt, Nick, *Greater London*, 2012
Barron, Caroline, *London in the Later Middle Ages*, 2004
Bill, Peter, *Planet Property*, 2013
Boughton, John, *The Rise and Fall of the Council House*, 2019
Bucholz, Robert and Joseph Ward, *London*, 2012
Clunn, Harold, *The Face of London*, 1970
Cohen, Phil, *On the Wrong Side of the Tracks*, 2013
Cruickshank, Dan, and Peter Wyld, *The Art of Georgian Building*, 1975
David, Terence, *John Nash*, 1973
Dorling, Danny, *All That Is Solid*, 2014
Esher, Lionel, *A Broken Wave*, 1981
Glanville, Philippa, *London in Maps*, 1972
Hanley, Lynsey, *Estates: An Intimate History*, 2007
Hatherley, Owen, *A New Kind of Bleak*, 2013
Hingley, Richard, *Londinium: A Biography*, 2018
Hobhouse, Hermione, *Lost London*, 1971
——, *Thomas Cubitt*, 1971
Inwood, Stephen, *A History of London*, 1998
——, *City of Cities*, 2005
Jackson, Alan, *Semi-Detached London*, 1973
Jenkins, Simon, *Landlords to London*, 1975
——, *Companion Guide to Outer London*, 1981

Kynaston, David, *The City of London*, 2011

Marriott, Oliver, *The Property Boom*, 1967

Mayhew, Henry, *The Unknown Mayhew*, ed. E. P. Thompson and Eileen Yeo, 1971

Minton, Anna, *Ground Control*, 2009

———, *Big Capital: Who Is London For?*, 2017

Moore, Rowan, *Slow Burn City*, 2016

Nairn, Ian, *Nairn's London*, 1966

Olsen, Donald, *The Growth of Victorian London*, 1976

Palmer, Alan, *The East End*, 1989

Pevsner, Nikolaus, *The Buildings of London*, various dates

Picard, Liza, *Restoration London*, 1997

———, *Dr Johnson's London*, 2000

———, *Elizabeth's London*, 2003

———, *Victorian London*, 2005

Porter, Roy, *London: A Social History*, 1994

Rasmussen, Steen Eiler, *London: The Unique City*, 1934

Sheppard, Francis, *Infernal Wen*, 1971

Sinclair, Iain, *Lights Out for the Territory*, 1997

———, *London Overground*, 2016

Stedman Jones, Gareth, *Outcast London*, 1971

Summerson, John, *Georgian London*, 1945

Thorold, Peter, *The London Rich*, 1999

Travers, Tony, *London's Boroughs at 50*, 2015

Weinreb, Ben and Christopher Hibbert, *London Encyclopaedia*, 1983

White, Jerry, *Metropolitan London*, 1982

———, *London in the 20th Century*, 2001

Wright, Patrick, *Journey Through Ruins*, 2009

Zamoyski, Adam, *Holy Madness*, 1999

Index

Abbey Mills pumping station 164
Abbott, Diane 299
ABC teashops 200
Abercrombie, Sir Patrick 240, 242, 245, 279
Abercrombie plan 242–4, 246, 249, 334–5; GLC updating 263–4, 278, 279; LCC approval and partial implementation 250–51, 254, 255, 258–9, 277
Aberdeen, John Hamilton-Gordon, 1st Marquess of 220
abortion 260
Ackroyd, Peter, *London: The Biography* 301
Act of Supremacy (1534) 44
Act of Union (1707) 92
Acton 206
Adam, John 122, 124
Adam, Robert 122–3, 123–4, 132, 220, 221, 227
Adams, John 118
Addison, Christopher, 1st Viscount 222–3
Addison, Joseph 105
Adelphi buildings 122, 123, 221, 338
Admiralty Arch 196
Aeneas (mythological figure) 8
Aethelbert, King of Kent 17
Aethelwulf, King of Wessex 19

'affordable' housing 312, 313, 322, 329
Agar Town 143
Agas, Ralph 51
Agincourt, Battle of (1415) 39
air pollution 77, 87, 186, 244–5, 324, 337; Great Stink (1858) 164, 259; 'pea-souper smogs' 259
al-Qaeda 304
Alaric I, King of the Visigoths 13
Albemarle, George Monck, 1st Duke of 67
Albemarle, Christopher Monck, 2nd Duke of 84
Albemarle Street 84, 199
Albert, Prince Consort 156, 170–71
Albert Bridge 284
Albert Hall 171, 199, 323
Albury House 220
Aldermaston marches (CND protests) 262, 291
aldermen (City of London) 25, 28, 32, 34–5, 50, 64, 82, 338
Aldersgate 126
Aldgate 11; Holy Trinity Priory 27, 45–6
Aldwych 8, 15, 21, 197, 221, 284
Alexander, John 171
Alfie (film) 261
Alfred the Great, King of Wessex 19–20, 41, 83, 120